Hiking Hidden Gems
in AMERICA'S
NATIONAL PARKS

FALCON®

An imprint of Globe Pequot, the trade division of
The Rowman & Littlefield Publishing Group, Inc.
4501 Forbes Blvd., Ste. 200
Lanham, MD 20706
www.rowman.com

Falcon and FalconGuides are registered trademarks and Make Adventure Your Story is a trademark
of The Rowman & Littlefield Publishing Group, Inc.

Distributed by NATIONAL BOOK NETWORK

British Library Cataloguing in Publication Information available

Library of Congress Cataloging-in-Publication Data

Names: Alvarez, Ted, author.
Title: Hiking hidden gems in America's national parks / Ted Alvarez.
Description: Essex, Connecticut : Falcon, [2024] | Includes index.
Identifiers: LCCN 2024004359 (print) | LCCN 2024004360 (ebook) | ISBN 9781493070770
  (paper) | ISBN 9781493070787 (epub)
Subjects: LCSH: Hiking—United States. | Day hiking—United States. | Walking—United States.
  | Backpacking—United States. | National parks and reserves—United States. | Trails—United
  States. | United States—Description and travel. | United States—Guidebooks.
Classification: LCC GV199.4 .A444 2024 (print) | LCC GV199.4 (ebook) | DDC 796.510973—
  dc23/eng/20240212
LC record available at https://lccn.loc.gov/2024004359
LC ebook record available at https://lccn.loc.gov/2024004360

Printed in India

(opposite) The aurora borealis as seen from Gates of the Arctic National Park and Preserve.

Hiking Hidden Gems
in AMERICA'S NATIONAL PARKS

Ted Alvarez

ESSEX, CONNECTICUT

Arches National Park

Death Valley National Park

Contents

Great Basin National Park   Kenai Fjords National Park   Mount Rainier National Park

Saguaro National Park

Virgin Islands National Park

Yellowstone National Park

Introduction

Be honest: You are here because you want easy answers. You're not reading this page. Instead, you flipped through to the park you're planning a trip to this summer, or next year. Maybe I stopped you in your tracks with a beguiling photograph on the way. But be real: You're checking the table of contents or the index first, looking for an out-of-the-box hike that guarantees solitude.

I mean no judgment. I'm like you. I've spent most of my reporting career feeding your craving for just-add-water solitude to cover my own addiction (and my rent). I'm always thirsty, and I want it on tap. Finding a wild spot you've never been to before and gulping it down with no one around is a helluva drug—one perhaps only surpassed by the anticipation you get before you offer it up to the masses wrapped with a map or GPS track to boot. I've done this by consulting rangers, grilling guides, hounding wizened old-timers, squinting at obscure maps, and often tossing myself into the field to see for myself.

I know, I'm a monster. But I live on both sides of the debate. For the longest time, I argued that it was important for me to spoil your favorite secret place so that it could earn the ardent voices needed to protect it. National parks remain one of our best ideas, but recent events have shown that when the winds shift, our sacrosanct ideals can (and should) always come up for reconsideration.

Later, after watching a few of my favorites get loved to death and hearing the pleas of park personnel brought to their knees by hashtags and drones, I completely flopped to the other side. The uptick in wilderness enthusiasm seemed to outpace any need for advocacy; our vast wildernesses no longer seemed boundless, and I worried that some of our favorites couldn't stand the glare of so much attention any longer.

Both facile theories inflate my (or anyone's) power to influence the future and flatten so many nuances of this debate. More importantly, they ignore the fact that these places shouldn't and can't ever be gate-kept. New people will discover, reclaim, and return to these places. All we can do is greet them with enthusiasm, share knowledge, and keep our ears and hearts open with an invitation to join us on the trail. Many of these noobs will come up with the brilliant ideas we'll need to keep this great thing called national parks at its best for humans and nature for another 100- or 200-odd years.

Let's address the central tension and irony expressed by this book. Any hidden gems revealed herein risk losing their status the minute eyeballs hit the page. To share them is to literally risk exposing them and undermine the whole stated purpose of the title.

But I don't believe that. Even if they're discovered, they're still gems. My sincere desire is that you recognize the trips included here as starting points that motivate you to go deeper on your own. The best adventures aren't given: They are found by you, when you least expect it, in a forgotten corner of wilderness you landed in by mistake, accident, or craft. That is the real goal of this book: not to impart knowledge of secret places you haven't encountered (they're all on the internet), but to inspire and empower you to get to know a wild place, learn from it, and become a lifelong student searching for the soul of national parks with your own feet. Discovering your own hidden gems—either alone in a desolate valley or wide-eyed in a crowd as awestruck as you—never gets old. As the worn adage goes, hike your own hike.

If you love parks, it's also imperative that you cultivate this skill and attitude. While park attendance has seen steady growth since the foundation of the national park system in 1916, visitation has exploded in the last decade, with a pandemic-influenced drop essentially erased by 325.5 million visits in 2023 (2019 holds the record at 327 million). In the abstract, this is wonderful: We need vibrant constituencies to protect and expand our parks. All communities must find their place in "America's Best Idea," reclaim their heritage in it, and advance how national parks work for everyone.

The dark side is our trails and park spaces are getting hammered, and the fine people who keep our perpetually resource-strapped and underfunded park service going can't hope to keep up. You've experienced the fallout: avalanches of trailhead trash, serpentine traffic, quota limitations, and backcountry permits that sometimes feel as hard to come by as Oscar nominations.

Access versus preservation: This tension will govern the national park discourse in the coming decades. It will demand patience, sacrifice, and resilience from everyone who loves these places and has experienced their transformative power. The parks are working on solutions, some of which might bring growing pains. Parks like Arches, Mt. Rainier, and Rocky Mountain already require ticketed entry or reservations to access them by car, and more will follow suit. Extend grace to park personnel, plan, and have backup plans for backup plans. In moments of frustration, remember that any day spent outside beats doing almost anything else.

You can also eschew marquee, iconic parks and opt for obscure ones. Over a quarter of all park visits cluster in the top eight parks. All parks offer deep rewards (explored in detail in this book). If you asked me my favorite, I'd have to choose the newest one I visited.

For me, that's Gates of the Arctic, the least visited in the system, which I explored for the first time while writing this book. My ten-day excursion required expedition-grade planning and truckloads of grit, but it lived up to the legend: stellar scenery, humbling wildlife close encounters, crushing solitude. Deathbed-quality memories for us all.

Notice I said "us." Though I was in search of the most solitary, hidden experience a national park can provide, I didn't go alone.

I went with a tight-knit crew of four of my best friends and family, who sacrificed precious time and money to accompany me on a wild-hair exploration of the quietest, meanest park in the system. And I'm convinced the gifts of Gates resonate more because they were shared.

To wit: Our near tragedy became our biggest triumph. One morning, I explored an empty valley of peaks and lakes with our guide Trevor, my cousin Jonathan, and my friend Travis. Meanwhile, my sister and my friend Rob hung back in camp to rest after a backbreaking slog up to the Arrigetch Peaks. The problem with separating: For the last two days, a mother grizzly bear and two cubs kept foraging on a tundra slope near our camp. They never seemed interested in us, and both parties gave each other a wide berth—perhaps between 600 yards and a half mile.

My sister had slept in bear country before, but this did little to soothe Rob's self-described "bearanoia." I wanted either the guide or me to stay behind since we'd both encountered Alaskan browns before, but Trevor insisted it would be fine and came with me, leaving the group with bear spray and instructions for the satellite device we used to text each other.

On a scramble up slippery boulders, the exploration party got the text message we least wanted to see: "BEARS IN CAMP." We rolled down the slope we just climbed, desperate to return in case help was needed. At the same time, we took a circuitous route: Willow thickets boxed in our camp on the most direct approach, and we couldn't risk surprising the bears and making a fraught situation worse. We ran into Rob and Elissa on this detour; they pointed out where mom and cubs retreated, far up a mountainous slope to a cave where they denned. It was striking how chill they were—especially after I learned what transpired.

While Elissa napped in her tent, Rob climbed a high ridge to attempt to relax with a crossword puzzle. He looked up and over at camp and saw nothing, then focused on solving the mysteries of Will Shortz. When he next looked up several minutes later, mother and cubs were sniffing at the foot of my sister's tent.

"One can never forget the feeling of being sniffed from a foot away with nothing but nylon between you and a snout," she later told me. Time slowed down for the Grizz (not the bear—Elissa, who earned that nickname early in childhood for her grouchy morning temper).

"Each moment as it happened felt like its own event. My hackles rising, hearing Rob Smith screaming 'Elissa!!! Bears!!!' from a football field away, the moment of deciding to unzip the tent, grab the spray, and look out all at once."

The noise made the bears scoot from camp, and they showed no further interest in these strange visitors. Our guide told us the bears here see so few people that they don't associate us with anything, and mild curiosity almost always becomes aversion. A few days later, we would see a possible papa bear many miles away, fording the wide, shallow Alatna River and appearing the size of his mate and progeny combined. When we reported the encounter to a ranger, she mentioned that other parties in the Arrigetch reported mom and cubs all summer; she never approached, but she always lingered somewhere in the valley.

Encroaching males will often kill cubs when given the chance so the female will go into heat and they can then mate with her. The ranger theorized that the female might be using human presence as a deterrent to males, since bears here typically avoid people whenever they can. She didn't seem to associate humans with anything else, but it still brought concern: As remote as Gates is, more and more people visit every year, bringing increased impacts and unintended consequences with them. They tend to concentrate their presence on Arrigetch Peaks. We had it entirely to ourselves, but that's becoming the exception.

Our experience in Gates with the bears contains all the complicated and conflicting messages and feelings I want to explore in this book, only some of which I fully understand and can express. More will come as I dwell on this memory and others, but a few rise above others. Solitude bears incredible power, but it means little without other people. Everyone deserves to seek out wilderness for its own

A brown bear print stamped into the bank of the Alatna River.

sake, and yet we must allow it to persist and thrive without us. My mind knows I have more to fear from the Grizz than the grizz, but my body doesn't feel that way.

My sincere hope is that you join me in exploring these questions yourself, looking for answers in rocks, trees, and waters untouched and not. Please share them with me and everyone you know.

Let's get hiking.

The Gates expedition crew. From left: Jonathan Pease, Ted Alvarez, Rob Smith, Elissa Alvarez, Travis Dobson.

How to Read This Book

You'll notice there are no maps in this book, and that route descriptions vary in detail. This is by design: The point is to get you inspired to go deeper and fill in the gaps with your own research and preparation. This builds safe, well-rounded adventurers—plus it's fun! Most people who get into trouble or have a less-than-stellar time do so because of a lack of prep or education. There's more than enough here to immerse yourself in any park, but keep going: Once you start, you'll get hooked.

This book is also not a substitute for the essentials of any hike. Do not attempt any hike without a topo map or GPS (better is both), the 10 Essentials, and preferably consultation with experts like park rangers, guides, and other official personnel. Pay close attention to permitting, as rules change often. Make sure to check online before your hike. When in doubt, ask: Always confirm logistics or routes with official NPS material or personnel—third-party sources can be helpful, but many come with errors or outdated information. Also, national parks are sensitive places that experience extreme conditions; trips, trails, and entire parks can be subject to unforeseen closures and restrictions (especially in our era of increased traffic and climate impacts). We've listed each national park's website, which is the best place to start and end your planning process.

The parks in this book are broken into distinct sections. The introduction offers an overview of the park's highlights—you should come away understanding its unique traits, rewards, risks, and character. Some parks contain **Zones of Interest**: whole areas that warrant further exploration and beg you to dive deeper and find your own adventure. Zones often have starter trips, but it's best to break out a map and start exploring. **Hikes** are established routes—self-explanatory, though they vary between official trails and unofficial routes. **Hidden Gems** represent a singular spot, fact, or experience that will blow your mind. Some are clues nudging you to attempt to discover them yourself.

The Rules of Solitude

With parks enduring such high levels of visitation, finding solitude often relies on behavior more than location. Follow these rules for the best chance of skipping out on crowds and finding a pure experience. Some are no-brainers, and others demand you step outside your comfort zone to access their benefits.

1. **Go in shoulder and off-seasons.** Most parks experience one or more high seasons (usually summer, but not always), but few get swamped year-round. Though you may sacrifice access to facilities or certain big-ticket attractions, and certain seasons increase risk or discomfort, this is usually the easiest way to find quiet.
2. **Avoid the weekend.** Another easy one. Monday to Wednesday usually guarantees a drop in visitation anywhere you can think of. This loses some effectiveness in high seasons for some parks, and getting out of the grind is tough for most folks, but it goes a long way to securing permits, parking, and privacy.
3. **Stay the night.** If you're reading this book, you have plans to get out of the car. That's huge: Most park visitors don't, and those that do are usually day hikers. Backpacking helps reduce

company. Most parks maintain permitting systems to further limit crowds, but plan in advance to get them (some offer limited first-come, first-served options).

4. **Go the distance.** Everyone loves short and sweet, but the longer you go, the less likely you are to see people on all but the most popular routes. It's also an opportunity to see gains in exercise and fitness.

5. **Embrace the suck.** Bad weather, route difficulty, challenging access, rough roads or trails—learning how to seek out and enjoy what others suffer through is a solid ticket to finding an empty place. But it's not an excuse to put yourself in danger. Know your abilities and limits, and understand the risks.

6. **Get off the trail.** Leaving the trail and going cross-country can earn you spectacular solitude in the most crowded parks. Many national parks designate cross-country zones for this purpose. But be sure to check in with rangers on permitting and places where this is allowed. Observe Leave No Trace principles, taking extra care to mitigate your impact, and be sure you are a competent navigator. Don't use an off-trail trip as your first opportunity to orienteer with a map, compass, or GPS.

7. **Be map savvy.** Spend lots of time learning how to read and understand trail maps. Learning how to link trails and read terrain on a topo map can unlock all kinds of emptiness. Use official USGS quads or similar. Park maps lack enough detail for all but the most casual hikes.

8. **Look for wilderness substitutes.** Parks rarely exist in isolation from other wildlands. They're typically surrounded by national monuments and forests, state parks, BLM land, and wilderness areas that feature many of the same attributes with fewer crowds. Prominent examples include Gros Ventre (Grand Teton), Never Summer (Rocky), Cedar Breaks (Bryce), and Cumberland Gap (Smokies).

Acadia National Park

Maine | nps.gov/acad | Visitation: 3,879,890

When I lived in concrete-bound New York City, stepping over pizza rats on the subways or squinting at the sliver of sky between skyscrapers, I first caught a true whiff of the wild I was missing from out West in Maine's Acadia National Park.

Located primarily on Mount Desert Island but spread between the mainland and nineteen islands on Maine's coast, the oldest national park in the eastern United States isn't Yellowstone east of the Mississippi. But it has a grandeur you can't find anywhere else: sweeping vistas of jagged cliffs plunging into the crashing surf of the Atlantic, serene forests cloaking tranquil ponds, and lofty summits boasting views of a craggy coastline dotted with picturesque lighthouses.

Acadia owes its spectacle to the ancient collisions and cataclysms that inform its geology. Volcanic activity forged Acadia's rocky bones over 500 million years ago. Thick ice sheets covered the resulting granites, shales, and basalts that form the park's complex bedrock over the last 2 to 3 million years, peaking 18,000 years ago. The glacier's geologically speedy retreat left the terrain of gray and pink granite cliffs, rounded bare mountaintops, and U-shaped valleys we see now. Piles of rock, sandy and cobbled beaches ground from stone, and large sentinel boulders known as erratics remain today to mark their passage, scooped out and dropped in place by the frozen hands of the last ice age.

Cadillac Mountain, famously the tallest mountain on the Eastern Seaboard and the first spot to see the sunrise, owes its profile and popularity to these processes. Somes Sound is also frequently referred to as the only place in the eastern United States where one can witness the deep, steep, glacially carved valleys filled with water known as fjords. (Technically, Acadia's more gentle, sloping sides and lack of depth classify them as fjards.)

This dramatic geology sets the stage for a wealth of biodiversity. From the intertidal zones to the coniferous and deciduous forests, Acadia's theater of life stays active throughout the year. White-tailed deer amble through the piney understory, while peregrine falcons launch from cliff faces to trace arcs and dive in the sky above at speeds faster than any other animal. Though rarely seen, moose, lynx, bobcats, and black bears patrol the forest's secluded reaches, while tide pools along the craggy coast nurture a vibrant, miniature world of starfish, anemones, periwinkles, barnacles, and crabs. Each season ushers in a new cast of characters, from the migratory birds of summer to the seals and whales that frequent the park's waters in the colder months. (In summer, you might catch an adorable, clownish puffin bopping around on the outer islands.)

Cadillac Mountain is the first place in the United States to see the sunrise.

Acadia also serves up heaps of human history. Native Wabanaki people hunted, fished, and tilled the soil for over 12,000 years. They etched their presence into the landscape, leaving shell middens and tool fragments. European colonization brought severe change: Forests were felled for timber, mountains mined for granite, and fishing settlements soon speckled the coastline.

By the late nineteenth century, America's elite transformed Mount Desert Island into a summer haven, building grand cottages. John D. Rockefeller Jr. himself laid the foundation for the park's iconic carriage roads, which today offer visitors a tranquil journey through the heart of Acadia.

Influential figures like George Dorr, the "Father of Acadia," and philanthropist Rockefeller championed protection for the area. Both donated significant swaths of land, and their efforts helped create the first national park east of the Mississippi, originally christened Lafayette National Park in 1919 before adopting Acadia in 1929.

Each year, droves of nature enthusiasts swarm what is effectively a pocket park—at 50,000 acres, it's one of the smallest. Parking lots fill up fast in summer, and leaf peepers revel in autumn's fiery hues of orange, red, and gold. And who can fault them? In the same day you can disappear into a golden forest, top out on a peak with a seaside view, and enjoy a delicious crustacean plucked not far from the tide pool you just poked around in. Consider the lobster roll, served with a side of deep nature.

But despite its popularity, there are opportunities aplenty to carve out pockets of solitude, especially for those willing to take on some of the more strenuous options on the park's 125 miles of trail. Few visitors venture beyond sightseeing along the 27 miles of the Frederick Law Olmsted–designed Park Loop Road. Even popular trails like the Precipice, Jordan Cliffs, or Valley Cove, while demanding, offer rewards worthy of their challenge and breaks from road-bound throngs.

But with a little effort and know-how, you can catch a bigger whiff of wilderness in Acadia that approaches the best of the West.

ZONES OF INTEREST

Schoodic Peninsula

The Schoodic Peninsula is Acadia National Park's only portion on the mainland, situated an hour's drive northeast from busy Mount Desert Island (or MDI in Mainer). While it shares the same dramatic geology as Mount Desert Island, only 10 percent of park visitors ever see Schoodic's rugged coastline, dense spruce and fir forests, pink granite outcroppings, and stirring ocean views. A 6-mile, one-way loop road that winds around the peninsula gives you easy access to photo ops, 7 miles of hiking trails, and picnic areas.

Schoodic Point, at the peninsula's southern tip, provides a front-row seat to the raw power of the Atlantic Ocean. With no reefs or barrier islands to slow them, waves crash against the granite coastline at full speed. It's an excellent spot for picnicking,

Without barrier islands or reefs to protect the shore, Schoodic Peninsula absorbs open-ocean waves at full speed.

bird-watching, or absorbing the hypnotic rhythms of the sea. In contrast, the short, family-friendly Wonderland Trail deposits you on a protected, rocky beach with excellent tide pools to explore at low tide.

Isle au Haut

The 10,000-acre "high island" sees 25 percent of the park's visitors. With fewer than eighty residents, the teensy namesake lobster town offers little in the way of amenities beyond a general store and a single seasonal food truck. But 18 miles of silent, mixed-use trails take hikers to the barren beaches, thick woods, and sea-sprayed cliffs that typify Acadia.

Isolation comes with a catch. The island is located 6 miles south into the Atlantic from the mainland, so visitors first need to get to Stonington (1.5 hours from Bar Harbor); you'll then hop one of two tiny mailboats (*Mink* or *Otter*). The boat lands in the town harbor year-round and Duck Harbor seasonally from May to October. Duck Harbor is your best bet to get immersed in the island's best scenery right away. There are no cars on the island; all locomotion is by foot or bike.

HIKES

Bald Peak and Parkman, Gilmore, and Sargent Mountain Loop

Buckle up: This grand loop summits four thrilling peaks in 5.4 miles, but eastern Mount Desert Island crowds largely stay away because of its leg-crunching ascents and descents that'll have your knees begging for mercy. Still, the scenery is worth every bit of toil.

Begin at the Lower Hadlock Pond parking area and head toward the Bald Peak trailhead, where a steep uphill climb will set your heart racing and soon deposit you on 974-foot Bald Peak. Drink in the distant views of islands dotting Somes Sound before pressing on to Parkman Mountain. The trail meanders along the ridge, treating you to wide views of the peaks ahead of you and Penobscot and Cedar Swamp Mountains to the east.

Having planted your flag on Parkman Mountain, descend gently on the Grandgent Trail for a bit before a tough section brings you to open 1,036-foot Gilmore Peak. Descend once again, this time toward the giant of your journey, Sargent Mountain.

The hump to Sargent requires you to push through encroaching trees and branches over rough, uneven trails. But your final summit puts you atop Acadia's second-highest peak (1,373 feet) and rewards you with sweeping views of eastern MDI highlights Cadillac, Jordan Pond, and the Bubbles erratics against the backdrop of Somes Sound and the western peaks beyond.

To return to your starting point, proceed southeast from the Sargent Mountain summit. Here you'll find the Grandgent Trail that connects to the Hadlock Brook Trail, a more leisurely route through forests and alongside streams. It offers a calm finish to a challenging hike, leading you back to Lower Hadlock Pond.

Sargent Mountain is the second-tallest peak in Acadia.

Beech Mountain via the Valley Trail

While Beech Mountain and its old fire tower remain a popular summit to bag, tackling it on the longer Valley Trail/Beech South Ridge Trail gives you more privacy and access to an entrancing forest for only a few more miles (3.6 round-trip).

Begin at the Valley trailhead, accessible from the Park Loop Road. Start hiking south, and soon you'll find the trail gradually climbing through a lush hardwood and spruce forest marked by large, moss-covered boulders.

As you continue along the Valley Trail, you'll encounter a fork. Take the right path toward Beech South Ridge Trail, where you'll conquer most of your incline for the day. Shortly, you'll find yourself on the south ridge of Beech Mountain, standing 839 feet above sea level. Pause for a moment to catch your breath under the disused fire tower (it's typically closed) and appreciate the sweeping views of Long Pond, Somes Sound, and the Cranberry Isles and Isle au Haut dotting the Atlantic Ocean beyond. Return by going north on the busier Beech Mountain Trail.

The Perpendicular Trail to Mansell Mountain

The Perpendicular Trail up Mansell Mountain is an exciting and challenging alternative to the dizzying Precipice Trail on the island's east side. Known for its unique human-made elements—including iron ladders and a stone stairway—the Perpendicular Trail offers an excellent mix of history, physical challenge, and rewarding views.

Get to the parking area near the Long Pond trailhead and begin hiking on the Cold Brook Trail, following it for 0.2 mile to reach the start of the Perpendicular Trail, which routes you toward the Mansell Mountain summit.

The Perpendicular Trail lives up to its name. In a short 1.3 miles, you'll ascend 1,000 feet. What makes this trail particularly unique is the stone stairway, a remarkable feat of trail engineering. Constructed during the Great Depression, the Civilian Conservation Corps built 300 stairs as part of a project to create jobs and stimulate economic recovery. They provide hikers with a steep but manageable ascent.

Beech Mountain gives you sweeping views of Somes Sound, the Cranberry Islands, and beyond.

As you ascend, you'll pass through forests of spruce and fir, cross chattering brooks, and skirt boulders and rock ledges, creating a diverse and engaging trek.

After you've mastered the stairs and a little more uphill trudging, you'll reach the junction with the Mansell Mountain Trail. From here, it's a short climb to the summit, sitting at 949 feet. The summit is mostly forested, so look out for a spur below it that leads to an overlook of Long Pond.

After admiring the views, continue over the summit and descend via the Mansell Mountain Trail. This trail will lead you to the Great Notch Trail. A right turn on the Great Notch Trail will bring you to the Long Pond Trail. Turning right on the Long Pond Trail will take you back to the trailhead and your starting point.

Western Head/Cliff Trail Loop

Immerse yourself in Isle au Haut's isolation while touring this mellow 3.6-mile loop's secluded pocket coves and jagged seaside cliffs. You can begin from either behind the campground at the Duck Harbor Landing or the ranger station near the town landing.

Secluded Duck Harbor on Isle au Haut is one of the quietest places in Acadia.

From the ranger station, head southwest on the main road for 1.5 miles until you reach the trailhead for the Western Head Trail. This trail will take you through a dense spruce forest before the terrain starts to open to coastal views.

After 2 miles, you'll reach the Western Head, a rocky outcrop that offers breathtaking views of the Atlantic Ocean afar and pounding surf and sea breezes.

Continuing from the Western Head, you'll connect with the Cliff Trail, which bounces along the cliff tops. The Cliff Trail can be narrow and rough in places, with some minor rock scrambles. The path winds through dense forest, skirts tidal pools, and leads you across ledges with more dramatic ocean views.

Follow the Cliff Trail until you meet the Western Head Road. From here, it's an easy 1.5-mile walk back to the ranger station.

HIDDEN GEM

For most, hiking Isle au Haut consists of one day bookended by choppy-if-scenic boat rides. But lucky people can camp overnight at the **Duck Harbor Campground,** which has five sites limited to six people. Three-sided lean-to shelters provide a roof, floor, and an accompanying picnic table and fire ring. There's a water pump and composting toilet, but otherwise this is a primitive backcountry experience. For a step up in amenities and uniqueness, you can also book a stay at the Robinson Point Lighthouse. Both options deliver sweeping, stay-awhile views of the sea and some of the best night skies on the East Coast.

Arches National Park

Utah | nps.gov/arch | Visitation: 1,482,045

Arches does what it says on the tin: over 2,000 arches, the greatest density in the entire world. There are bigger, wilder, and emptier desert parks, but few have the capacity to transform casual visitors into aspiring desert rats so quickly. Majesty abounds the minute you crest the park road and round onto its elevated plateau.

The otherworldly red-rock moonscape of Arches National Park, situated in eastern Utah just beyond the Colorado border, contains more than arches. Stone spires reach toward the heavens, massive balanced rocks teeter precariously on eroded pedestals, and expansive rock fins form surreal labyrinths.

Arches' gritty past began around 300 million years ago when a salt bed formed beneath the current region as an ancient sea evaporated. Over time, sediment washed down to cover the salt bed and harden into rock. The unstable salt layer shifted and buckled under the weight, pushing the rock into domes and basins. Water and ice, heat and cold all worked to sculpt these layers into the fantastical landforms we see today.

You can see the beginnings of this formation in desert varnish—the black streaks that mark where water begins pouring down cliff faces. They point to where water sneaks into cavities and freezes, breaking off chunks of sandstone bit by bit until a hunk of rock becomes a fin and then an arch. If the beginning of an arch happens over thousands and even millions of years, we can often see the end of an arch in real time. In 1991, a huge section cleaved off the bottom of 300-foot Landscape Arch, the longest arch in the world. And in 2008, Wall Arch crumbled completely; now it's a pile of ruddy boulders under open sky and a broken bridge.

In between the rocks life persists, tenacious and diverse. Juniper and pinyon pine find root in harsh terrain, providing shelter for creatures like the kangaroo rat and desert cottontail rabbit. Red-tailed hawks and golden eagles soar high above the rock formations, their keen eyes scanning for rodents. In this stark environment, the most minute forms of life—a lichen, a beetle, a lizard—feel like a small miracle.

If you look down, you'll also see impressive canyon formations in miniature. The bumpy, brown and green and black fuzzy undulations found in patches of sand is a living soil composed of algae, lichens, mosses, and bacteria. Known as cryptobiotic crust, it can take hundreds of years to form. Admire but take special care not to step on it.

Double Arch glows under some of the darkest skies in the country.

Arches has been a crossroads for thousands of years. Ancient Puebloans left their mark in the form of petroglyphs, while later Ute and Paiute tribes passed through the region. In more recent history, ranchers, prospectors, and settlers arrived, adding their own chapters to the story.

Most trails in Arches are short but rewarding: Less than 50 miles of trail cross the park, and backcountry opportunities are limited. You'll be sharing trails most of the time. Still, the iconic Delicate Arch Trail is a must-do for newcomers. For all the tourists who visit, the view that ended up on Utah license plates and state line welcome signs retains all its power in person, usually silhouetted against bluebird skies with the white La Sal peaks cresting on the horizon.

Most desert parks dwarf Arches, a scant 76,000 acres, by a wide margin, and its proximity to I-70 and charming Moab makes finding solitude a challenge. Crowding has gotten so intense that as of spring 2022, reservations are required for drive-in visitors to the park (you can always bike in). Timed-entry tickets to enter Arches National Park for the month of April are typically released in January of each year.

Spring and fall are the most comfortable seasons for exploring, with milder temperatures and swelling crowds. The massses continue into summer's intense heat, but winter can offer a uniquely serene experience, with snow-dusted arches and crisp, clear skies.

ZONES OF INTEREST

Fiery Furnace

Fiery Furnace's labyrinth of narrow sandstone canyons contains towering sandstone formations, deep fissures, and secret arches, offering one of the most unique and adventurous experiences in the park away from the selfie-sticked crowds. But there's a catch: Access requires a permit, which you can get from the Arches Visitor Center, or a ranger-guided tour. The ranger-led tours are recommended, especially for first-time visitors, as the route's complex maze-like structure can be quite challenging and easy to get lost in.

Fiery Furnace's maze-like passages require scrambling experience and patience to navigate.

Inside, you'll weave through narrow slot canyons, some of which open into hidden amphitheaters. High above, blue sky creates a stark contrast to the deep oranges and reds of the sandstone (from whence the area gets its name when it glows at sunset). At your feet, small pockets of lush green vegetation persist in miniature oases.

Hiking here involves scrambling over sandstone, navigating narrow passages, and hopping across gaps. The total distance is 2 miles with moderate elevation gain, but the tough terrain and slow pace can make the hike last 2 to 3 hours or more. But you'll also get the chance to see rarely glimpsed Surprise Arch and creepy Skull Arch.

HIKES

Tower Arch

Tucked away in the Klondike Bluffs region, Tower Arch delivers an off-the-beaten-path trek through diverse landscapes to a classic, quiet arch in an otherwise bustling park.

Start at the Klondike Bluffs parking area, accessed via a 10-mile dirt road off Salt Valley Road. The road is usually passable with a regular passenger vehicle, but after heavy rains, a high-clearance vehicle may be necessary.

Hulking Tower Arch remains off the beaten path at the end of a rough dirt road.

The trail's 3.4-mile showstopper loop takes hikers on a dynamic trail through a few steep and rocky sections, sandy patches, and the occasional moderate scramble. Depending on your pace and how often you stop to enjoy the scenery, plan for around 2 to 3 hours round-trip.

You start in an expansive high desert terrain scattered with sagebrush and junipers, set against a backdrop of red and orange sandstone formations. As you ascend a sand hill, the landscape transitions into dramatic fins and boulders. Along the trail, you'll see the Marching Men—a group of tall, isolated fins that resemble a procession of soldiers—and the Parade of Elephants, a rock formation that, with a bit of imagination, looks like a line of pachyderms strung trunk-to-tail.

The trail ultimately winds through a series of more inspiring rock formations to reveal Tower Arch. The arch itself spans 92 feet and stands 43 feet high. Its name comes from the towering sandstone pinnacles flanking either side. Depending on the time of day, the arch and towers glow in the warm hues of the sun.

Sand Dune Arch

This delightful, family-friendly hike leads through a slot canyon to Sand Dune Arch, another impressive example nestled between towering sandstone fins. You'll find the trailhead just past the turnoff for the Delicate Arch, located in a large parking area. The relatively short length (0.3 mile) and easy terrain make this jaunt perfect for families with young children.

The trail meanders into a gap between large sandstone fins to reach a patch of soft, red sand deposited over time from the eroding sandstone. The trail ends at the Sand Dune Arch, a small but picturesque arch tucked in the fins' shadows. All the loose sand gives younger visitors a chance to play in a fun, natural sandbox. The tall fins provide some shade and create a cooler microclimate, making this hike a great option on hot days.

The Primitive Loop at Devil's Garden

While Devil's Garden is the longest trail in the park at 7.9 miles and quite popular, crowds drop off beyond Landscape Arch at 1.6 miles. Starting from the Devil's Garden trailhead, the route follows

Devil's Garden Primitive Loop features sandstone ramps with steep drop-offs.

The Milky Way rising behind iconic Delicate Arch.

the main trail to Landscape Arch before veering onto the Primitive Trail. As its name suggests, the Primitive Trail is more rugged and less marked than the park's other trails, and continuing requires decent route-finding skills and comfort scrambling past drop-offs and balancing on slim fins. Your reward is another selection of arches and rock formations few see, including the brooding Dark Angel tower.

HIDDEN GEM

While throngs flock to see Delicate Arch at all times of day (photographers especially prize the golden glow of sunrise and sunset), the park is open 24 hours. Catching **Delicate Arch at midnight** gives night owls a chance to have the most famous hunk of rock in the Southwest to themselves. Finish dinner in Moab, fill your thermoses with coffee, and prepare to see this icon as few do: silhouetted against a sugary Milky Way or bathed in soft moonlight.

Sun sets on the distinctive eroding cliffs of South Dakota's Badlands National Park.

Badlands National Park

South Dakota | nps.gov/badl | Visitation: 1,046,400

Every culture to encounter this forbidding crossing—Lakota, French, Spanish, American—cursed it with a name translating to "Badlands." Understandable: Imagine crossing the wavy, rolling prairies of what is now South Dakota on foot or horse for days only to encounter a sinking maze of crumbling gullies, sinkholes, chasms, and hills striped in eerie colors.

Sprawling across 244,000 acres in South Dakota, Badlands National Park's moniker may come from an epithet. But while cursing under their breath at the prospect of crossing it, early visitors must've also been overwhelmed by its austere beauty. Over millennia, the forces of water and wind shaped sedimentary layers of clay, sand, and silt into a spectacle of buttes, pinnacles, and spires. Ranging in colors from subtle pastels to vibrant reds and oranges, these layered formations come alive when the low-angled light of sunrise and sunset paints them in an ethereal glow.

The oldest layer, the inky Pierre Shale, was an ocean floor when dinosaurs roamed 65 to 70 million years ago. The clay, silt, and sand that settled onto that ancient bottom compressed and solidified into the shale we see today. In its dim recesses, the Pierre Shale harbors the remnants of ammonites and baculites—early marine mollusks that once drifted lazily through those prehistoric waters.

Resting atop that are the Yellow Mounds, remnants of yet another sea that gradually receded, creating marshes that trapped and preserved plants and animals in layers of sediment. Aged between 34 and 37 million years, their warm hues pop against the landscape in a watercolor wash of ochre, mustard, and lemon. The color derives from an iron-hydroxide mineral called goethite.

The fossil-rich Brule Formation constitutes the final section. Its crumbly, chalk-like facade comes in shades of gray, tan, and white. About 30 to 34 million years old, this formation owes its existence to the tumultuous rivers and floodplains of the Oligocene. These torrents drowned, washed away, and otherwise collected fossils that give us glimpses into the lives of the large mammals of that era: ancient horses, camels, rhinoceroses, and saber-toothed cats. Each layer contains a paleontological playground where important discoveries are made every year.

The inhospitable badlands host plenty of life forms. Prairie dogs chatter in expansive colonies, bison and pronghorns graze on the mixed-grass prairie, and bighorn sheep scale the rugged terrain with ease. Birds find refuge here—hawks soar overhead, while songbirds add melody to the windswept landscape. The more than sixty species of tall and short grasses preserved on half of the park's terrain serve as a relic, too: Though we think of the Midwest as prairie country, the kind that once dominated the interior United States is nearly gone.

Human history goes back at least 11,000 years. The ancestors of Indigenous Lakota Sioux lived and hunted here, following the rhythms of the land. Later, homesteaders arrived, lured by the promise of free land, only to struggle against the harsh conditions in these "starvation claims." The park also has a more recent history as a bombing range during World War II.

Modern visitors to Badlands National Park will find a variety of experiences to suit their tastes. For the adventurous, there are trails that offer intimate encounters with the park's unique formations, such as the Notch Trail or Castle Trail. The short Fossil Exhibit Trail gives visitors the easiest way to travel through time (and spy a saber-tooth skull). The Badlands Loop Road offers stunning views for those who prefer to explore by car.

The park is open year-round. Spring brings wildflowers and newborn bison. Summer, though hot, is the most popular time to visit. (This isn't the beach or a glacier, but don't forget your sunscreen: I experienced one of the worst sunburns of my life on an all-day hike when I idiotically forgot it.) Fall offers cooler temperatures and vibrant colors, while winter presents a stark beauty, with snow accentuating the park's contours.

The Wall, a prominent 60-mile-long escarpment, divides the park into North and South units, each at different elevations. The North contains the most trails, but the South (also called Stronghold) and Palmer Creek Unit offer remote backcountry experiences.

Any hiker who gets lost within the strata of time at Badlands can't help but feel acutely aware of the procession of time and the ways it shifts physical matter, always adding or subtracting: rock, dirt, bone. It took 500,000 years for erosion to reveal the badlands, at one inch per year. And they aren't permanent: In another 500,000 years they'll be gone.

ZONE OF INTEREST

The Badlands region, especially the area known as **the Stronghold Unit**, is of significant cultural and historical importance to the Oglala Lakota people. Before European colonization, the Great Plains region was home to many Native American tribes, including the Lakota, who relied on the land's resources for their livelihoods and emerged as the dominant tribe in the region as colonists arrived.

The relationship between the Oglala Lakota Tribe and the Badlands is rooted in centuries of history, cultural significance, and ongoing stewardship. It's rich and complex, and often fraught with tensions both modern and historical.

The Lakota consider all the Black Hills, including the Badlands, as *Paha Sapa*: a sacred homeland from which all their people

The Stronghold Unit hosted the Ghost Dance, a spiritual movement among Native American tribes in the late nineteenth century.

originated. The landscape features in their creation stories, and certain areas within the park, including sites not accessible to the public, are used for traditional ceremonies and spiritual practices.

In the 1868 Fort Laramie Treaty, the US government promised the Lakota ownership of the Black Hills. However, after the discovery of gold, the United States reneged on the treaty and forcibly removed the Lakota to reservations, leading to the Black Hills War of 1876–1877.

In 1976, a significant portion of the Badlands was returned to the Oglala Lakota Tribe but is jointly managed with the National Park Service. This area, known as the South Unit, comprises the Stronghold and Palmer Creek Units. The park service and the tribe have a Memorandum of Agreement for managing the lands, with the goal of developing it into the first Tribal National Park.

The Oglala Lakota's relationship with the Badlands today is characterized by ongoing efforts to preserve their cultural heritage, protect sacred sites, and manage the land in a way that respects their traditions and the ecosystem. While progress has been made, issues like resource management, land rights, and economic development continue to pose challenges.

HIKES

Saddle Pass Trail

This trail offers adventure wrapped in a short, 0.7-mile round-trip hike. Find the marked trailhead in the Badlands National Park's eastern section, along the Badlands Loop Road (Highway 240), between the Burns Basin Overlook and Conata Picnic Area.

The trail begins on flat prairie before abruptly ascending the Badlands Wall, cutting through the layers of sedimentary rock and giving hikers the chance to climb 200 feet up through the geological story of this place. The path can be steep and slippery with loose gravel, making it a moderate to strenuous hike despite its short length.

Absorb Badlands geology on a short but steep climb up Saddle Pass.

As you climb, you'll have close views of the peculiarly eroded buttes and pinnacles characteristic of the park, while the panorama of the vast prairie lands stretches out behind you.

At the top of the Saddle Pass Trail, you'll reach a junction with the Castle Trail and the Medicine Root Trail, giving you an opportunity to extend your hike. The Castle Trail offers a longer, moderately challenging hike through mixed-grass prairie and striking badland formations, while the Medicine Root Trail winds through the prairie lands, where you might spot grazing bison and prairie dogs.

Medicine Root Trail

Starting at the Saddle Pass trailhead along the Badlands Loop Road (Highway 240), the moderate Medicine Root Loop weaves through the mixed-grass prairie ecosystem for 4 miles round-trip, distinguishing it from the typical badlands scenery dominated by rocky formations.

The trail begins by intertwining with the Castle Trail and then diverges southward, leading you across the undulating prairie. The flat trail makes for a pleasant, leisurely walk that traverses a sweeping sea of prairie grasses that shift in color with the seasons—from vibrant greens in the spring to golden hues in the fall. Patches of wildflowers, such as prairie roses and coneflowers, add splashes of color to the landscape.

As you traverse this trail, keep an eye out for bison grazing in the distance, prairie dogs chattering near their burrows, or hawks soaring overhead. If you're lucky, you might catch a glimpse of a coyote or a badger.

The trail ends as it rejoins the Castle Trail, which you can follow back to the trailhead or extend to explore more of the park's geological marvels.

Sheep Mountain Table

Sheep Mountain Table is one of the more remote and less-traveled hikes in Badlands National Park, offering a unique chance to experience the park's scenic beauty in relative solitude.

The trail is in the Stronghold Unit of the park, which is co-managed with the Oglala Lakota Tribe and situated within the Pine Ridge Indian Reservation. Access to this part of the park requires driving down a series of gravel and dirt roads. The dirt road leading to Sheep Mountain Table can become impassable in wet conditions, and a high-clearance vehicle is recommended.

Bighorn sheep graze on the tallgrass prairie.

From the trailhead, the hike to the top of Sheep Mountain Table is 7 miles round-trip. The trail is primarily a flat, dirt road that takes you atop the large namesake mesa. While the hike doesn't involve a significant elevation change, its length can make it challenging for some.

As you trek along the trail, you'll be treated to an immersive experience of the Badlands' unique geology and wide-open vistas. You'll encounter mixed-grass prairies, rugged badlands formations, and a diversity of plant life. This part of the park pops in the spring when wildflowers burst into bloom.

Panoramic views from atop Sheep Mountain Table offer sweeping, miles-long vistas of the Badlands on clear days. At such distances, the jagged peaks, deep canyons, and expansive prairies become otherworldly.

Unlike the park's main unit, this area doesn't have established visitor facilities, so ensure you bring all necessities, including water, food, sun protection, and a map or GPS for navigation. Cell service can be unreliable in this area.

Remember that the Stronghold Unit is on the Pine Ridge Indian Reservation, so be respectful of this fact and adhere to all rules and regulations. There may be areas of cultural significance to the Oglala Lakota Tribe that are off-limits.

HIDDEN GEM

Badlands is the rare Lower 48 park where going off trail is often encouraged—and it brings rewards in the form of solitude and plentiful wildlife. For self-sufficient and experienced backpackers, the 22-mile, three-day **Sage Creek Wilderness Loop** has all that and more. *Caution:* You'll need excellent route-finding, map, and GPS navigation skills, and you must bring in all your water.

The description that follows is merely a rough selection of potential destinations and landmarks; navigating your way there and carving your own path is part of the discovery. Find the trailhead at the Conata Picnic Area and head southwest through high prairie while surrounded by iconic badlands spires for a few miles.

Disappear into the Badlands on the largely off-trail Sage Creek Loop.

After a few more miles, you will reach Deer Haven, an oasis of junipers in the largely treeless landscape. Camp here, and on day two climb a narrow ridge to stand atop The Wall. Descend and venture into the prairie of Sage Creek Basin proper, which you'll cross for a bit more than 3 miles. Hike west from here into Tyree Basin, and spend the next night here.

For your final day, find a gap in the badlands formations: This is Sage Creek Pass, which after crossing will deliver you to a fence line you can follow until you reach a north–south fence line you'll need to duck under to continue. Drop into Conata Basin for your final 3-ish miles of hiking back to the Conata Picnic Area.

Ocotillo ("little torch" in Spanish) blooms red from March to June in Big Bend.

Big Bend National Park

Texas | nps.gov/bibe | Visitation: 509,129

Growing up in Texas, I always looked north and westward for wilderness and adventure. Drives for hours in any direction brought suburban lawns, planned communities, golf courses, or gigantic city buildings bounded by concrete rivers jammed with cars. Escape far enough and you'd find rolling farms dotted with cows, or vast plains or rocky scrub and desert—but always cornered by barbed wire or fencing. It was all pretty, but far from wild.

Facts bear this out. Despite its size and famous motto, Texas is in the bottom five states for percentage of public land—more than 95 percent is private.

I never went far west enough. Along the remote southern border of Texas, where the Rio Grande snakes between the United States and Mexico to bisect the Chihuahuan Desert, a rugged set of mountains and river floodplains converge. Here Big Bend National Park preserves stark beauty, rich history, and profound silence in a state where that's in short supply.

Big Bend's geological story is still under construction. But we know it began some 500 million years ago, as sediments deposited by an ancient sea compacted into limestone. Over millions of years, volcanic activity, uplifting, and erosion sculpted the terrain into a diverse topography that includes the jagged peaks of the Chisos Mountains and the sunbaked limestone canyons of the desert. The park holds a fossil record that spans millennia, featuring dinosaur bones and sea creature imprints that tell a story of constant transformation.

Native peoples inhabited this region for thousands of years, leaving behind rock art, artifacts, and structures. The Comanche Trail, used by Native American tribes for trade and travel, cuts through Big Bend. Spanish explorers and missionaries arrived in the sixteenth century, followed by ranchers and miners who all left their mark on the landscape.

The crossroads of multiple climate zones in the vast Chihuahuan Desert supports hardy yucca, prickly pear, and ocotillo plants that splash green against the tawny desert sand, blooming vibrantly in spring. This desert gives way to the greener, cooler highlands of the Chisos Mountains and stands of juniper, oak, and pinyon pine. Along the Rio Grande, the riparian ecosystem's reeds and willows offer refuge for the park's wildlife.

Javelinas rustle through the underbrush, roadrunners dart across trails, and Mexican black bears chomp on berries. Big Bend is a vital migratory pathway, and over 450 species of birds have been recorded here, from tiny hummingbirds to golden eagles.

Extreme heat and distance from cities mean few visitors stray from Ross Maxwell Scenic Drive. But more than 150 miles of trail serve hikers. Those who stay the night get the best treat: In this International Dark Sky Park, stargazers can revel under an unobstructed and pure celestial dome sprinkled with stars, planets, and the milky streak of a galaxy close and bright enough to touch.

While the heat of summer can be intense, the park thrives in spring and fall when temperatures are milder. Winter also has its own stark charm, with cooler weather and fewer visitors.

When I first arrived in Big Bend, I'd been to wild spaces all over the world. But by gazing into deep time in the rocks that flanked me or the night sky blooming above, I experienced a homecoming of sorts into the wild, beautiful heart of Texas I'd missed.

HIKES

Marufo Vega Trail

The Marufo Vega Trail is a 14-mile loop through rugged desert terrain, with broad views of the Rio Grande and the Sierra del Carmen in Mexico. The trail is strenuous and often desolate; hikers must

Hikers can spy Mexico's Sierra del Carmen range in the distance.

come prepared with plenty of water, sun protection, a detailed map, and considerable self-sufficiency.

Begin your journey at the trailhead near the Boquillas Canyon Overlook, off the main park road. The trail descends immediately into an arroyo, weaving its way through the Dead Horse Mountains' rocky terrain. Early on, you'll encounter a spur trail leading to an overlook of the Rio Grande—an excellent detour if time allows.

Around 3.5 miles in, the trail splits into the loop section. Here, you can choose to go either clockwise or counterclockwise. If you go clockwise, you'll find more shade in the afternoon (helpful in desert heat).

The southern half of the loop brings you closer to the Rio Grande. This portion of the trail provides sweeping views of the river with Mexico's Sierra del Carmen as the backdrop. From the arid, rocky desert landscape, you'll descend into a riverine environment where the Rio Grande glistens under the sun.

The northern half of the loop cuts back into the desert, through the foothills of the Dead Horse Mountains. The terrain here can be strenuous, with several ups and downs, but it offers expansive views of the park and the distant Chisos Mountains.

The two halves of the loop converge back at the split, from where you'll retrace your steps through the arroyo to the trailhead.

Upper Burro Mesa Pouroff

This trail looks unassuming at the beginning but quickly turns into an interesting box canyon before blossoming into a massive rock bowl formed over millions of years. If they time it right, visitors can see water pouring hundreds of feet to fill the pool below. But even dry, the smooth stone bowl astounds.

You'll find the trailhead for Upper Burro Mesa Pouroff off the Ross Maxwell Scenic Drive past the Sotol Vista Overlook when coming from the north.

The round-trip length of the Upper Burro Mesa Pouroff trail is 3.8 miles. The trail first descends into Javelina Wash, then follows the wash uphill into a narrow box canyon before dropping

To catch a spectacular waterfall, hikers should visit Upper Burro Mesa after a heavy rain.

into a slickrock grotto. The trail can be rocky and uneven at times, and a moderate amount of scrambling is required.

Desert scrubland dotted with plants like lechuguilla, ocotillo, yucca, and various types of cacti dominates the route. As you progress, you'll witness a spectacular display of layered sedimentary rock formations, offering shades of red, orange, and brown. The hike ends at the main feature: the Burro Mesa Pouroff itself—a massive cliff where water pours off through a crack during heavy rains, creating a waterfall. It's a dramatic and impressive sight.

Outer Mountain Loop

The Outer Mountain Loop is one of the most challenging and rewarding backpacking routes in Big Bend National Park. It's a three-day, 30-mile journey that will take you through some of the park's most iconic landscapes, from the high Chisos Mountains to the desert lowlands and back.

The journey starts at the Chisos Basin trailhead, located near the park's visitor center. From here, you'll hike along the Pinnacles Trail, climbing steadily through forests of juniper, oak, and pinyon pine. At around 3.8 miles, you'll reach the juncture with the Boot Canyon Trail, where you can take a short detour to see the distinctive Boot Rock formation.

The trail then descends into Juniper Canyon. The vegetation thins as you move lower, transitioning to desert plants like yucca, sotol, and lechuguilla. Seven miles from the trailhead, you'll reach the designated campsites in the Juniper Canyon zone where you can set up camp for the night.

On the second day, you'll continue down Juniper Canyon before linking up with the Dodson Trail. Here, the landscape opens, offering expansive views of the surrounding desert and the distant Chisos. The Dodson Trail is exposed and can get hot, so start early and carry plenty of water.

Around the halfway point of the Dodson Trail, you'll pass Fresno Creek, a potential water source, but it's unreliable and should not be depended on.

The Dodson Trail ends at the Homer Wilson Ranch, a historic site with a blue box that serves as a water cache location (you'll need to stash water here in advance). From here, you'll head up into the Chisos Mountains again via the Blue Creek Trail. This is a tough climb, especially after a long day, but you'll be rewarded with alpine landscapes and cooler temperatures.

There are designated campsites in the Blue Creek zone for your second night. This is also a good place to cache water ahead of time.

The final day of the Outer Mountain Loop is a strenuous uphill hike along the Blue Creek Trail, back into the Chisos Mountains. The red-rock canyon around you slowly gives way to a greener, lush environment as you gain altitude.

The Blue Creek Trail links up with the Laguna Meadow Trail, which will take you back to the Chisos Basin. This final stretch offers some fantastic views of the mountains and the basin below, a fitting end to a challenging journey.

The Outer Mountain Loop is a test of endurance and preparation. Self-sufficiency and awareness of extreme desert conditions remains paramount. Always check in with the park rangers before and after your trip and let someone know your plans.

HIDDEN GEM

Seeing the hidden oasis of **Pine Canyon** at its best requires luck and timing. The seasonal cascade thundering over the sheer walls of Pine Canyon generally flows only after substantial rainfall, which typically occurs during the monsoon season from July to September. The waterfall quickly drains off—a double-edged sword, since the same heavy rains that birth it can render roads muddy and impassable.

Pine Canyon Trail is located off Glenn Spring Road, a rough and rocky dirt road that requires a high-clearance vehicle for safe passage. From Panther Junction Visitor Center, head southeast on the main road, then turn left onto Glenn Spring Road and continue for 6 miles to the Pine Canyon access road, which is marked by a sign. From there, it's another 4 miles to the trailhead.

Pine Canyon Trail's round-trip hike of 4.8 miles typically takes around 3 to 4 hours to complete. The hike begins with a gradual uphill climb through desert scrub and then ascends to the mouth of Pine Canyon over a steep and rocky path.

Initially, you'll traverse open deserts of cacti, yucca, and ocotillo. As the trail ascends, juniper and pinyon pine begin to appear, giving way to a forest of towering ponderosa pines as you reach the

Lush pine canyon's desert oasis bursts with color in the fall.

mouth of the canyon. The higher elevation and cooler, damper conditions here provide a lush contrast to the arid desert below. Even though it's the desert, black bears are often seen here.

The pièce de résistance of the trail comes at the sheer cliff at the end of the canyon where, in the right conditions, a seasonal waterfall plunges dramatically into a rock-strewn basin below. The contrast of the waterfall against the sheer, reddish-brown cliff face framed by the greenery of the canyon makes for a magical sight.

Biscayne National Park

Florida | nps.gov/bisc | Visitation: 571,242

Biscayne's wide expanse of swamps, mangroves, seagrass beds, and coral reefs stretch across forty-two islands at the southern tip of Florida—and most of the time, the Miami skyline punctuates the horizon. This is a place where the line between civilization and wilderness has always blurred.

Threatened and endangered species like the West Indian manatee and the American crocodile sidle up to shipwrecks, lighthouses, and military forts. The park protects a rare combination of aquamarine waters, emerald islands, and fish-bejeweled coral reefs. Evidence of 10,000 years of human history spans prehistoric tribes to pineapple farmers, but it's possible the creation of the park itself resulted in some of our most disagreeable behavior: blimp rides, roads bulldozed out of spite to discourage conservation, and poisoned family dogs.

When the fighting ended in 1968, 173,000-acre Biscayne National Park emerged to protect the third-largest barrier reef system, which hosts over 500 species of fish. Limestone bedrock and fossilized coral reefs showcase an oceanic geology spanning eons.

Since 95 percent of the park is water, hiking boots don't go as far as fishing, boating, or snorkeling. Anglers especially can cast for sport fishing prizes like bonefish, tarpon, grouper, and snapper. Dirt-bound visitors' best bets are the Elliot Key Loop Trail, which offers both Atlantic and bayside views over an easy 1.1-mile out and back, and the Boca Chita Key's 0.5-mile trail, which opens to a secluded cove. Limited first-come, first-served campsites (boat-in only) on both Elliot and Boca Chita give visitors the chance to stargaze and wake up to sunrise on the beach.

ZONE OF INTEREST

Maritime Heritage Trail

Biscayne's premier trail isn't visible. The Maritime Heritage Trail takes you under the park's clear, warm waters, where visibility often exceeds 50 feet. In the only underwater archaeological trail in the park system, snorkelers can explore the remnants of six shipwrecks that span a century and a wide variety of vessel types. Vibrant marine life surrounds the sunken ships, including hard and soft corals, sponges, and a diverse community of fish species.

The six sites on the trail are the *Arratoon Apcar*, *Mandalay*, *Alicia*, *Lugano*, *Erl King*, and *Half Moon*. Each offers a unique opportunity to see a piece of oceangoing history marooned and frozen at the bottom of the sea, now home to a gallery of colorful sea life.

Biscayne's manatees are threatened by boats, habitat loss, and pollution.

The Maritime Heritage Trail is accessible by private boat or by hiring a concession-operated boat. Boat rentals and guided tours are available from the park's Dante Fascell Visitor Center.

The trail can be visited year-round, but the best time is during the summer months when the water is warmest and the sea conditions are usually calmer. It's hotter and tours slow down, but it's also less crowded.

HIDDEN GEM

Completely encircled by Totten and Old Rhodes Keys, the mangrove lined channels in quiet **Jones Lagoon** harbor jellyfish, stingrays, and many kinds of nesting and wading birds, including the rare and unique-looking roseate spoonbill. On a stand-up paddleboard or kayak, paddlers can spy shoals of fish and baby sharks in placid waters sometimes only a few inches deep. Skilled and experienced kayakers can attempt the 7-mile crossing from the mainland, but the nonprofit Biscayne National Park Institute offers guided tours.

Look for baby sharks in Jones Lagoon's mangrove nurseries.

Black Canyon of the Gunnison National Park

Colorado | nps.gov/blca | Visitation: 357,069

Picture the famous canyons of the American Southwest, and the mind journeys to mile-wide vistas of striated, terraced sandstone piled like layer cakes to meet the horizon. At sunset or sunrise, the stone glows in hues of salmon and tangerine and chalk, begging for someone to pose on a promontory with arms outstretched into the endless rising blue.

Colorado's Black Canyon of the Gunnison feels more like a forbidding fortress where mythical quests go to die. Peer over the edge and you'll see vertical black monoliths of gneiss and schist riven with pinkish pegmatite streaking the walls like lightning frozen in place. If you squint 2,500 feet below, you'll see the foamy green seam of the Gunnison River dropping an average of 34 feet per mile. At the top, the canyon narrows to a span just over a thousand feet; at the river, the canyon walls contract to 40 feet across—tight enough to pin a school bus in midair. There are deeper canyons and steeper canyons, but few this steep and deep.

And there are few that are this dark: In some spots, the sun shines on the canyon floor for barely 30 minutes a day, earning this slit in the earth its evocative and unnerving name. If the Grand Canyon's signature trait is size, then Black Canyon's is sheer impenetrability.

Those barriers to entry stem from the ultra-hard gneiss and schist bedrock, which has largely foiled water, wind, and time for eons. Baked and pressurized in the earth's guts 1.8 billion years ago, metamorphic stone was thrust upward 60 million years ago by the same forces that created the immense earthen platform known as the Colorado Plateau. Around 30 million years ago, large volcanoes erupted on either side of the uplifted plateau, burying it in ash that would compress into a layer of light and soft rock called tuff. Trickles of rain became rivers like the Gunnison. It took the Gunnison 2 million years to carve its way through some of the oldest rock in North America, adding about an inch every hundred years.

The canyon didn't let up for people. Only its rims show evidence of human occupation; the Ute people who lived in the area since well before written history avoided the inner canyon. Common sense played a part: Why risk tumbling off a ledge or into a thicket of poison ivy the size of a tree when all the key resources could be found in riparian areas along the rim or downstream beyond the canyon?

At its slimmest, Black Canyon narrows to 40 feet across.

Early trappers stuck to those areas, but prospectors and miners began to probe the canyon in search of gold and minerals. The first recorded exploration of the canyon was by Captain John Williams Gunnison in 1853, but his crew was rebuffed and spread the word that it was impassable. The river took his name, but it would be another sixty-three years before a determined Grand Canyon adventurer and photographer named Ellsworth Kolb would "shoot the rapids" and traverse the whole thing. It took him four tries and multiple smashed boats before he pulled his boat out to glory at Delta Bridge.

Ellsworth's expedition came at a time when competing interests had already arrived to tame the impassable Black Canyon. His focus on recreation and ecology (and his dedication to recording it all with cumbersome photographic equipment like the "cinematograph") helped the canyon's natural and geological potential overcome trains, tunnels, irrigation projects, and other extractive and industrial interests to become a national monument in 1933 and a national park in 1999.

Beyond preserving access, this also safeguards the diverse plant and animal communities that have a much easier time navigating the canyon than we do. On the canyon rims, pinyon pine, juniper, and scrub oak create a habitat for mule deer, bobcats, and coyotes. Black bears, elk, bighorn sheep, and mountain lions roam the higher elevations, hidden among the aspen and spruce-fir forests. River otters and beavers frequent both the riparian areas and the river bottom. Birds of prey, including the peregrine falcon, fly above the canyon, while the Gunnison River's cold, clear waters shelter a gold-medal fishery for rainbow and brown trout.

Black Canyon's intimidating natural fortifications and remote location keep it relatively low on the popularity list. But with a bit of Ellsworth-ian boldness, adventurers can experience the chasm in its purest state and feel as if they are the first human to enter its inky depths.

ZONES OF INTEREST

South Rim

Like the Grand Canyon, a visit to Black Canyon of the Gunnison is divided into the South Rim or the North Rim; like the Grand, most visitors go to the South.

The South Rim gives you the best view of two of the best-known showcases of tumultuous, grinding erosion: the Painted Wall and the Giant's Staircase. Compared to the yawning Grand Canyon, visitors can glimpse both in surprising intimacy thanks to the tightness of the canyon walls.

The iconic, visually striking Painted Wall is named for the streaks of intrusive igneous pegmatite crosshatching the cliff face. They formed over a billion years ago, when molten rock intruded into existing hard gneiss and schist, then cooled and crystallized into large-grained minerals like quartz, feldspar, and mica. At about 2,250 feet from river to rim, this towering rock face stands as the highest cliff in Colorado, topping the Empire State Building by 800 feet.

To view the Painted Wall, stop by the Painted Wall View along South Rim Road. You can access the overlook via a paved, generally wheelchair-accessible trail 250 yards from the parking area.

From this vantage point, you can also see the Giant's Staircase—a series of cliffs descending like steps or terraces, each several hundred feet tall. It's easy to picture some beastly kaiju or Godzilla striding out of the depths to come snack on the speck-size humans dotting the rims.

While the South Rim is easier to access and thus more frequently visited, the North Rim and the Inner Canyon offer the best rewards for intrepid travelers and are less crowded because of their more remote and rugged nature.

The North Rim

Unlike the South Rim, the North Rim is characterized by more remote and challenging access. It's open seasonally, usually from mid-April to mid-November, depending on snow conditions. There is no bridge between the rims, so the drive from South Rim to North Rim is 2 hours long.

North Rim Road, a gravel road off CO 92 near the town of Crawford, leads to the North Rim. The road can be rough, making it less suitable for low-clearance vehicles or large RVs (which helps cut down on crowds).

There are no services (like food or gas) on the North Rim, so plan on bringing everything you need (Crawford is your last shot). Primitive camping is available at the North Rim Campground on a first-come, first-served basis. The North Rim has an occasionally staffed ranger station and several lookout points with spectacular views into the canyon, like Exclamation Point and Green Mountain. The North Vista Trail offers a strenuous hiking experience with rewarding panoramic views, including the highest point in the national park, Green Mountain.

The Inner Canyon

Adventuring into the Inner Canyon is the most overwhelming way to experience the area's extreme forces of nature—but it's a heady challenge and a strenuous backcountry experience. The park has several established routes, but none of them are maintained trails: Routes are rugged, steep, and unmarked but for informal and possibly unreliable cairns; hikers must obtain a Wilderness Use Permit from the visitor center before attempting any route into the Inner Canyon.

Only experienced hikers in good physical condition with the necessary gear (including water purification systems and heat and sun protection) should consider it. Route-finding skills and comfort with exposure are key: Loose rock and terrifying drop-offs litter every route down, and rescue here is difficult and can take time. Be prepared for self-rescue situations, including overnight stays.

The Gunnison Route is the easiest and therefore most popular route to descend into the Inner Canyon from the South Rim. We said easi*est*: The route careens 1,800 feet down over a deceptively short 1 mile, but hikers should plan on at least 2 hours each way. (Also keep an eye on Colorado's fickle weather: Frequent afternoon thunderstorms can slick the rock and make the trip exponentially more difficult and terrifying.)

At the bottom, however, surprisingly lush banks line the frothing Gunnison, and looking up at the skyscraping black cliffs from here offers a delirious, inverted spectacle. Sandy beaches in between slippery boulders provide overnight accommodations and the rare chance to see bright stars focused and heightened through a narrow slit of night sky (additional backcountry camping permit required).

HIKES

North Vista Trail

The North Vista Trail is a remarkable trek on the North Rim offering some of the most breathtaking views in the park and is probably the most rewarding hike short of descending into the canyon itself. At 7 miles round-trip and with a manageable elevation gain of 800 feet, it's a comfortable day hike for most (though you can opt for the shorter, 3-mile round-trip hike to Exclamation Point). For those who continue to the end, you'll be rewarded with an exhilarating climb to the highest point in the national park: Green Mountain.

The trail begins near the North Rim Ranger Station on a well-defined path traveling west along the rim, gradually ascending. At 1.5 miles, the Exclamation Point overlook provides jaw-dropping views into the narrowest, deepest part of the canyon where the tiny ribbon of the Gunnison River glints far below.

Past Exclamation Point, the trail continues to climb and becomes more challenging, with steeper grades and some loose rock. The path winds through stands of pinyon pine, juniper, and scrub oak, and you'll find occasional benches to rest and enjoy the views (or look for deer, birds of prey, or possibly a black bear).

The final ascent to Green Mountain consists of a series of steep switchbacks. At the summit, a sweeping, bird's-eye view of the surrounding landscape greets you: Black Canyon spreads out like a crooked vein below, and on clear days you can see the San Juan Mountain Range, the West Elk Mountains, and the Uncompahgre Plateau.

Chasm View Nature Trail

While technically on the North Rim, this trail is accessed through the South Rim Road. It's a short, easy 0.3-mile round-trip walk

The Gunnison River carved the Black Canyon over 2 million years.

The quieter North Rim allows access to the park's highest point.

Steep, treacherous S.O.B. Draw earns every bit of its name.

through bird-larded pinyon and juniper forests to a few grand overlooks. Because of the added travel time to reach this location from the South Rim, it's typically less crowded.

S.O.B. Draw

This trail's knee-knocking, profanity-provoking scramble into the depths of the Black Canyon might be the most accurately named hike in the national park system. The unmaintained, 1.5-mile one-way route rapidly tumbles down 1,800 feet of loose, jumbled rocks and dizzying cliffs. "Hiking" here is a bit of a stretch: The reality involves more crawling, slipping, and cautious sidestepping. Many times, I chose between tiptoeing along a ledge with a 60-foot drop-off or hugging a crevice choked with poison ivy. (I often chose ivy. For this reason, you may want to wear long sleeves and pants, even in summer.)

But should you accept the challenge, S.O.B. gives you more than bragging rights over beers. Few trails in the park offer as much solitude: I can still smell the tang of the Gunnison from my empty beach while watching the sun briefly flit from rim to rim.

The trail begins near the North Rim Campground. From the starting point, you'll follow the canyon rim west, passing Balanced Rock. The trail veers right, descending a steep talus slope into the draw. Here's where the "fun" starts. You'll need your hands for balance and support as you navigate through a hot mess of boulders, loose rocks, and slippery scree.

There aren't any significant landmarks, per se, as the draw's real calling card is its relentless steepness and tricky footing. The only way is down. If you start wondering whether you've made a poor life choice, rest assured—you're probably on the right path.

Reaching the Gunnison River at the bottom is a cause for celebration, but hold off on kissing the flat ground. The return trip flips the script and doubles your time as you climb back up that 1,800-foot-tall mountain of shifting rocks. Summon your inner mountain goat: Use hands and always maintain three points of contact to help keep your balance.

The real treat comes when you haul yourself back onto the rim, sweaty, dusty, and victorious. And the memory of the Black Canyon's ominous lower reaches will long outlast your well-deserved beers back in town.

HIDDEN GEM

Accessed from the North Rim, the **Long Draw Route** is one of the least-used routes into the Inner Canyon. This is because it's a bit of a nightmare: The demanding 1.7-mile trek one-way drops you like a stone into the river, maintaining a constant gradient of 40 degrees. At one point, you'll lose 1,800 feet in 0.5 mile. Your reward is a front-row seat to the Narrows: the tightest, darkest, and most dramatic section of the canyon.

The Paiute believed Bryce's hoodoos were wicked humans turned to stone as punishment.

Bryce Canyon National Park

Utah | nps.gov/brca | Visitation: 2,461,269

Bryce Canyon can't hide its topsy-turvy, fairy-tale whimsy. Fairyland Canyon, Thor's Hammer, Hat Shop, Queen Victoria, and Sinking Ship are a few of the imaginative place names bestowed on the canyon's ornate formations by visitors, each seduced into dreaming as if picking shapes out of the clouds.

The thousands of crimson-colored hoodoos—towering limestone spires—make Bryce feel less like other canyon parks' cold shrines to geological history and more like a portal to a dimension where rock and stone feel infused with living spirits chittering and giggling among themselves when we're not looking.

Located in southwestern Utah, Bryce Canyon is a series of natural amphitheaters carved into the eastern edge of the Paunsaugunt Plateau. Each amphitheater's cacophony of color, texture, and shape started 65 million years ago just as the dinosaurs exited. Layers of sediment accumulated on the seafloor that once covered the region. Over millions of years, tectonic activity caused this sedimentary rock to rise, forming the Colorado Plateau. It was then cut by wind, water, and especially frost, which wormed its way into the stone as water and expanded as it froze. This happened frequently through eons, since Bryce's combination of high altitude (7,000 to 9,000 feet) and hot southwest sun conspires to swing temps both above and below freezing on the same days more than half of the year.

Two thousand years ago, Early Native American groups like the Ancestral Puebloan and later Fremont cultures inhabited the area (though not permanently, given the harsh conditions). Their mysterious disappearance in the twelfth century remains a cliffhanger in the annals of archaeology. The Paiute Indians came next and called the hoodoos "Legend People": those turned to stone by the trickster Coyote for their wicked deeds.

In the mid-1800s, Mormon pioneers moved in, including Scotsman Ebenezer Bryce, for whom the park was named. Bryce once described the labyrinthine region as a "helluva place to lose a cow," an understated take on the practicalities of living in this bizarre landscape.

Bryce Canyon houses an intriguing array of flora and fauna, most especially Utah prairie dogs standing sentry outside their burrows. They nearly became extinct in the 1920s, but continued conservation efforts within the park brought them back from the brink. Over 175 species of birds are also park residents, including the bullet-fast peregrine falcon.

Spend several nights in Bryce on a 23-miles route under the canyon rim.

The park also hosts bristlecone pines, the oldest trees on the planet. The isolation and aridity that bars us from thriving here has helped these trees survive for millennia. Their slow growth during short growing seasons at high altitudes makes their wood dense and therefore resistant to the insects, fungi, rot, and erosion that plague other trees. Extracting sustenance from nutrient-poor, limestone earth keeps them high above the thick stands of mixed forests that burn easily.

Bryce's accessibility brings plenty of drive-up splendor. Seeing the hoodoos blush under the early morning sun at Sunrise Point and continuing down the relatively short Navajo Loop Trail from there takes you through the slot canyon of Wall Street, where the towering walls block out the sky. It's backcountry wonder at front-country prices.

Everyone knows this. The mild spring or fall cuts into crowds a bit, and winter's freezing temps and whipping wind saps them further, though snow contrasting sharply with the red hoodoos arguably improves the view. Nighttime brings extreme rewards, too: Bryce's high altitude, low humidity, and distance from cities create some of the darkest night skies in the country. Ranger-led tours or solo expeditions can help illuminate the 7,000-plus stars lighting up the landscape, no moon required.

With only 20 miles of canyon and 60 miles of trail, Bryce is a pocket park among national parks in the western United States. But its supernatural magic looms large, and with some creativity hikers can craft sneak routes so quiet you might hear the hoodoos whispering as you pass.

HIKES

Swamp Canyon Loop

The name "Swamp Canyon" might seem odd in this arid environment, but it comes from the relatively lush vegetation supported by springs and seeps in the canyon. Its moderate 4.3 miles round-trip present a less-crowded way to experience the park just off the main scenic drive.

The trail descends 800 feet from the rim—an easy down you'll have to sweat for on the way back up. Make sure to save enough water for the return.

The trail starts at Swamp Canyon Overlook. Admire the view and then drop down into the canyon through a series of switchbacks that level out along the canyon floor. The trail takes you through dense forests, meadows, and the park's signature hoodoo formations. The "Wall of Windows" in the Bryce Amphitheater is a striking formation of pinnacles and arches. Halfway through the hike, you'll find yourself in a serene and isolated amphitheater

Swamp Canyon is named for its spring-fed greenery.

surrounded by ponderosa pines and cliffs. Mule deer, prairie dogs, and a variety of bird species begin poking their heads out here.

The elevation is over 8,000 feet, so it's essential for hikers to prepare for altitude, changing weather conditions, and sun exposure.

Riggs Spring Loop

The Riggs Spring Loop allows hikers to experience both the rim and canyon ecosystems beneath. Plus, from Yovimpa Point at the start of the trail, you can see three states: Arizona, Nevada, and Utah. At 8.8 miles, the trail is strenuous but rewarding and an excellent option if you're looking for solitude and more extended exploration.

The trail descends 2,200 feet from the rim to the canyon floor from Yovimpa Point, weaving through dense, fragrant fir and spruce forests. The path heads northward, curving east to reach Riggs Spring, named for a cowboy who once used the spring to water his cattle.

The trail then circles Corral Hollow's shady, treed series of campsites with views of Bryce's looming pink cliffs in the background. It then climbs back up to rejoin itself near Yovimpa Pass. Along the trail, you might see elk, mule deer, and (rarely) mountain lions. Bird-watchers might spot the northern flicker, Steller's jay, Clark's nutcracker, and perhaps a golden eagle.

Riggs Spring Loop has several designated backcountry campsites (a backcountry permit is required), including at Riggs Spring and Yovimpa Pass. Riggs Spring and Yovimpa Spring can serve as water sources, but availability can be unreliable so prepare to carry enough water for the entirety of your hike.

Under-the-Rim Trail

As the longest single trail in Bryce Canyon National Park, the Under-the-Rim Trail gives hikers a unique opportunity to bite off a huge, less-visited chunk of this mystical park in one go. The trail spans roughly 23 miles from Bryce Point to Rainbow Point and has a total elevation change of 3,000 feet. It's best experienced as a multiday trip.

Ricocheting between 6,800 and 9,115 feet in elevation for its duration, the Under-the-Rim Trail weaves through deep forests, crosses meadows, and offers constant stellar views of the park's famous hoodoos. You will be close enough to touch and admire the layers of pink Claron Formation limestone that give the hoodoos their unique coloration.

The trail can be accessed at several points along the main park road, allowing you to hike smaller sections if you prefer. Notable waypoints include Agua Canyon, Swamp Canyon, Whiteman Connecting Trail, and Right Fork Yellow Creek.

Several backcountry campsites along the trail include Right Fork Swamp Canyon, Yellow Creek, Iron Spring, and Sheep Creek (among others). A backcountry permit is required for all overnight trips.

Water can be found at several points along the trail, including Yellow Creek, Right Fork Yellow Creek, and Iron Spring. However, sources can run dry, especially in summer months.

HIDDEN GEM

If you've come this far, it's worth visiting **Grand Staircase Escalante National Monument**—arguably the biggest, baddest section of desert action in the Southwest. As a site that courts controversy over land use (ATVs vs. hikers vs. conservationists vs. industrialists), its borders are perpetually growing and shrinking depending on the administration in charge (after being halved in 2017, it's been restored to a size just larger than Delaware).

This vast playground of high desert plateau, river-carved cliffs, and labyrinthine slot canyons was the last place mapped in the Lower 48, and the gravitational pull of its undiscovered allure still tempts hardy adventurers. Accessible adventures like Coyote Gulch abound, but it gets better and better as you level up your skill set in navigation, desert travel and safety, off-road driving, and canyoneering. Those looking to graduate might want to give intermediate slots Peek-a-Boo and Spooky Canyon a shot. But do your research and make sure you're prepared (especially against flash floods).

Buckskin Gulch is one of the premier slot canyons in Grand Staircase Escalante National Monument.

Canyonlands features hundreds of miles of wild desert trails to explore.

Canyonlands National Park

Utah | nps.gov/cany | Visitation: 800,322

Vast and imposing, Canyonlands brings a sprawling mess of top-tier canyon country to get lost in, upriver on the Colorado from the Grand Canyon—every bit as grand as the Grand, but with 4 million fewer visitors. In fact, it's the least visited of Utah's Big Five despite being the largest, though sections of it are barely more than 30 minutes from the red-rock mecca of Moab.

Canyonlands lacks a distinctive centerpiece feature like Arches' vaulting bridges, Zion's Narrows or spires, Capitol Reef's stacked beehives, or the Grand's showstopping maw. Instead, it features a broad sampling of the surreal beauty that occurs when Utah's sandstone country crashes into the sky. Colorful canyons, teetering towers, sentinel mesas, shipwrecked buttes, and arcing fins and arches all exist here, sculpted by the unrelenting persistence of the Colorado River and its tributaries. Here, you can get a heaping dollop of them all to yourself.

Established in 1964, Canyonlands' 337,598 acres splits into three districts: Island in the Sky, Needles, and the Maze. Though they are part of the same park, each district offers a distinct character and adventures.

Island in the Sky is the easiest district to access and provides panoramic views from an elevated mesa. Here, you can take a relatively gentle mosey to Mesa Arch, an excellent "bang-for-your-buck" hike. For a moment of solitude, consider the Murphy Point Trail, which ends with a showstopper view.

The Needles district offers more challenging hikes and a closer look at the colorful sandstone spires that give the district its name. The standout Chesler Park Loop Trail feels like the set of a sci-fi film (close: sleeper hit *Galaxy Quest* was filmed in nearby Goblin Valley State Park).

The Maze, the most remote district of Canyonlands, is the domain of the intrepid. Its trails are long, convoluted, treacherous, and often require four-wheel drive to reach. It's a place for those who prefer their solitude served with a side of risk and commitment.

No roads directly link the districts within the park. Comprehensive exploration of Canyonlands requires strategic planning and a penchant for road trips. Resilience, self-reliance, and a talent for careful improvisation are as valuable as the audiobooks or podcasts you'll need for tarmac time.

The drives are never boring. From the road, you can see how every layer in the sandstone cliffs of Canyonlands tells part of a 300-million-year story. Like much of the Southwest, it begins in the Permian period, with sediments from ancient mountains, tropic seas, and wind-blown sands slowly compressing into stone. Over eons, the relentless work of the Colorado and Green Rivers sliced the flat sedimentary rock layers into a labyrinth of canyons. This ongoing erosion process continues to reveal the history of the earth's crust layer by layer.

Much later, Native American cultures thrived here. From Archaic peoples to Ancestral Puebloans to Fremont people to contemporary Ute and Navajo tribes, every culture left its mark on the canyon.

Petroglyphs and pictographs, including the famed "Holy Ghost" panel, are scattered throughout the park. The arrival of cowboys and outlaws like Butch Cassidy added a different flavor to the history, turning Canyonlands into a backdrop for real-life Western dramas.

The park's varied elevation and precipitation create diverse microenvironments, from the riparian river corridors to the dry desert uplands. Blackbrush, Mormon tea, and bunchgrasses spread across the lower basins, while pinyon pine and juniper woodlands claim the higher terraces. Biological soil crust, also known as cryptobiotic soil—a bizarre, knobbly, dark crust—plays a crucial role in preventing erosion and helping plant life. (When in Canyonlands, take care and "Don't Bust the Crust.") As for wildlife, a surprising abundance from mule deer to mountain lions to red foxes to desert bighorn sheep thrives here. Bird-watchers can spot everything from ravens to peregrine falcons.

Spring (April to May) and fall (September to October) are the most temperate seasons to visit Canyonlands. Summer brings oppressive heat, and some roads can be impassably muddy in winter. It can also get bitterly cold, especially at 6,000-foot Island in the Sky.

ZONE OF INTEREST

Horseshoe Canyon

Detached from the main body of Canyonlands National Park, Horseshoe Canyon was added to the park in 1971 and is home to some of the most significant and well-preserved ancient rock art in North America, including the mesmerizing Great Gallery. The Great Gallery is one of the most famous and best-preserved examples of Barrier Canyon–style rock art in the country. Adjacent to

The Holy Ghost panel in Horseshoe Canyon features life-size rock art up to 8,000 years old.

the Maze, it also gives visitors a taste of that zone's remote beauty without the perilous learning curve and risks.

The hike to the Great Gallery is a round-trip of 7 miles and starts from the Horseshoe Canyon trailhead, a remote site accessed by graded dirt roads (30 miles from UT 24 or 47 miles from Green River). The trail descends 750 feet from the canyon rim to the canyon floor. The first half is a 3.5-mile walk along a sandy wash with towering sandstone cliffs rising on either side.

From the canyon floor, the trail moves along the dry riverbed and meanders between steep canyon walls. Be prepared for walking in soft sand and minor scrambling over boulders.

As you make your way through the canyon, you'll encounter a series of rock art panels, including the Horseshoe Shelter, Alcove Gallery, and the High Panel. Each has its own unique array of fascinating pictographs and petroglyphs, some of which are 8,000 years old.

The climax of the trail is the Great Gallery, one of the best examples of ancient rock art in the country. This impressive panel stretches over 200 feet and features more than eighty figures, including the famous human-size "Holy Ghost" figure.

Backcountry camping is not allowed within Horseshoe Canyon, but you can camp at the west rim trailhead where there are basic facilities. There are no reliable water sources in the canyon; carry all the water you need.

HIKES

Syncline Loop

The Syncline Loop's strenuous, challenging 8.3 miles wrap around the Upheaval Dome, a unique geologic structure within Canyonlands National Park whose origins are still debated among geologists. Steep sections, elevation changes, and route-finding challenges dog hikers throughout, but the solitude and views are among the best in the Island in the Sky.

Beginning at the Upheaval Dome parking area, the trail splits shortly after starting and you can choose to go either left or right. The left path descends steeply into a canyon and provides more shade, but it is a challenging descent. The right path is a more gradual descent but is more exposed to the sun. We recommend taking the left path and hiking the route clockwise.

As the trail loops around, it brings you to the inner syncline, a U-shaped bend in layered stone. It then continues along the rim of the mysterious Upheaval Dome. Some geologists believe the dome was caused by salt deposits from an ancient sea layer becoming plastic and "bubbling" up to create the dome; others believe it's a partially collapsed impact crater from an ancient, gigantic meteorite.

The trail rejoins itself to complete the loop. Whichever direction you choose, expect some scrambling over rocks and steep sections. A final scramble before the dry washes that lead you to the trail's end requires balancing on fridge-size boulders. We find it easier to climb than descend these, but your mileage may vary.

There are two designated backcountry campsites along the Syncline Loop: Syncline Valley and Upheaval Canyon. Both sites require a backcountry permit, which can be obtained from the park. Water is scarce on this trail. Some may be available at the Green

Large rock formations rise from the valley floor on the Syncline Loop.

River, but it's not reliable and would require a significant detour to reach. As a result, hikers should be prepared to carry all the water they'll need for the hike.

Elephant Canyon/Druid Arch

This 11-mile round-trip trail in the Needles district of Canyonlands National Park climaxes at Druid Arch, a natural sandstone bridge shaped like the monoliths at Stonehenge. The view of the arch with a blue-sky backdrop and surrounding red-rock landscape is well worth the steep sections, technical scrambling, and exposure to the elements that mark this hike as difficult.

The trail begins at the Elephant Hill trailhead, which is reached by a technical four-wheel-drive road—a small adventure. From there, you will descend into Elephant Canyon, following the sandy washes that wind through the colorful sandstone needles and spires that give the district its name.

The trail is well marked, but there are a few side canyons that can confuse first-time hikers. When in doubt, follow the cairns and the beaten path that snakes through packed soil paths and sandy wash bottoms. The journey through Elephant Canyon itself features tall, striped sandstone spires lining it throughout.

Druid Arch rises at the west end of Elephant Canyon.

As you approach the end of the trail, you'll encounter a section that requires some ladder climbing and scrambling to reach the base of Druid Arch. Druid Arch was named by a park ranger in the 1930s because its shape reminded him of Stonehenge, built by the druidic cultures of ancient Britain.

There are several designated backcountry campsites in the Elephant Canyon area, including EC1, EC2, and EC3. They require a backcountry permit, which can be obtained from the park.

At the risk of sounding like a broken record: Water is unreliable along this trail. Seasonal water may be found in potholes, but it is not always present and must be treated before use. It is best to carry all the water you will need for this hike.

Murphy Loop

The Murphy Loop is a 10.8-mile moderately difficult loop trail in Canyonlands National Park's Island in the Sky district, with wide, sweeping vistas and views of Candlestick Tower, a stand-alone formation that rises dramatically from the White Rim.

Starting from the Murphy Point trailhead, the trail quickly descends via a series of switchbacks into the Murphy Basin. You'll be walking on a mix of slickrock, packed dirt, and sandy washes. The trail is well marked with cairns, but always be aware of your surroundings; it's easy to stray in canyon country.

The loop itself traverses the heart of the Murphy Basin before looping back around and ascending the same switchbacks to the trailhead. Along the way, it offers outstanding views of the Green River, Candlestick Tower, the White Rim, and the surrounding canyon country. The trail also offers a rare view of the "Island in the Sky" mesa from below.

There are several camping areas along the Murphy Loop, including Murphy Hogback and Murphy A and B. All require a permit for overnight stays. Take a guess about water sources (hint: no reliable water sources available along the trail).

If the Murphy Loop seems a bit ambitious, the 3.6-mile out-and-back Murphy Point Trail follows the same initial trail from the trailhead before splitting off to a viewpoint overlooking Murphy Basin, the Green River, and Candlestick Tower. It provides a taste of the dramatic views the longer loop offers without the significant descent and ascent.

HIDDEN GEM

True desert rats, welcome to heaven. The **Maze district of Canyonlands** is the most remote and least-accessible section of the park, a natural labyrinth and dream destination for solitude seekers comfortable with a genuine wilderness experience. However, hiking in this area is challenging and recommended for only the most experienced desert hikers.

Accessing the Maze district requires more time and effort compared to other parts of Canyonlands. The Hans Flat Ranger Station, the main access point to the Maze, is a 2- to 3-hour drive from Green River, Utah. From there, the canyons are another 3 to 6 hours by high-clearance, 4WD vehicle.

Because of its remote nature, you must be self-reliant and prepared for emergencies. There are no amenities such as food or gas in the Maze district, and water sources are extremely limited. Be sure to bring plenty of food, water, gas, and any other necessary supplies with you.

Backcountry permits are required for all overnight trips in the Maze. They can be reserved up to four months in advance, and it's recommended because of limited availability.

The vast, imposing Maze district demands caution and preparation from even experienced hikers.

Landmarks like the Chocolate Drops, Maze Overlook, and the Harvest Scene (one of the most famous and well-preserved petroglyph panels in the park) tantalize hikers worldwide.

The Orange Cliffs Unit along the western edge of the park provides sweeping views over the surrounding landscape. The Doll House area, only reachable via multiple days of strenuous hiking or a difficult 4WD route, boasts sandstone spires that resemble intricately carved dolls' houses.

Hiking in the Maze requires a high level of self-sufficiency and backcountry skills rare for the Lower 48. There is little to no cell phone service, and help could be days away. Navigation, water procurement, inclement weather, and injury risks grow exponentially in such a remote location. Be deeply experienced and prepared, and always check in with park rangers and emergency contacts.

Seemingly barren Capitol Reef hides a historic orchard along its scenic byway.

Capitol Reef National Park

Utah | nps.gov/care | Visitation: 1,268,861

A lesser-known gem of the American Southwest, Capitol Reef's red slickrock terrain and layered cliffs remain as wild and empty as an Ed Abbey fever dream. Solitary desert adventures await hikers of all skill levels.

Cap Reef surpasses Canyonlands in visitation. But it still feels wilder than the rest of Utah's famous Big Five, and my hunch is that most of the newbies rarely leave the main drive (beautiful) or the easy-access trails near Fruita and the visitor center. The park's huge, challenging, and largely unmaintained backcountry (there are only 40 miles of official trail) still provide chances to encounter the mystical Southwest as if you were the first person there—until you encounter petroglyphs thousands of years old, unnamed, unmarked, and unremarked upon in guidebooks.

At the heart of Capitol Reef is the Waterpocket Fold, a 100-mile-long wrinkle in the earth's crust. Imagine a giant invisible hand reaching up from the earth's core, scrunching the crust like a thick wool rug. This fold brought layers of rock from different eras cheek by jowl, creating a spectrum of color and form that makes the essence of what we see in Capitol Reef.

From soaring sandstone cliffs of the Navajo formation (glowing red and orange in the sun) to the grayish-white domes of the Entrada sandstone (thought to resemble the US Capitol's domes) the park's geology is a vivid, three-dimensional timeline of the earth's past. Sedimentary layers representing over 200 million years of geological history are exposed, derived from long-dead seas, desert dunes, and shifting tectonic plates.

Capitol Reef offers sanctuary for the flora and fauna present in much of high desert Utah. Junipers, pinyon pines, and blackbrush fill lower valleys, while ponderosa pines, aspens, and mountain mahogany adorn higher elevations. In the spring, desert wildflowers like Indian paintbrush and desert mariposa lily provide splashes of color against the crumbled landscape. Desert bighorn sheep tiptoe on cliff faces, and you can listen for the soft hoot of a great horned owl as dusk settles. Smaller critters like the kit fox, Utah prairie dog, and canyon tree frog each play a vital role in the ecosystem. Golden eagles, peregrine falcons, and white-throated swifts patrol the park's airways.

From petroglyphs to old homesteads, Capitol Reef offers an intimate connection to our human past. The Fremont people, a contemporary group to the Ancestral Puebloans, left petroglyph panels revealing an ancient language of symbols, anthropomorphic figures, and animals etched into the patina of the canyon walls.

Upper Muley Twist Canyon is named for the gyrations made by mules navigating the canyon.

Mormon pioneers came later, settling in the Fruita Historic District to plant orchards of cherries, peaches, and apples that still bear fruit. You can visit their old schoolhouse, catch a glimpse of daily life, or pick some fruit in the right season.

Capitol Reef is a place of contrasts and hidden treasures. One moment you're driving through an arid desert, the next you're strolling beneath shady cottonwoods in a verdant valley, or standing at the edge of a vast canyon, the land dropping away beneath your feet.

There are jaw-dropping vistas like the edge-of-the-world panorama from the Cassidy Arch Trail, or the surprise of finding a verdant oasis at the end of the Sulphur Creek Trail.

Even with growing visitation, most of Capitol Reef is a vast, unmaintained backcountry that few visitors have the gall to penetrate—everything is a "zone of interest." It requires backcountry smarts and skill, but some of these routes are surprisingly manageable, as moving through sandy washes and up sticky slickrock ramps helps travel go easier.

Spring and fall usually offer the most pleasant weather. Summer can be insanely hot, but if you're ready to brave the heat, the park is at its quietest. Winter brings stark, snow-dusted rocks capping the deep reds and oranges of the landscape.

(Another useful feature about Capitol Reef: The much-referenced "water pocket" refers to the frequent holes or tinajas that collect water. Between that and several perennial streams and rivers, water can be more accessible here than in some other desert parks.)

Getting off and backpacking through the backcountry to climb the park's towering cliffs or night hike under the glow of the Milky Way injects Capitol Reef into your soul. It's the place I trusted to take my own mom on her first big multiday backpack, deep into Lower Muley Twist Canyon. In her 60s, she'd scarcely camped before or visited canyon country, but as we slinked through slot canyons and shouted to no one in canyon alcoves big enough to house a jumbo jet, her words still echo in my head: "Let's keep going!"

HIKES

Upper Muley Twist Canyon (Upper Muley Twist)

This adventurous trail explores the remote red-rock wilderness of Capitol Reef's Waterpocket Fold. It combines panoramic views, countless natural arches, and the serenity of a less-traveled trail. The stretch along the rim of the Waterpocket Fold, with its panoramic views across Capitol Reef National Park, is particularly epic. On a clear day, you can see the Henry Mountains glinting in the distance to the east.

The profusion of natural arches requires a keen eye to spot. Some are right beside the trail; others are nestled into the cliffs. The canyon's name dates to pioneer times when ranchers would drive their cattle through the area. Often led by mules, the narrow canyons forced the animals to twist and turn sharply to fit.

From the Upper Muley Twist Canyon trailhead (located 2.9 miles south of the Burr Trail Road), the trail starts heading southeast along a dry wash. The path here is sandy and flanked by imposing sandstone walls. After 1.5 miles, the canyon splits, and you'll veer left (northeast).

As the trail ascends from the wash onto the slickrock of the Waterpocket Fold, you'll find yourself immersed in a landscape of domes, knobs, and cliffs. The trail then follows the rim

Visitors to Halls Creek Narrows need to prepare to get wet.

of the fold for 3 miles, offering broad views of the longer Water-pocket Fold. This is where you'll encounter the parade of natural arches—more than a dozen, the distinctive, large Saddle Arch standing out most.

The trail then loops back down into the canyon, and you'll hike the remaining distance through the wash. The descent into the canyon gives you a different perspective on the rock formations you passed earlier.

Halls Creek Narrows

Halls Creek Narrows, a remote backcountry hike in Capitol Reef National Park, lets you explore a stunning slot canyon and absorb the profound solitude present in the park's vast wilderness. I've hiked it twice and never encountered another person.

The Narrows themselves are a spectacular slot canyon where the walls squeeze shoulder-tight and loom overhead, obscuring the sky above. Walking through these narrows can feel like moving through a sculpted maze lost to time, water, and wind.

The trail begins at the Halls Overlook trailhead, reached by a 57-mile drive from the visitor center along Notom-Bullfrog Road and then Burr Trail Road. From the trailhead, you'll descend 800 feet down the Halls Overlook switchbacks to reach Halls Creek.

Once you reach Halls Creek, the trail turns into a sandy wash as it weaves its way south. You'll be hiking through open desert and along the bed of Halls Creek. As you advance, the creek starts to carve deeper into the Waterpocket Fold, creating a tightening canyon.

At 10 miles in, you'll reach the Halls Creek Narrows, where the canyon walls start to close in. This is the most dramatic part of the hike. The narrows continue for 3 miles, with the walls reaching up to 500 feet high and closing to a few feet apart in places. The narrows often fill with water that can be shoulder deep or deeper; it may require swimming, and with limited light reaching the canyon floor, it's always freezing. Take care to stay out of the narrows if there's even a hint of rain in the forecast, especially during monsoon season in June through August.

Backcountry camping is allowed in the Halls Creek area with a permit. There are no designated campsites, so hikers will need to find an established site or follow at-large camping regulations. Halls Creek usually has water, but as with any desert environment, water levels can fluctuate. It's always a good idea to bring plenty of water, and a filter or treatment system is essential (filters are best since they cut down on sediment and gunk).

Lower Spring Canyon

Spring Canyon is named for the occasional springs found along its length—remnants of the ancient rivers that once flowed through these canyons, slowly wearing down the rock to form the dramatic landscapes we see now.

The Lower Spring Canyon Trail showcases the vast beauty and solitude of Capitol Reef National Park while offering close-up views of the Waterpocket Fold, towering sandstone cliffs, wild rock formations, and seasonal waterfalls pouring off the rim like silver ribbons.

The trail is an 8.8-mile point-to-point hike that begins at the Chimney Rock trailhead and ends at UT 24. Its one-way nature requires a shuttle or a car at the exit point or retracing your steps, which keeps crowds at bay for most of its length. It also requires a knee-deep river ford at its conclusion near the road. The narrowness of the canyon also provides a cool respite from the desert sun.

Lower Spring Canyon showcases Capitol Reef's relative abundance of water.

The trailhead starts near Chimney Rock, a significant landmark in Capitol Reef National Park. From here, the trail winds down to Chimney Rock Canyon and follows it southwest. After 2.5 miles, you'll arrive at the junction with Spring Canyon, where you'll turn right (west) and head into Lower Spring Canyon.

Lower Spring Canyon is a treasure trove of sandstone cliffs, water-carved rock walls, and hidden alcoves. The trail takes you through the wash of the canyon, so it's relatively flat and easy to navigate, though there's no defined trail.

You'll find one challenging spot halfway through the trail, where a large chockstone (a boulder wedged in a narrow spot in the canyon) blocks the way. It requires a bit of scrambling to get past, but it adds to the sense of adventure.

The canyon gradually widens as you continue downstream, and you'll start seeing more vegetation, like cottonwood trees, indicating that you're nearing the end of the trail. In fall, they burst into golden coins. You'll reach the park's main road, UT 24, marking the end of your journey, after a short river ford.

Backcountry camping is allowed in Spring Canyon with a permit. There are no designated sites, and campers must set up in previously disturbed areas, at least 0.5 mile from roads or trailheads and 100 feet from water sources. Seasonal streams offer water sources, but their flow is unpredictable and depends on recent rainfall. Plan on bringing all the water you'll need for the hike.

HIDDEN GEM

Set apart and to the north of the main park in a more remote, less-visited section, the **Cathedral district** of Capitol Reef National Park doubles down on solitude in a place already renowned for it. Jaw-dropping monoliths rise above the desert floor, resembling gothic cathedrals. At sunrise and sunset, they cut into the horizon like a mythic palace out of *Dune* or *The Dark Crystal*. Volcanic dikes and crags interrupt the ubiquitous sand and sandstone, and the Cathedral and Hartnet Roads are typically only passable for high-clearance, 4WD vehicles—and sometimes not even those when wet conditions turn the bentonite clay substrate to quicksand.

Neither roads nor routes here are maintained. But the combination of short hikes and stops along the 57-mile dirt Cathedral Valley Loop Drive will thrill like few desert places can. There's a primitive campsite (Cathedral Valley Campground) with six spots located midway through the drive. There's no reservations or fees, but also no water—bring everything you need.

The Temple of the Sun is just one of the many impressive towers present in the remote Cathedral district.

Carlsbad Caverns National Park

New Mexico | nps.gov/cave | Visitation: 394,121

Above: The vastness of the open sky and the aridity of the Chihuahuan Desert, a vast dun-colored landscape of barren mountains, spiky plants, and scant water extending from southeastern New Mexico to outside Mexico City. Below: Enormous subterranean chambers fanged with stalactites and stalagmites, the black depths coated in glimmering crystal clusters or phallic blooms of limestone.

The formation of Carlsbad Caverns is complex but can be boiled down to three elements: a restless sea, eroding limestone, and acidic water. Two hundred and fifty million years ago, this region was part of a shallow sea. Over eons, marine remains of shells, coral, and skeletons accumulated on the seafloor, forming a dense layer of limestone.

Then, 6 million years ago, hydrogen-sulfide-rich water from nearby oil and gas fields met the groundwater, creating sulfuric acid. This acidic mix began to dissolve the limestone, creating cavities that grew into vast chambers and elaborate networks of tunnels. There are bigger and deeper caves, but few possess formations of such ornate beauty—including gypsum "chandeliers" that hang 18 feet from the ceiling. It's an extremely dense selection of caves: 117 known in the system, with Carlsbad and Lechuguilla acknowledged as the most significant. Many regard the off-limits Lechuguilla as the most scientifically important cave in the world.

Before Carlsbad Caverns was a national park, Indigenous people of the region knew of it. Artifacts dating back over a thousand years have been found in and near the cavern entrances. It wasn't until the late nineteenth century that settlers rediscovered the caves, initially drawn by the massive clouds of bats spiraling out of the natural entrance at dusk.

Hiking in Carlsbad Caverns is more of a descent than a trek across. The park offers self-guided tours of the caverns along a well-lit, paved trail. You can descend 750 feet below the surface, meandering through chambers as wide as football fields and filled with an array of dripping columns, neck-craning amphitheaters, stalactites, and stalagmites.

The main draw is the Big Room—the largest single cave chamber by volume in North America, covering an area of 8.2 acres (4,000 feet long, 625 feet wide, and over 250 feet tall). Inside, it resembles a grand natural cathedral, where stalactites hang like chandeliers and stalagmites rise from the ground like giant candles.

Carlsbad's Big Room features an array of stalactites, stalagmites, and flowstones.

The park features two distinct ecosystems each uniquely adapted to its environment (desert and subterranean landscape). Three hundred and fifty species of birds, mule deer, and foxes live above, but the undisputed stars of the park live underground. Each evening from May to October, visitors can witness the spectacle of hundreds of thousands of Brazilian free-tailed bats exiting the caverns in a swirling, spiraling exodus to hunt for insects until daybreak.

While most visitors to Carlsbad Caverns National Park are drawn to the cave systems, the park also has several aboveground trails that are often overlooked and therefore less crowded. But there are ways to lose yourself in the depths, too.

HIKES

Slaughter Canyon Cave Trail

Slaughter Canyon Cave is a non-developed cave that requires a ranger-guided tour to access. It's far less visited than the main cavern but still hosts a wealth of impressive formations, including the Monarch, one of the world's tallest columns at 89 feet. You must book your tour ahead of time and be prepared for a strenuous hike, with 1,000 feet of steep and rocky elevation change.

The trail to the cave starts with a steep climb through the scrubby desert before descending into the mouth of the cave. Inside, you'll explore the rugged beauty of the cave, navigating

Rattlesnake Canyon, one of Carlsbad's aboveground wonders.

rocky terrain using only headlamps for light. There are no established campsites or water sources in the area, and visitors should carry all water and food.

Rattlesnake Canyon

Rattlesnake Canyon is a challenging 6-mile round-trip hike that offers solitude and spectacular views. From the trailhead, the trail climbs steadily through the canyon, offering vistas of the surrounding desert and the distant Guadalupe Mountains beyond.

You'll follow the path as it weaves through juniper and scrub oak, crosses dry streambeds, and goes around or over boulders. As the canyon narrows, the trail becomes more rugged and requires some scrambling to proceed. The end of the canyon, where you turn around to head back, is marked by high, steep walls of buff-colored limestone.

There are no established campsites or water sources along this trail. Always carry plenty of water, especially during warmer months.

HIDDEN GEM

Spider Cave Trail ranks as one of the most strenuous tours offered at Carlsbad Caverns National Park. Visitors on the tour will belly crawl, leap over pits, and duck under numerous obstacles. You will get dirty and muddy, and it's not for the claustrophobic. The tour starts at the main building where you drive 0.25 mile to the trailhead. A 0.25-mile hike through the desert leads to a descent into the cave.

The first bit is a test piece for real caving: It requires a 30-foot crawl through a progressively narrowing tunnel to the first room. From there, a ranger will guide you through a series of cramped passages that lead to up-close views of cavern formations. It's a real adventure that mimics the types of expeditions that first explored this cave, and you must be fit, prepared, and not afraid of tight spaces or the dark.

The view from Inspiration Point on Anacapa Island showcases Channel Island's rugged coastline.

Channel Islands National Park

California | nps.gov/chis | Visitation: 328,746

Channel Islands exists in tandem with the Galapagos. Both are chains of islands strewn in the cold currents of the Pacific, oases of endemism and biodiversity found nowhere else on the planet. One of them is a three-day sail from the coast of Ecuador. The other is an hour-long boat ride from Los Angeles, California. And yet eleven times more people find their way to Yosemite every year.

Lucky us. The five islands of the park are a collection of isolated fragments of land that linger in the Pacific Ocean, graced with cliffs that plunge into azure waters where waves pound secret caves into their sides.

Formed from the tectonic clash of the Pacific and North American Plates, the islands emerged from the ocean around 25 million years ago and have rarely been connected to the mainland. These islands, each with its distinctive character, are time capsules, retaining elements from the mainland lost to time and evolution. On the land, dizzying sea cliffs back up to sprawling grasslands, foggy mountain peaks sink to serene sandy beaches, and each island tells a different story about evolution and survival in isolation.

That isolation led to over 150 unique species of plants and animals developing here and nowhere else on earth. Marquee specimens include the diminutive, cat-size island fox, the large island scrub-jay, and a variety of endemic plants that defy the salty sea air and arid soil to bloom in vibrant annual displays. Underwater, kelp forests fill with playful sea otters and rainbow-hued Garibaldi fish. Seasonally, blue whales troll the open ocean for rich shoals of plankton. The fossil record on these islands shows the presence of pygmy mammoths.

Despite their remoteness, the Channel Islands bear the archaeological imprints of 13,000 years of human habitation. The Chumash and Gabrielino Tongva nations left rustic remains of their villages, middens, and intricate shell beadwork. Spanish explorers arrived, followed by ranchers and farmers. The wars of the twentieth century brought the US Army, which used the islands for lookouts and munitions practice.

The area's natural gifts soon gained outside attention, and the islands of Anacapa and Santa Barbara became a national monument in 1938; in 1980, it upgraded to national park status and expanded to include the other islands and all the waters extending a mile offshore. Echoes of the park's long relationship with humans remain on many of the islands, but raw nature dominates.

Each island offers unique opportunities for exploration. Santa Cruz Island, the largest of the five and California's biggest overall, is a hiker's dream, with trails that traverse rugged mountains and descend to secluded beaches; however, 75 percent of it is managed by The Nature Conservancy and requires special permission to visit. On popular Anacapa Island, you can explore the lighthouse, bask in panoramic views from Inspiration Point, and marvel at Arch Rock, a natural bridge sculpted by the sea. Spring and early summer enchant when the islands burst with wildflowers. All transportation to the islands is by park concessionaire boats and planes or private boat, regardless of the time of year, though concessionaires often cease service to the smaller, more distant islands in the winter months.

ZONE OF INTEREST

Santa Rosa Island

Though Santa Rosa Island is the second largest of the Channel Islands and the second-largest island in California, it takes three times as long to reach as Santa Cruz. Far fewer visitors enjoy its comparable wealth of sandy beaches, expansive grasslands, rugged canyons, dramatic cliffs, and Torrey pine forests, some of which contain the oldest and largest Torrey pine trees in the world. The higher elevations offer panoramic views of the Pacific Ocean and other Channel Islands.

Get to Santa Rosa Island via park concessionaire boats (Island Packers) from Ventura Harbor or with a private boat. The journey takes 2.5 to 3 hours. Remember, all landings are dependent on sea conditions.

Reservations should be made in advance for boat transportation. It's recommended to stay for multiple days to fully explore the island, so camping is the best option. The empty beaches offer fantastic camping in a lost paradise—but timing is key: They close for

Remote Santa Rosa Island features a wealth of grassy hills, sandy beaches, and hidden canyons.

large parts of the year for seal pupping and nesting seabirds. Your best bet is between mid-September and mid-December. You must pack in everything you need, including water, as there are no services on the island.

Once you have parked on Santa Rosa, a world of trails offers days upon days of varied exploration. Hiking 5 miles round-trip on the Cherry Canyon Trail to Black Mountain allows you to traverse riparian woodlands to high-elevation island chaparral over a 1,200-foot climb. The 4-mile Torrey Pines Trail offers up-close views of the rare Torrey pine, Becher's Bay, and the Santa Rosa plains. East Point to Ford Point is a 10-mile round-trip hike that offers a remote beach experience complete with great opportunities for viewing wildlife, particularly seals and sea lions at Sandy Point.

The Water Canyon Campground is a hub of sorts, with many trails leading directly out of this landing point. A short walk from the campground leads to a beautiful sandy beach, a great place to relax after a day spent crushing it on longer trails. Lobo Canyon is a spectacular canyon with wind- and water-sculpted sandstone cliffs, a year-round stream, riparian vegetation, and a spectacular coast at its mouth. With the opportunity to see fossils and shells embedded all along its walls, it's well worth the effort.

HIKES

Santa Cruz Island: Smuggler's Cove

A favorite hike on giant Santa Cruz is the Smuggler's Cove trail. Starting from Scorpion Anchorage, you'll head inland on the Scorpion Canyon Loop before branching off toward Smuggler's Cove.

This trail is 8 miles round-trip and traverses a mix of coastal bluffs, rolling hills, and groves of island oak. You'll then descend into the secluded Smuggler's Cove. The cove is an idyllic spot with a historic olive grove and a quiet beach perfect for a picnic and some wildlife spotting.

There are several camping options on Santa Cruz Island; the nearest to this trail is Scorpion Ranch Campground. As with Santa Rosa Island, you will need to carry all your water as there are no reliable sources.

Quiet Smuggler's Cove offers great chances to spot seals, sea birds, and more.

Santa Rosa Island: Black Mountain

The moderate Black Mountain Trail offers a mix of island habitats, from riparian canyons to grasslands and high-elevation island chaparral. The trail is 5 miles round-trip with a little over 1,200 feet of elevation gain, making it a great option for intermediate and experienced hikers.

Starting from Water Canyon Campground, after landing at Becher's Bay, you'll take the trailhead that starts in Cherry Canyon. The trail winds through a canyon filled with a riparian habitat featuring native willows and island oaks. You'll begin ascending, cross several small streams, and then begin a steady climb up a ridge. Continue climbing through grasslands and up to the high-elevation chaparral. Shortly after, you'll top out on Black Mountain. On a clear day at the summit, you'll have a 360-degree view of the Pacific Ocean, Becher's Bay, and Santa Rosa Island, with its diverse topography of canyons, beaches, and other mountains. Return the way you came.

San Miguel Island: Point Bennett

The westernmost in the Channel Islands chain, San Miguel is the most remote and often experiences the toughest weather, keeping crowds extremely low. Additionally, you can hike only its centerpiece 15ish-mile round-trip trail to Point Bennett on a guided, ranger-led tour. But those who brave the 3- to 4-hour ferry and grueling hike get to see one of the largest collections of wildlife seen anywhere in the world.

Reach San Miguel Island via the park's concessionaire boats (Island Packers) from Ventura Harbor. It's remote location and limited services make reserving your spot well in advance crucial. Once you are on the island, the hike to Point Bennett is only allowed with a National Park Service guide. Be sure to check the schedule for guided hikes, which typically take place once a day.

Visitors should be well prepared. The island has no food, potable water, or services, so you need to bring all necessary supplies. The weather is also more unpredictable here than on the eastern islands, so layers, wind protection, and rain gear are a must.

One of the largest populations of northern elephant seals hauls out on Point Bennett.

The trail to Point Bennett passes through beaches, dunes, and bluff edges. As the island is heavily influenced by the sea, the environment is harsh but stunning, with wind-sculpted landscapes and cool, foggy weather.

Starting from the ranger station, the guided hike moves west across the island. You'll hike over shifting sand dunes and along the edges of bluffs, with the sea on one side and the island's interior on the other. The trail continues to the western tip of the island, ending at Point Bennett.

Once at Point Bennett, you'll witness one of the world's largest gatherings of seals and sea lions, with up to five different species present and numbers that can reach into the tens of thousands during peak seasons—sometimes as many as 80,000. In fact, you'll hear it before you see it: The low barks and growls of enormous northern elephant seals greet you like rolling thunder long before you spy them lolling about the beach itself.

HIDDEN GEM

Channel Islands National Park's volcanic origins have resulted in a coastline riddled with sea caves, arches, and rock formations that are **best explored by sea kayak.** Santa Cruz Island boasts the highest concentration of sea caves in the world and allows beginner-to-expert paddlers chances to see the dramatic coastline's precipitous cliffs, kelp forests, and rich marine life through clear blue water.

Arrange boat transportation through Island Packers from Ventura Harbor. If you want to bring your own kayak, you'll need to make a separate kayak reservation, as space is limited.

For most people, booking a guided tour with an authorized kayak outfitter is recommended. Guided tours typically include all necessary equipment, including kayaks, paddles, helmets, and life vests. They also provide valuable guidance and safety instructions for navigating the caves.

Most kayak tours begin at Scorpion Anchorage on Santa Cruz Island, which offers easy access to many sea caves. Your exact route and the caves you can explore depend on sea conditions and

Arch Rock and sea caves beckon experienced kayakers to Channel Islands.

Bright lichens and algae color Painted Cave.

your group's experience level. Departing directly from Scorpion Anchorage provides access to a high concentration of navigable sea caves appropriate for beginners. Advanced kayakers can attempt Painted Cave on the northwest coastline of Santa Cruz Island. One of the largest and deepest sea caves in the world, it's named for the colorful lichens and algae on the walls.

Congaree hosts the tallest deciduous forest in the United States.

Congaree National Park

South Carolina | nps.gov/cong | Visitation: 250,114

In the heart of South Carolina, Congaree's Deep South dreamworld of huge trees, river-born swamps, and chorusing wildlife remains an unsung unit in the national park system, often eclipsed by its distant siblings. But it remains distinct and extraordinary: Rather than being carved by the violent eruptions of volcanoes or grinding of tectonic plates, Congaree bows to the slow, constant flow of water.

Congaree isn't quite a swamp as many assume; instead, it's the biggest remaining tract of bottomland hardwood forest. Over millennia, as the Congaree and Wateree Rivers seasonally spill over their banks, they deposit sediments that leave a floodplain of fertile soil. That soil supports the tallest deciduous forest in the United States, with some trees soaring over 160 feet. Bald cypress and water tupelo trees have risen from the waters over centuries, planted in the marsh on broad, flared bases.

When the water recedes, the forest floor fills with a wild concoction of ferns, vines, and wildflowers. Bobcats, deer, armadillos, river otters, snakes, turtles, fish, and more than 200 species of birds make their living between here and the canopy.

Long a vital hunting and fishing ground for Native American tribes, the forest endured the logging and prospective development plans of European settlers before grassroots efforts culminated in its designation as a national park in 2003.

Congaree National Park serves hikers, bird-watchers, and canoeists. The Boardwalk Loop Trail, a 2.4-mile journey into the heart of the forest, is an easy stroll that offers intimate encounters with the park's towering trees and teeming wildlife high above the waters and sensitive flora.

For a more immersive experience, paddling the marked canoe trail on Cedar Creek lets you glide silently beneath the forest giants along an aquatic artery, the canopy far above filtering sunlight into golden shards in the surface fog. The 15-mile route over blackwater can be split into many variations between Bannister Bridge and the Congaree River. It's also likely your best chance to spot an alligator.

Congaree is accessible all year, with each season offering unique charms. Spring floods breathe new life into the forest, attracting migratory birds and awakening a symphony of frogs and insects. Autumn boasts vibrant hues, while winter brings a quiet beauty and the chance to hear barred owls hooting "who-cooks-for-you!"

A plain-bellied water snake swims through the swamps of Congaree.

The marquee parks of the West offer big vistas and grand sights. Congaree National Park's charms exist on a more intimate scale: in looking up at the ancient canopy or breathing in the scent of loamy earth, looking for the changes brought by the slow ebb and flow of the floodplain.

HIKES

Oakridge Trail

The Oakridge Trail is a 6.6-mile loop trail, perfect for those who prefer solitude in a higher and drier area of the park that contrasts with the famous floodplain. Beginning and ending at the Harry Hampton Visitor Center, the trail meanders through mixed hardwood oak, hickory, and pine forests. You'll pass some of the largest loblolly pines in the park and cross creeks on sturdy bridges. You can take the trail in either direction, but going clockwise gives you a gradual introduction to the park's biodiversity.

Campsites are available at the Longleaf and Bluff Campgrounds, but be aware there are no water sources along the trail.

Kingsnake Trail

The challenging Kingsnake Trail roams off the beaten track for 11.7 miles, traversing some of the most remote areas of the park, giving you a chance to enjoy real quiet. Starting from the South Cedar Creek Canoe Landing and ending at the Bates Ferry trailhead, it winds through cypress-tupelo sloughs, bottomland hardwood forests, and pine ridges. The trail is well marked but can be a bit challenging because of length and occasional wet and muddy conditions.

Beyond tall trees, you'll find yourself passing through areas of younger growth and traversing creeks. If you're lucky, you might spot river otters or a shy bobcat. This trail is especially known for its snake sightings (hence the name), so look down; be cautious but also appreciative. There are no established campsites or reliable water sources along this trail, so come prepared.

River Trail

The River Trail is a 10-mile out-and-back trail that ends at the Congaree River, the lifeblood of the park. You'll start this trail from the Boardwalk Loop, then follow the Weston Lake Loop Trail until the River Trail branches off to take you through dense, old-growth forest and swampy areas, ending at the sandy banks of the Congaree River. You'll see plenty of the park's famous cypress trees, and on reaching the river, you'll be rewarded with beautiful views of the waterway and, with some luck, an otter or alligator sighting.

Elevated walkways keep hikers above the floodplain.

Crater Lake National Park

Oregon | nps.gov/crla | Visitation: 559,976

I call a certain class of parks stop-and-stare parks. They're built around a showstopping central feature that commands all attention and eyeballs. Crater Lake National Park is perhaps king of the stop-and-stare parks: As soon as you crest Rim Drive, you're slapped in the face with a vivid, unbelievable blue that makes the sky dull in comparison. It all sits in a symmetrical bowl 20 miles around and 6 miles across, with Wizard Island rising from the middle like a fantastical fortress. It is impossible to look away.

At 1,943 feet deep, Crater Lake is the deepest in the United States and the fifth deepest in the world. Fed entirely by rain and snow and without inlet or outlet streams, it's also one of the clearest and purest lakes anywhere—you can see to a depth of 130 feet. The lack of pollution, extraordinary depth, and cold temperatures contribute to this clarity. There's a small species of zooplankton found in the lake (*Mysis relicta*) that helps maintain water clarity by consuming algae.

Crater Lake formed over a geologically swift period of 420,000 years, when magma along the Cascade volcanic arc welled up to create 12,000-foot Mount Mazama (which would've made it the tallest in Oregon). About 7,700 years ago, Mount Mazama erupted in an earth-shattering display of volcanic power and the mountain collapsed in on itself, leaving a gaping caldera in its wake. Over centuries, rain and snow filled the basin, giving birth to Crater Lake. While elevations in the park extend to 9,000 feet, the water level sits at a near constant 6,000 feet.

Its isolation and depth created an ecosystem like no other, home to unique aquatic species that have adapted to its cold, dark depths. But the park extends well beyond the lake, though, to include over 180,000 acres of wilderness. Stands of mountain hemlock and whitebark pine dot the landscape, harboring black bears, Roosevelt elk, marmots, and a chorus of bird species. The lake itself hosts only two species of fish, rainbow trout and kokanee salmon, introduced into the lake in the late nineteenth and early twentieth centuries. Introduced around 1915, crayfish threaten the endemic Mazama newt.

The history of Crater Lake is deeply intertwined with the Indigenous people of the region, especially the Klamath Tribe. The Klamath people and their ancestors have lived in the area of Crater Lake for thousands of years, and the lake remains a significant site in their spiritual tradition.

According to Klamath legend, Crater Lake was created during a great battle between Llao, the chief of the Above World, and Skell, the chief of the Below World. The two entities resided in Mount Mazama and Mount Shasta, respectively, and the Klamath perceived the eruption of Mount Mazama as a battle between these supernatural beings.

Crater Lake is the deepest lake in the United States.

Llao fell in love with a beautiful Klamath maiden but was rejected by her. In anger, Llao began to hurl rocks and flames at the Klamath people. Skell, seeing the destruction, rose to their defense and a tremendous battle ensued. The earth shook, and the sky was darkened by smoke and ash.

In the end, Skell was victorious, and Llao's body was thrown back into Mount Mazama. The great mountain collapsed onto Llao, imprisoning him there for eternity. The deep pit that remained filled with rain and snow over the years, forming Crater Lake. The Klamath people saw the lake as a sacred site and a portal to the spirit world.

The Klamath believed the feature known as Wizard Island was Llao's head surfacing from the depths, a remnant of the epic battle.

Prospectors encountered the lake in 1853, and in 1902 it became the fifth national park. Most visitors focus on the mesmerizing blue mirror of the lake itself and stick to the views along the 22-mile Rim Drive that traces the entire circumference of the lake, and it doesn't have a bad angle. Hopping a boat to visit Wizard Island is popular, too.

While the park is open year-round, accessibility varies. Late July through early September is the best time to visit if you want to take in all the park has to offer, including boat tours and access to all trails and roads. Winter brings its own isolated beauty, but many services and roads are closed.

Finding solitude often means turning your back on the entrancing azure orb and venturing into the old-growth woods, meadows, and peaks of the backcountry. While they may lack the visual awe of the lake itself, they are no less mesmerizing.

HIKES

Pinnacles Trail

This family-friendly route takes hikers through a fascinating geological landscape in a scant 0.8 mile. To get there, take East Rim Drive for 7 miles past the park's headquarters. You'll find a parking lot for the trailhead near Lost Creek Campground.

As you walk the trail, the Pinnacles soon pop into view. This series of spindly, needle-like formations formed when hot ash

Crater Lake's pinnacles are minerals left by old fumaroles.

and pumice spewed out of the volcano during its climactic eruption. Much of this material filled the ancient river valleys, and as the softer material eroded away, these harder formations remained standing.

The trail is an out and back that runs along the rim of Wheeler Creek Canyon and is easy to navigate, mostly flat, and should take an hour.

Plaikni Falls

At 2 miles round-trip, Plaikni Falls is a relatively easy, family-friendly hike that leads you to a beautiful waterfall set in a lush, old-growth forest. The trail is almost entirely flat with only a 100-foot elevation gain. It's worth noting that it's the rare trail in the park that is wheelchair accessible.

To get to Plaikni Falls, you'll need to start from the Rim Drive, the main road that encircles Crater Lake. The trailhead is located 2 miles southeast of the Phantom Ship Overlook and is clearly signposted.

Enchanting Plaikni Falls lies at the end of a short, family-friendly hike.

The Plaikni Falls Trail weaves through an old-growth forest characterized by its towering trees, shady canopy, and cool, damp undergrowth. The trail itself is well maintained, consisting of packed dirt with some gravel sections. The ground is carpeted with ferns, and in the spring and early summer an array of wildflowers, including lupines, asters, and Indian paintbrush, sprout throughout. The falls themselves are tucked into a stony alcove, and they cascade down a moss-covered rock face into a small pool.

Union Peak

The longest maintained trail in the park, the 9.8-mile Union Peak hike climbs an ancient, eroded shield volcano and features a fun scramble to attain the panoramic views of the surrounding region from the exposed summit.

Start from the Pacific Crest Trail (PCT). The closest parking is at a pullout on OR 62 near the junction with the road leading to the Pinnacles Overlook. The trailhead is 1.7 miles from the parking area along the PCT. The Union Peak Trail initially follows the PCT, traveling at a gentle incline through a serene old-growth forest of mountain hemlock and Shasta red fir.

The craggy summit of Union Peak involves some minor scrambling over a rocky slope, but it's manageable for most hikers with some experience. You'll win 360-degree views of the southern Oregon Cascades, including Crater Lake, Mount Thielsen, Mount Bailey, Mount McLoughlin, and on a clear day, California's Mount Shasta.

Mount McLoughlin looms behind Crater Lake's Union Peak.

Though conditions can be extreme, winter brings solitude and beauty to Crater Lake.

HIDDEN GEM

Winter dumps an average of 44 feet of snow on Crater Lake each year, making it one of the snowiest places in America. With most roads, facilities, and services closed, **winter in Crater Lake** attracts far fewer crowds. Their loss: The sheer white of pristine snow surrounding the intense blue of the lake makes for a serene, quiet, and otherworldly experience. The surface of the lake is often still, reflecting the surrounding snowy rim like a gigantic mirror. The trees wear heavy cloaks of snow, their branches sparkling against the steel-gray sky.

All that snow means the Rim Drive around the lake closes to vehicular traffic, opening opportunities for cross-country skiing and snowshoeing. Independent, hardy travelers can traverse the West Rim Drive, and the park offers free ranger-led snowshoe walks on weekends from late December through the end of March, weather permitting.

A bit of caution, though: Winter conditions can be extreme. Dress warmly and prepare for wild changes in weather. Check the forecast and consider the road conditions. The park's north entrance is typically closed to cars from early November to late May, so the only access during this period is through the park's west and south entrances.

Cuyahoga Valley
National Park

Ohio | nps.gov/cuva | Visitation: 2,860,059

Without the imposing grandeur flaunted by the Grand Canyon or Yellowstone, Cuyahoga Valley is not the most scenic national park. But Cuyahoga's green oasis of hardwood forest, wetlands, and tumbling waterfalls bloomed from an urban industrial dumping ground so polluted its namesake river once caught fire. This transformation from such inauspicious circumstances marks it as perhaps the most miraculous park.

Long before Europeans set foot on the North American continent, tribes like the Erie, Mohawk, and Iroquois roamed the lands surrounding the *Ka-ih-ogh-ha*, "crooked river" in Mohawk. Native peoples fished, farmed, and flourished on its resources without exhausting them.

But after colonization, the Civil War helped Cleveland grow exponentially, and the Ohio and Erie Canal cemented its position as an industrial powerhouse. During the height of the Industrial Revolution, the river provided power and convenience to the mills, factories, and urban settlements that sprouted like mushrooms along the river's winding path. Unchecked dumping of industrial waste soon cloaked the river in grime, chemical runoff, and a perpetual oil slick. The crowning indignity came when the Cuyahoga River caught fire in 1969, burning for 30 minutes and causing $50,000 worth of damage. In truth, it had caught fire before *at least nine time*s—but this was the first time anyone cared.

The flames of the Cuyahoga helped ignite a nationwide movement for environmental justice, paving the way for legislation including the Clean Water Act and the establishment of the Environmental Protection Agency. This wave of advocacy took hold on determined locals in the 1970s, who began dreaming of turning a scarred industrial hinterland into a national park. They took painstaking efforts to rehab the polluted river and restore the land, slowly making room for the resurgence of diverse flora and fauna.

In 2000 Cuyahoga National Park earned national park status, preserving 33,000 acres of forests, rolling hills, working farms, and wetlands along a 22-mile stretch of river improbably sandwiched between Cleveland and Akron. A river that once bubbled with pollutants and raw sewage now teems with over 60 species of fish and more than 200 of birds. A 125-mile network of hiking trails invites visitors to lose themselves in the hardwood forests of oak, hickory, and maple trees or

Brandywine Falls is one of many impressive waterfalls in Cuyahoga National Park.

peer at its numerous waterfalls. The park's wetlands hum with frogs and insects, while herons stalk through the reeds. In the meadows, you might catch a glimpse of white-tailed deer grazing or hear the playful chatter of river otters in the marshes.

While the river's redemption marks a rousing victory for nature, it also serves as a model for how wild spaces can be restored and preserved in urban places, serving the interests of people and nature through compromises that allow both to thrive. Wandering through Cuyahoga's steep, glacier-cut ravines or tracing the curves of its sinuous river, you never forget that civilization and wilderness commingle here, making it more precious.

HIKES

Salt Run Trail

This path undulates through a cathedral of trees, ambles along babbling brooks, and unveils forgotten facets of Ohio's history on a 3.3-mile loop trail, packing a one-two punch of scenery and topography into modest length and moderate difficulty.

Starting and ending at the Pine Hollow parking lot, located on Quick Road in Peninsula, Ohio, the Salt Run Trail begins with a descent into a beech, maple, and oak forest. Under dense foliage, the Salt Run stream gurgles along the route; in fall, that foliage explodes into red, orange, and gold hues. In spring, look for salamanders in shaded pools. In summer, you'll witness a carpet of wildflowers, including trilliums, Dutchman's breeches, and jack-in-the-pulpits.

A highlight is Kendall Ledges, a glacially carved sandstone escarpment dating back to the Devonian period 350 million years ago. Watch for woodland creatures and various bird species that make these ledges their home.

As the trail continues, it climbs and dips, mimicking the contours of the land, giving hikers a good workout. Toward the end of the trail, you'll come across an expansive wetland area. This wetland is a biodiversity hot spot with frogs, salamanders, herons, and a host of water-loving birds and plant species.

Wetmore Trail

At 4.5 miles, this moderate loop remains off most hikers' radar since it bears a reputation as a trail meant for stock. And while you'll need to watch for horses, equine traffic is low, especially in the off-season.

From the trailhead located off Wetmore Road, near Peninsula, the path plunges you into a landscape that alternates between mature forests, with towering canopies of oak, maple, and hickory trees, and wetlands and meadows. The trail is named for the

Glaciers carved Kendall Ledges during the ice age's retreat.

Wetmore family who once resided in the Cuyahoga Valley. The remnants of the Wetmore homestead and their cemetery can be found nearby.

Blue herons stalk the shallows of Wetmore Bog.

The Wetmore Trail undulates through a series of ascents and descents before reaching Wetmore Bog, which serves as a vibrant habitat for a rich variety of aquatic plant and animal species. Bird-watchers can look for songbirds, woodpeckers, and the occasional hawk.

Tinker's Creek Gorge Loop

The Gorge Loop Trail is a 1.8-mile moderately trafficked loop that showcases a mixed hardwood forest of oak, hickory, maple, and tulip trees. Depending on season, wildflowers or fall foliage will color your route.

The trail starts on a leisurely path and soon leads you into a series of inclines and declines that can get muddy and slippery after rainfall. The Great Falls of Tinkers Creek cascades over a shale cliff; impressive in summer, it's more so in winter, when the falls often freeze into giant icicles.

Carved by the same water that cascades down the Great Falls, the sandstone and shale cliffs of the gorge itself are some of the most impressive in Ohio, often referred to (semi-hilariously) as the "Grand Canyon of Cleveland." An overlook, which is part of the

In winter, the falls at Tinker's Creek turn to giant icicles.

Gorge Loop Trail, presents a wide overview of the entire gorge; it's made especially stunning when ablaze in autumn.

Death Valley National Park

California, Nevada | nps.gov/deva | Visitation: 1,099,632

If the American West is a land of natural juxtapositions, Death Valley is the place where landscapes that are at once starkly beautiful and mercilessly punishing reach a frightening apex. In this place superlatives reign: the hottest, driest, and lowest points in North America all rub shoulders here, creating an arena of unnerving extremes.

Sprawled across 3.4 million acres of California and Nevada, Death Valley's immense wilderness is the biggest park outside Alaska, a paradoxical paradise where desolation shares space with delicate desert blooms. As the most parched realm in North America, a paltry 2.36 inches of rain fall annually. It sports the "hottest" title, having recorded a skin-scorching 134 degrees Fahrenheit in 1913—a record that could break each year as climate change drives global temperatures higher and higher. However, many experts doubt that record and instead point to twin readings of 130 degrees recorded in 2020 and 2021. Don't expect that record to hold for long.

The valley floor at Badwater Basin, a surreal salt-encrusted wasteland, rests 282 feet below sea level, making it the lowest point in the continent. Toss in the snowy peaks of the Panamint Range, which top out at over 11,000 feet, and you have a place where sunbaked abyss and frigid peaks exist in bizarre proximity.

Death Valley's staggering temperatures and dryness stem from a unique combination of geographical and atmospheric conditions. The high peaks of the Sierra Nevada wring out most of the incoming Pacific moisture, and the Panamint Range to the west of Death Valley forms a significant barrier that blocks what little remains from reaching the valley floor. Meanwhile, the valley's deep, elongated, and enclosed structure enables air to get trapped and heated efficiently: As sunlight enters the valley, it warms the ground, which in turn heats the air near the surface. This hot air rises but is unable to escape the high mountain barriers surrounding the valley. As the air gets pushed back down, it compresses and warms through a process known as adiabatic heating.

Death Valley's sparse vegetation doesn't help matters. Plants can absorb some heat from the atmosphere—but in Death Valley, there's nothing to absorb it. The clear, dry air allows for a larger amount of sunlight to penetrate and heat the surface, as there's little humidity or pollution to scatter or diffuse it.

Nighttime brings relief from the heat and reveals wondrous sights above. The International Dark Sky Association designates Death Valley as a "Gold Tier" Dark Sky Park, meaning that on a moonless night, the shimmering Milky Way can be seen clearly. Not far from the megalopolises of Las Vegas or

In addition to being the largest park in the Lower 48, Death Valley is a land of beautiful extremes.

Los Angeles, the unpolluted darkness is so profound that one could mistake a shooting star for a wayward spacecraft.

While it's not well understood, every geological process that exists helped create Death Valley. Volcanic eruptions, earthquakes, uplifted mountains, ice age flooding and lake formation, and extensive erosion conspired over millions of years to form this undulating panorama of salt flats, sand dunes, badlands, canyons, and barren mountains.

None of that has stopped humans from occupying Death Valley since time immemorial. Long before the first Europeans set foot here, the Timbisha Native Americans made this unforgiving land their home. The 1849 Gold Rush brought a flood of fortune-seekers through the valley (some of whom granted the park its name after they found themselves stranded here for two months, losing a member of their group in that time). But the area's mineral wealth would remain untapped until miners and mule teams started hauling borax from the salt pans during the "borax booms" of the late nineteenth century.

Today, multitudes throng to Death Valley in all seasons to stand below sea level in Badwater Basin, march up Zabriskie Point, or take selfies next to the triple-digit numbers displayed on giant thermometers at Furnace Creek. Those are worth a visit. But with so much trackless, harsh backcountry on offer, it's quite easy to veer off those worn tracks and escape crowds.

The very nature of Death Valley's beauty lies in its inhospitality. People die here every year, especially in the crushing summer heat when the ground gets hot enough to cause third-degree burns on bare soles. Fall through spring is much more hospitable, though unpredictable weather and a lack of water can still make the park dangerous. The margin for error in Death Valley is much smaller than your average park, especially in the gigantic and rough backcountry. Do your research and be exceptionally well prepared with redundant food, water, and supplies, and you'll easily avoid joining the unlucky souls who keep this park's name accurate.

ZONE OF INTEREST

Racetrack Playa

Racetrack Playa, home to the world-famous "sailing stones" of Death Valley National Park, is a fascinating destination for those adventurous enough to make the journey. Getting there isn't a walk in the park, though—figuratively or literally.

Located 27 miles south of Ubehebe Crater and not accessible via any paved roads, the trip requires a high-clearance, 4WD vehicle to navigate rough terrain and roads of hard-packed dirt often scattered with tire-piercing stones. The drive can take up to 2 hours each way, and checking road conditions at the visitor center before heading out is paramount, as rains can render the roads impassable.

Once you reach the Racetrack Playa, you'll be greeted by a flat, 3-mile-long dry lakebed. Near the southern end, you'll encounter the moving rocks, some weighing several hundred pounds, with long, straight trails spooling in their wake. For decades, this puzzled scientists and visitors alike, lending a sense of eerie mystique to the valley.

Racetrack Playa's sailing stones confounded scientists for decades.

A research team led by Scripps Institution of Oceanography at UC San Diego solved the mystery in 2014. They discovered that when the playa receives rain, it can form a shallow, temporary lake. If the temperatures drop below freezing (common during winter nights), the water can freeze into thin sheets of ice.

As the day warms, the ice breaks up into large floating panels. Light winds can then push these ice panels, with the embedded rocks, across the playa. The movement of the rocks and ice, along with the water underneath, creates the tracks. When the ice melts, and the water evaporates, the rocks are left with the trails behind them, giving the illusion that they've skirted across the desert floor of their own volition.

Remember that the Racetrack Playa is a protected area. While the sailing stones are an incredible sight to see, it's important to leave no trace—don't move or disturb the rocks, as their tracks are fragile, and the phenomenon takes years to form.

HIKES

Eureka Dunes

Situated in the remote Eureka Valley, these towering dunes are the tallest in California. Like a mirage, they rise from the valley floor, creating a dramatic contrast against the rugged limestone wall of the Last Chance Range that cradles them to the east.

Start from Stovepipe Wells and take CA 190 west past the sprawling desert plains, rolling dunes, and stark mountain ranges. After 33 miles, make a left onto Scotty's Castle Road. After 7 miles, turn right on Ubehebe Crater Road and leave paved roads behind for the gravel track of Death Valley/Big Pine Road.

Continue for 41 miles on this gravel track, passing the abandoned sulphur Crater Mine. Keep an eye out for wildlife: This raw, remote stretch is home to a range of creatures from kangaroo rats to desert bighorn sheep.

After your long and dusty ride, Eureka Dunes will spring into view, a crescendo of sand rising dramatically from the desolate

Eureka Dunes' tallest rise to 700 feet.

desert floor. The dunes sea spans an area of 3 square miles and reaches heights of 700 feet. Venture into the dune field as far as you wish and listen for the low-frequency hum or boom that occurs when the sand avalanches down a dune face. Be careful where you step: A close look at your feet can reveal endemic Eureka dune grass, shining locoweed, or the Eureka evening primrose—which have all adapted to this sandy environment.

Services are virtually nonexistent in this primitive area. You should arrive prepared with ample water, food, sun protection, and a spare tire (or two!). Check road conditions before you leave, as the tracks can become difficult after weather events. It's also worth noting that while standard SUVs can generally handle the road to Eureka Dunes, a 4WD vehicle is recommended.

Fall Canyon Trail

Known for its beautifully colored and sculpted narrows, Fall Canyon offers a challenging yet rewarding hike in the northern part of the park.

From Stovepipe Wells Village, take CA 190 heading north for 33 miles until you reach the well-marked turnoff for Scotty's Castle. Turn left onto the unpaved but well-maintained Titus Canyon Road.

Fall Canyon ends in an impressive pouroff.

The trail narrows as you venture, and imposing canyon walls rise on either side of you. Look out for sculpted rock formations and watch the wall hues change from yellows and browns to purples and reds.

At 2.2 miles into the canyon, you'll run into a large, dry waterfall, 15 to 20 feet high. Most hikers turn around here, but those with good scrambling skills and comfort on rock can stem their way up this chimney and continue up the canyon. The trail becomes increasingly challenging from this point onward, with additional dry falls and scrambles.

The length of the Fall Canyon Trail varies depending on how far you choose to go. Many people choose to turn around at the dry fall, making it a 4.5-mile round-trip hike, but you can extend it to 6.5 miles round-trip if you continue beyond.

In addition to water, food, and sun protection, be aware of the potential for flash floods. Check the weather forecast before setting out and avoid entering the canyon if there is a risk of rain.

Corkscrew Peak

Notable for its distinct, twisted peak and panoramic views, Corkscrew Peak works as an alternative to popular Wildrose and Telescope Peaks.

From the Furnace Creek Visitor Center, head north on CA 190 for 33 miles. Keep an eye out for the junction with Daylight Pass Road. Turn right and continue for 8 miles until you reach Hell's Gate, a saddle with expansive views into Death Valley and across to Nevada. Here, park in a small gravel lot on the left-hand side of the road. There is no official trailhead or sign for Corkscrew Peak, but the trail begins on the right side of the road, initially rolling downhill toward a wash, then up along the base of the mountain. A cairn-marked path will guide you toward the peak, but remember, this is a route, not a defined trail, and part of the fun is in finding your own way.

Ascend past desert shrubs, creosote bush, clusters of Mojave yucca, and barren rock as you climb higher. Mineral-rich rocks glow along this section in reds, yellows, and purples. Halfway up,

After 2.5 miles, you'll arrive at a signed parking area for Fall Canyon. The trailhead can be found on the left side of the wash.

Begin your hike by crossing the wash and finding the trail on the other side. Climb gently uphill toward the mouth of Fall Canyon.

Sunrise at Corkscrew Peak.

alluvial fan of sediment washed out of the canyon—a remnant and reminder of the powerful flash floods that can sweep through here.

Upon entering the canyon, high walls displaying mineral-rich layers of rock weave patterns of rust red, ochre, pink, and green, while a crack of blue sky rises overhead.

As you delve deeper into the canyon, the walls narrow, and the terrain becomes more rugged. Here, you'll encounter the eponymous "grottos"—overhanging alcoves worn into the canyon walls by water. Some of these grottos form narrow tunnels and chutes, inviting you to scramble and clamber. A word of caution, though: The rock can be deceivingly fragile. Tread carefully and avoid climbing on loose or unstable sections.

The canyon continues to narrow until it's impassable. This is your cue to turn around and make your way 2.2 miles back to your car.

you'll come to a false summit followed by a saddle. The real peak lies hidden behind, but you're close. After a challenging final ascent, reach Corkscrew Peak's true summit at a lofty 5,812 feet. You'll get incredible 360-degree views of Death Valley, the Grapevine Mountains, and Nevada's Amargosa Desert. On a clear day, you might spot Boundary Peak, Nevada's highest point.

The round-trip hike is 8 miles, with an elevation gain of around 3,000 feet. This is a strenuous and challenging hike that requires navigation skills in addition to Death Valley's usual challenges. You should undertake it only if you're physically prepared and carry plenty of water, sun protection, snacks, and a map or GPS.

Grotto Canyon

Down the way from the far more popular Mosaic Canyon, Grotto Canyon provides the same astonishing desert geology with a fraction of the crowds.

From Furnace Creek Visitor Center, head south on Badwater Road for 20 miles until you reach the clearly marked turnoff for Artist's Drive. This one-way scenic drive offers a painter's palette of desert hues, a sneak peek of the colorful geology ahead.

About a mile along Artist's Drive, you'll find a small parking area on your right. The mouth of Grotto Canyon is visible from the parking area. Head directly toward the canyon, crossing a broad

Death Valley hides many slot canyons like Grotto Canyon and Mosaic Canyon (pictured).

Superblooms in Death Valley are unpredictable, magical occurrences.

HIDDEN GEM

Death Valley may be completely defined by its harsh climate and ceaselessly rugged terrain of earth tones. But every so often this hard place bursts into a riot of color: Poppies, primroses, verbena, lilies, and dozens of other flower species carpet the valley floor and foothills, giving potent fragrance to the breeze with their blossoms. Welcome to **Death Valley's superbloom.**

A superbloom isn't an annual event; in fact, decades can pass without one occurring. It depends on the perfect confluence of seasonal conditions: Heavy autumn rains are required to wake dormant seeds that lie beneath the desert's surface. Winter must remain mild, followed by a calm spring without extreme heat or gusty winds. If this all occurs, a superbloom might explode sometime in late February and March.

To experience this natural marvel, you'll need to keep a close eye on the park's wildflower reports, which are updated regularly during the bloom season. If it happens, hurry! As ephemeral as they are beautiful, these rare blooms peak for only a couple of weeks.

Flowers can pop up anywhere in the park, but Jubilee Pass and Ashford Mill in the park's southern portion can be excellent viewing spots. In the north, consider Beatty Cutoff and the foothills of the Funeral Mountains. Along Badwater Road, near Badwater Basin, is another reliable site.

Visiting a superbloom requires responsible behavior. Stick to established paths and roadsides, and never pick the flowers. This ensures others can enjoy the spectacle and allows the plants to complete their life cycle, spreading seeds for future blooms.

Some years Denali is visible only one day out of three.

Denali National Park and Preserve

Alaska | nps.gov/dena | Visitation: 498,722

The Alaska Range, a 600-mile-long mountain arc in south-central Alaska, is an imperious rampart of rock and ice. It's alpine overload—one of the mightiest wildernesses out there, dotted with gigantic glaciers, threaded with huge rivers, and punctuated with more than forty peaks that tower over 10,000 feet.

A mountain among mountains anchors it all. Rising to 20,310 feet, Denali—or "The High One" in the native Koyukon Athabaskan language—is North America's literal apex, the tallest mountain on the continent. But even among the Seven Summits, it punches well above its weight: Geographically isolated, Denali's dramatic relief (the vertical height difference from base to summit) is greater than Everest's. Its daunting scale and palpable, hulking presence both humbles the observer and spurs adventurous spirits toward its technical and dangerous summit. You don't have to set foot on it to understand this: For hundreds of miles, Denali dominates the horizon, and within the park's borders it swallows everything.

That's if you're lucky enough to see it. All that incredible relief and stormy Arctic weather hide the peak often. A common rule of thumb says the mountain is out one out of every three days (though some years it can disappear for weeks on end). That said, I've been lucky enough to catch it in full, glorious sun for many days in a row. Plan for an extended stay to maximize your chances.

Denali owes its existence to a multimillion-year-old geological fender bender. Around 60 million years ago, the Pacific Plate began its slow-motion collision with the North American Plate, creating a titanic crumple zone, the buckling of which birthed the whole Alaska Range. Denali itself is a granite pluton, cooled and solidified deep within the earth's crust before being pushed to the surface. Its granite composition enables Denali to withstand the relentless weathering and erosive forces better than the surrounding sedimentary and metamorphic rocks. It's all draped in glaciers that forgot to leave at the end of the last ice age; in some places they're over 4,000 feet thick and snake on for more than 30 miles.

Denali's human history stretches back millennia. Indigenous Alaskans have lived here for over 11,000 years, with the Athabascan people referring to the peak as Denali long before the word "Alaska" ever appeared on a map.

A bull caribou strides over a ridge in Denali.

The more recent history of Denali is entwined with the allure of the gold rush and exploration. In 1896, a gold prospector named it Mount McKinley to honor then-presidential nominee William McKinley and win support for the gold standard. In 2015, the mountain officially regained its original name at the federal level, recognizing its cultural significance and Indigenous heritage.

Denali National Park's subarctic mosaic of spruce forests, kettle lakes, braided rivers, tundra at middle elevations, and glaciers, rock, and snow at higher altitudes houses loads of charismatic megafauna in populations that dwarf anything in the Lower 48: grizzly bears, caribou, wolves, Dall sheep, moose, wolverines, lynx, snowshoe hares, and over 160 species of birds. Spotting the paw print of a bear or hearing the distant howl of a wolf pack echoing across the valleys is relatively commonplace, and while seeing wildlife isn't guaranteed, in my experience it's more likely than in any other park.

I've watched a trio of grizzlies standing from their berry banquet to get a sniff at me from a safe distance across a large river; I've spied a pair of golden eagles locked in midair combat. I rounded a bend of the Nenana River to startle a lynx mid-sip, and an elusive wolverine once interrupted a bathroom break to bound down the moraine of the Muldrow Glacier right past me. Rangers balked at that one when I told them.

These encounters are plentiful in the backcountry, but they're also frequent on the Denali Park Road that threads its way 92.5 miles across the entirety of the wilderness. Access is what sets Denali apart from many Alaska parks: A well-organized system of buses takes visitors deep into the heart of the park, stopping at highlights and visitor centers but also at any point a hiker chooses. You can access the first 15 miles by private car, but many major sites are beyond that and require you to hop a green bus. They're operated by friendly, knowledgeable drivers who are adept at spotting wildlife and stopping at obscure drop-off points. (I'll never forget the driver who paused to let a wolf pup frolic and then take a 15-minute nap in the middle of the road, before he joined his impatient pack waiting on a nearby tundra bench.)

Denali gets more visitors than most Alaska parks, but the pacing and schedule of the buses space out the cruise-ship hordes, and most won't venture more than a few hundred feet from the road. You can exit one bus and wait for the next one with space; doing this renders popular overlooks like Polychrome Pass empty. As soon as the echo of the bus's motor fades past the next overlook, you'll be left alone to listen to the solitary wind and jump at every rustling bush. (Don't worry: It's probably an Arctic ground squirrel. Probably.)

ZONE OF INTEREST

Mount Eielson Visitor Center

Though it's a major stop on the Denali road, the Mount Eielson Visitor Center is a perfect jump-off point for beginners and experts alike, staffed with seasoned park rangers and experienced naturalists who can offer crucial, up-to-the-minute information and beta. (If you're backpacking, make sure and get your permit from the Backcountry Information Center in the bus depot before hopping a bus.)

The Mount Eielson Visitor Center is an ideal departure point for backcountry adventures.

Perched at an elevation of 3,733 feet and located at Mile 66 on the Denali Park Road, the center offers awe-inspiring panoramas of Denali from the get-go. Several day-hiking trips radiate from the visitor center, each providing a unique perspective on the Alaskan wilderness. If you're planning a day trip, be prepared to encounter varying landscapes—tundra meadows, dense spruce forests, and windswept ridges. Navigation is rarely straightforward, and carrying a topographic map and compass is recommended as there are few marked trails.

One of the most popular routes for day hikers starts at the Eielson Visitor Center and meanders along the Thorofare River bar. Traversing this 4-mile round-trip on an open river bar provides a vantage point for viewing grizzly bears, caribou, and wolves that often come to fish or cross the river.

For more ambitious backpackers, multiple multiday options fan out from the Mount Eielson Visitor Center. Before you shoulder your pack, remember that Denali is a trailless wilderness. You create your own path, and the park's backpacking is very strenuous but rewarding.

One of the favorite routes among seasoned backpackers is the traverse from the Eielson Visitor Center to Wonder Lake. This epic trek usually takes three to four days and covers 22 miles. The landscape you encounter is varied and breathtaking, with undulating alpine tundra gradually giving way to stately spruce forests and the meandering, rushing McKinley River. Don't be surprised if you come across a herd of caribou elegantly crossing the tundra or spot golden eagles soaring above the ridges.

While making your way through this route, the main challenge is river crossings, which should always be undertaken with caution. Always unbuckle your backpack when crossing a river to avoid getting dragged under by its weight if you happen to slip. Look for wide, braided sections of the river to cross, where the water is shallower and moves slower. High, dry tundra can make for fast travel; at lower elevations it can resemble a spongy mattress, and puddles and mud hide between slippery tussocks of grass. Whatever you do, try to avoid schwacking through alder and willow thickets. In general, travel in Denali and much of Alaska is slower; strong hikers shouldn't plan to clock more than 7 or so miles a day. The backcountry information center's exhortation to "accept wet feet" is a wise one.

When navigating Denali's utter wilderness, it is essential to treat the landscape with the respect it deserves. The weather can change quickly, so carry layers and be prepared for sudden snow or rainstorms, even in the summer.

Also: This is major bear country. Store all food and scented items in bear-resistant food containers. Make noise (loud talking or an occasional "hey, bear!" will do) while hiking to avoid surprising them, and always give them wide berth and right of way.

HIKES

Triple Lakes Trail

Triple Lakes Trail offers more than a trio of pristine, glacier-fed lakes. This 18.8-mile round-trip big bite journeys through spruce forests, hushed shorelines, rolling tundra, and glacier-cut valleys, all with the backdrop of the Alaska Range. And it's accessible by private car. It's the longest established trail in Denali, but you don't have to hike the whole thing to experience its wonders. (The point-to-point has a north and south entry point; we started at the northern point.)

From the visitor center, follow the park road westward for 0.8 mile until you reach the signed trailhead and parking lot on the left-hand side. The north–south traverse begins by snaking its way through a dense spruce forest. After around 2 miles, you'll catch your first glimpse of the northernmost lake.

Leaving the first lake behind, climb to sweeping views of the Yanert Valley followed by a steep descent to the serene second lake. Look out for beavers and waterfowl.

Triple Lakes offers a lengthy hike on the edges of Denali.

Continue through undulating terrain to land at the third and final lake. Approach carefully: This is a good place to catch a glimpse of a moose grazing near the water's edge. After a final uphill stretch, you'll emerge at the south trailhead and parking area, marking the end at 9.4 miles if you've got a second car shuttle. Otherwise, loop back.

Oxbow Loop

Nestled away from the high-adventure trails and extreme wilderness experiences lies mellow Oxbow Loop. A gentle 1.5-mile trail offers hikers a peaceful stroll along the Nenana River and through a cottonwood forest, presenting a quieter facet of Denali National Park in the front country.

Park at the Denali Visitor Center, near the park entrance. The trailhead is conveniently located here, making it easily accessible and perfect for those looking for a less strenuous exploration of Denali's diverse ecosystems.

Start by following the bank of the Nenana River, whose milky-white, opaque color comes from the glacial silt that the river carries. The trail then veers away from the river into thickets of white spruce and trembling aspen. Late summer brings bright colors to the understory and ripening berries.

The trail then returns to the river for a high view of the river's oxbow, a U-shaped bend in the river's course. Look out for the American dipper, North America's only aquatic songbird, often seen diving in the river for food.

Anderson Pass-Eielson Loop

To sample Denali's best rewards, you must strike out into the trailless backcountry. This Y-shaped trip combines the best parts of the popular Eielson loop with a climb to Anderson Pass, the only non-technical path across the Alaska Range. This 31.8-mile crown-jewel backpacking trip is raw Alaska, with all the awe-inspiring wildlife and soul-quieting solitude you could ever hope for.

The Muldrow Glacier borders the beginning of the Anderson Pass-Eielson Loop.

Ask the bus driver to drop you off at Grassy Pass, just beyond the Mount Eielson Visitor Center. From Grassy Pass, bushwhack to a ford of the Thorofare River (depth varies with weather and season) at mile 0.4. Reach Glacier Creek and head 1.1 miles south to a canyon in the Muldrow Glacier. You'll climb 150 feet southeast to a tundra bench adjoining Mount Eielson. Weave through blueberry patches for 2 miles, then drop to cross Intermittent and Crystal Creeks and ford calf-deep Glacier Creek above its confluence with Crystal Creek at mile 4.8.

Next, you'll hug the gravel pathways next to the Muldrow Glacier until the streambed widens into a braided gravel bar at mile 6.6; expect multiple crossings over the next 2.5 miles. Scout for a flat campsite near a tumbling creek near the 8-mile mark. You can day hike on day two 6 miles (one way) to Anderson Pass, where you'll be able to peer into the deep Alaska Range and spy the blue ice of glaciers. Explore as much as you're comfortable.

The next day follows Glacier Creek north to Crystal Creek; follow Crystal Creek a mile until Wolverine Creek veers left of a tundra bench. Get your calves ready for a 3.3-mile, 1,174-foot climb to 4,724-foot Contact Pass. At the top, you'll get sweeping 360-degree views of the Alaska Range, the Muldrow Glacier, and Denali itself lording above it all. Then drop a steep mile along Contact Creek to find flat, campable ground on the other side of the pass.

On your final day, follow the Thorofare River drainage 2.1 miles, scouting places to ford, before the river cuts west at 30 miles into your trip. Here, ascend a marshy bench, pass a small lake in 0.5 mile, then ford Gorge Creek at mile 31.7. Close the trip on a 653-foot climb on a user trail leading to the Eielson Visitor Center.

Pack old sneakers for plentiful river crossings and trekking poles for uneven terrain. Bomber rain gear and tents are a must; we got battered by a tent-flattening storm. Plentiful bears along this blueberry-covered route require you to bring bear spray and bear canisters. You can get free bear canisters at the permit office.

The trip is doable all peak season, but we did it in September, which brought fewer people, plentiful remnant berries, no bugs, and typically lower river flows. Caveat: You risk weathering the first winter storm.

HIDDEN GEM

Denali National Park, spanning over 6 million acres, is divided into **eighty-seven backcountry units.** Each unit provides a unique and unspoiled wilderness experience, offering ambitious adventurers a chance to forge their own path in the wild. It's also a great way to level up your backcountry abilities and get used to planning, reading, navigating, and moving over challenging backcountry terrain without trails to guide you. Doing so will require attuning yourself to the rhythms of the wilderness, adjusting to its unpredictability, and learning the balance between adventure and safety.

Before you set out into the backcountry, familiarize yourself with the different units and the unique challenges each presents. Information on these units is available at the Backcountry Information Center (BIC) located within the park. It's advised to study topographic maps and recent trip reports, and to speak with the rangers at the BIC, who have an intimate understanding of the park's changing conditions.

For backcountry camping, you must obtain a permit for the specific unit and dates of your trip. Permits can only be obtained in person and no more than a day in advance of your trip start date. This system is designed to prevent overcrowding and to minimize the impact on the environment.

A great option for the first-time backcountry hiker, Unit 8 is accessible via the park bus system. It features the Polychrome Glacier and a beautiful overlook on the park road, offering incredible views of the Alaska Range. Moderately challenging terrain gives newcomers a taste of backcountry hiking without throwing them into the deep end.

Denali's eighty-seven backcountry units offer unparalleled opportunities for wild camping.

Unit 34 encompasses Cathedral Mountain, a crumbling formation that pokes high above Denali's tundra. While accessible via the park bus system, the unit's rocky terrain and swift rivers demand experience.

Some units lie beyond the reach of the park road and are accessible only by air taxi services that operate out of nearby towns. These trips are often expedition grade and can range from the high peaks, steep-sided valleys, and swift rivers common in road-accessible units to full-on mountaineering in mazes of crevasses, seracs, and icefalls. Guides are recommended for fly-in trips for all but the most experienced backcountry travelers.

Dry Tortugas National Park

Florida | nps.gov/drto | Visitation: 84,285

The Dry Tortugas lie out beyond the southernmost tip of Florida, 68 miles west of Key West where the Gulf of Mexico and the Atlantic mix. A string of seven coral-and-sand islands, they appear on maps as specks in the sea.

The islands owe their existence to coral reefs, which grew and died over thousands of years, building up layers of limestone beneath the waves. As sea levels fluctuated, these layers were sculpted into islands, home to beaches of delicate sand and tropical-blue water. The "dry" in their name was given by early explorers who arrived thirsty and came away disappointed at the absence of freshwater. "Tortugas" comes from the Spanish word noting the abundance of sea turtles that call these waters home.

Arid name aside, the Dry Tortugas teem with life. The archipelago encompasses sandbars, seagrass beds, mangrove swamps, and the best-preserved coral reefs in the Florida Keys. Those rich ecosystems harbor dolphins and more than 250 species of birds—many of which are migratory species that use the scarce land as a critical stopover and much-needed rest spot on their transoceanic flights. It's also an important nesting site for the threatened green turtle and the endangered loggerhead turtle. The coral reefs and seagrass beds provide a home for a dizzying array of marine creatures, from brightly colored parrotfish to elusive nurse sharks.

Recorded history of the Dry Tortugas dates to the sixteenth century, when the Spanish adventurer Ponce de Leon explored the area. By the early nineteenth century, the United States built Fort Jefferson on Garden Key to help protect shipping lanes along the nation's Gulf Coast. Today, massive Fort Jefferson on Garden Key is the magnet for most visitors.

Getting to the Dry Tortugas is an adventure, as it's accessible only by boat or seaplane. Camping is available on Garden Key, where you can spend a night under the stars, lulled to sleep by the rhythm of the waves. The clear waters around the islands are perfect for snorkeling and diving, offering an up-close view of the park's marine life.

Given the tropical location, there's no bad time to visit Dry Tortugas (except hurricane season). Spring and fall offer the chance to see migrating birds, while the summer brings long days perfect for snorkeling and swimming.

Little Africa offers exceptional snorkeling.

The best way to experience Dry Tortugas? Get wet.

Loggerhead Key hosts one of the most isolated lighthouses in the United States.

ZONE OF INTEREST

Little Africa

"Little Africa" gets its name from the coral reef formation that, when viewed from above, is said to resemble the shape of the African continent. Located near Loggerhead Key, the westernmost island of the Dry Tortugas, Little Africa is known for its vibrant coral formations and diverse marine life.

The reef of Little Africa is relatively shallow, making it an excellent site for snorkeling in water with fantastic visibility, often 50 to 100 feet.

Little Africa is home to various corals, including brain corals, star corals, and sea fans. Snorkelers can also expect to see a variety of tropical fish like parrotfish, angelfish, and wrasses, among others. If you're lucky, you might spot larger species such as sea turtles, stingrays, or reef sharks.

Alligators are plentiful in Everglades National Park.

Everglades National Park

Florida | nps.gov/ever | Visitation: 810,189

Everglades doesn't enjoy a reputation for being a hiker's park. The uncharitable way to explain this is that it's a swamp, complete with all the mosquitoes, alligators, and rampant poisonous snakes and mud-sucking terrain that implies.

A better way to envision the Everglades is as a slow-moving river—one that feeds an astonishing array of subtropical ecosystems and wildlife unlike anywhere in the United States. It's hard to invoke the Everglades without leaning on the poetic words of Marjory Stoneman Douglas:

> *The miracle of light pours over the green and brown expanse of saw grass and of water, shining and slow-moving below, the grass and water that is the meaning and the central fact of the Everglades. It is a river of grass.*

Her tireless advocacy for the Everglades changed public perception of the park from a worthless swamp to a treasure trove of biodiversity. On the southernmost tip of Florida, it became the third-largest national park in the lower 48 states in 1947, covering a massive 1.5 million acres. It's the largest subtropical wilderness in the United States by far.

Complex hydrology defines the park. This vast, slow-moving river is 50 miles wide but only an average of 6 inches deep. During the wet season (May to November), heavy rainfall overflows Lake Okeechobee to the north, and the excess water is slowly released into the Everglades. The water then travels over the limestone bedrock and through sawgrass marshes toward Florida Bay in the south.

The resulting web of marshlands acts as a shallow sheet of water flowing over low-lying lands. The limestone bedrock beneath serves as a catchment area for this slow-moving river, while providing a natural filter for the freshwater above. That limestone bedrock came from millions of years of sea-level fluctuations coupled with the disintegration of tiny sea creatures. Overlaid with peat, that substrate supports a fantastic jigsaw puzzle of ecosystems—pinelands, cypress, mangroves, and, of course, the emblematic sawgrass marshes.

Each plays host to an extraordinary array of wildlife. American crocodiles sun themselves on muddy banks here and almost nowhere else in the Lower 48. Lithe Florida panthers disappear into the bush. More than 360 species of birds live here, including the regal heron, the vibrant roseate spoonbill, and the elusive snail kite. Manatees are often spotted in the brackish waters. Alligators are plentiful. Over 40 species of mammals, 300 species of fresh- and saltwater fish, 50 of reptiles—the list goes on.

The earliest human occupation in the Everglades dates to around 10,000 to 8,000 BCE, during the Paleo-Indian period when sea levels were much lower. By 500 BCE, the inhabitants of the Everglades, known as the Glades culture, had adapted to the wetland environment, becoming skilled at fishing and hunting small game and waterfowl. They built their settlements on tree islands and traveled through the marshes and rivers in dugout canoes. They also made pottery and used tools made from bone, shell, and wood.

In the sixteenth century, the arrival of Spanish explorers brought diseases that decimated Indigenous populations of South Florida. Over the centuries, the Everglades became a refuge for Indigenous people displaced by European colonial expansion, including the Seminole and Miccosukee tribes. When the United States acquired Florida from Spain in 1821, conflicts over land like the Seminole Wars forced many into the remote Everglades, while others were relocated to Oklahoma.

A small group of Seminoles and Miccosukees managed to resist removal and stayed in the Everglades, forced deeper and deeper into the wetland environment. They lived in chickees—open-sided huts with thatched roofs—and relied on hunting, fishing, and gathering wild foods. They also developed patchwork clothing, intricate beadwork, and unique ways of capturing alligators to bring them back live to camp for consumption (killing them on the spot would spoil the meat too fast).

Today, the unconquered Seminole and Miccosukee tribes continue to live in South Florida, including within the Everglades region. They maintain their distinct cultures and play an essential role in the management and preservation of the Everglades. Their history and ongoing relationship with the Everglades are integral to understanding the human story of this unique landscape.

Kayaking or canoeing Everglades' mangrove channels is an excellent way to navigate the park.

The Everglades invite the adventurer all year round, but keep in mind, there are two primary seasons: wet (May–November) and dry (December–April). If you're partial to less humidity and fewer mosquitoes, dry season is your best bet. Plus, wildlife viewing is prime as animals congregate at watering holes.

ZONES OF INTEREST

Paddling in Everglades National Park offers the best way to explore the park's labyrinthine mangrove tunnels, serpentine canals, and the vast, shallow grasslands. You can see alligators and crocodiles basking in the sun, manatees grazing in the seagrass, dolphins playing in the waves, and a variety of bird species, including ospreys, pelicans, herons, and egrets.

Everglades National Park offers numerous paddling routes, accommodating everything from short day trips to multiday excursions. Coastal paddling routes offer views of the Gulf of Mexico, the Ten Thousand Islands, and Florida Bay.

Camping is allowed at designated beach sites and ground sites along the Wilderness Waterway and other interior canoe routes. A backcountry permit is required for all overnight trips.

Hell's Bay Canoe Trail

Despite its intimidating name, idyllic Hell's Bay Canoe Trail winds 5.5 miles through mangrove tunnels and across small bays. It's well marked and suitable for kayakers of all skill levels, although navigating the twists and turns can be a bit tricky.

Start at the Hell's Bay Canoe trailhead off the main park road, just past the Pa-hay-okee Overlook. Follow the numbered PVC trail markers to make your way through the dense mangroves. The trail ends at a chickee (a raised, open-air platform for camping) in Hell's Bay, a perfect place for a peaceful night's rest. There are three chickees along the trail—Pearl Bay Chickee, Hell's Bay Chickee, and Lard Can Chickee. You must obtain a backcountry permit to camp.

Nine Mile Pond Canoe Trail

A more leisurely paddle, the 5-mile loop trail around Nine Mile Pond is perfect for novice paddlers and families. The trail is well marked with yellow and white poles.

To begin, head to the Nine Mile Pond Canoe trailhead, located off the main park road before the Flamingo Visitor Center. Follow the trail markers counterclockwise around the pond.

West Lake to Alligator Creek

For more experienced paddlers, the 10-mile round-trip paddle from West Lake to Alligator Creek provides a variety of environments, from open lakes to narrow, winding creeks.

Begin at the West Lake Canoe trailhead, paddling out into the lake, and then turn south to follow the shoreline. As you reach the south side of the lake, look for the entrance to Alligator Creek and follow the creek upstream.

HIKES

Snake Bight Trail

This 3.2-mile out-and-back trail (1.6 miles each way) meanders through mangrove forests and buttonwood trees, leading you to

The shaded Snake Bight Trail eventually leads to a view of Florida Bay.

an observation platform overlooking Florida Bay. As the name suggests, it's a great place to spot wading birds and the occasional snake.

Starting from the trailhead at the end of the Snake Bight Trail road, follow the trail south toward the coast. It's a straight shot with minimal elevation change. Mosquitoes can be plentiful, so bring bug spray and consider hiking this trail during the winter months when mosquitoes are less abundant.

Secluded beach campsites lie along the Wilderness Waterway in Everglades National Park.

Coastal Prairie Trail

This trail, often overlooked by visitors, takes you through 7.5 miles of scenic wetland prairies and mangrove swamps, ending at the historic Clubhouse Beach. Begin from the Flamingo area and head west following the trail along the coast of Florida Bay. The trail is mostly flat but can be muddy and wet during the rainy season. Clubhouse Beach itself offers a spectacular view of the Florida Bay, especially during sunset, and you can camp with a permit.

Otter Cave Hammock Trail

This loop trail, totaling just under a mile, offers a unique and easy trek through hardwood hammocks and past solution holes; you might spot its namesake otters if you're lucky.

From the trailhead, follow the path into the dense hammock. Expect to navigate some tight spots and to duck under tree limbs.

HIDDEN GEM

The most adventurous watermen can disappear into the heart of the Everglades on the **Wilderness Waterway,** a glorious 99-mile paddling route in Everglades National Park that stretches from Everglades City in the north to Flamingo in the south. This epic journey takes eight to ten days by canoe or kayak and winds through a varied landscape of mangrove-lined creek tunnels, shallow bays, narrow channels, and open Gulf waters.

While the route is mainly sheltered, there are more exposed parts, such as crossing large, open bodies of water like Whitewater Bay and paddling along the Gulf Coast, where the route is subject to wind and tides. It requires strength, planning, and navigational skills: Camping chickees are spaced 10 to 12 miles apart, and the waterway can be challenging to follow, especially in the mangrove areas. Bring detailed nautical charts or a GPS device, and be prepared to cross open water where conditions can change rapidly.

Gates of the Arctic National Park and Preserve

Alaska | nps.gov/gaar | Visitation: 11,045

"If you get in trouble, give us a call on the sat phone. There's no one else out here but you and the bears."

Those were the last words our rowdy bush pilot said to us before she kicked her pontoon out of the muck and clambered back into her 1960s-era De Havilland Beaver. The turboprop coughed to life and became a mosquito against the enormous polychrome peaks that crowded a horizon tufted with ominous clouds. Circle Lake's waters returned to plate glass, and I peered into a wall of rusting fall foliage where a trail should be, feeling as small as a person can be.

Even to someone accustomed to visiting the wildest places one can find on a map, Gates of the Arctic represents something beyond all reckoning. To venture into the least-visited national park in the country doesn't just mean losing yourself in it. Before you take a step into its spongy, trackless muskeg or confounding bush, you understand you will emerge a completely different person—if you emerge at all.

The challenges to travel here range from absurd to extreme. Mileages and distance mean nothing, as you can go from skipping like a Von Trapp over high-altitude tundra to spending 40 minutes trying and failing to get around a waist-deep bog. Snow could close out your sunniest day, just in time to set up camp on the soggy mattress of tundra that passes for a suitable site. The inescapable bush claws at you like demonic hands from an *Evil Dead* movie, mauling bare skin and pilfering items out of your pack. Each step presents a doomed gambit: slippery tussock or mucky hole? The terrain can make an industrialist out of the staunchest treehugger—or at least make you want to marry a trail builder. Grizzly bears are plentiful, and though they've earned the nickname "salad bears" because the ones here mostly subsist off veggies, that won't calm your nerves when you see their hulking shapes trundle down the mountainside toward your camp.

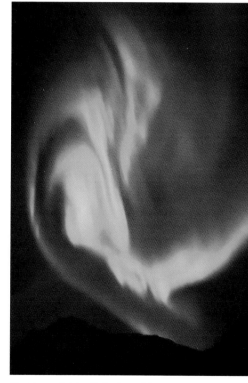

On clear nights, Gates' position well above the Arctic Circle offers excellent chances to see the aurora borealis.

Gates of the Arctic is the least-visited park in the United States.

So why go? Experiencing wilderness at this scale offers rewards that match the gargantuan effort. We spent several days basecamping and exploring under the Arrigetch Peaks, a fortress of impossible black spires erupting thousands of feet skyward out of the tundra. Wolf tracks guided us to the best path along the swift and clear Arrigetch Creek, and loons treated us to nightly serenades.

The bears at the edges of our valley soon became entertaining fixtures: After a close encounter where both species did everything right, the mom and her two roly-poly cubs stuck to scarfing willow buds on the vast tracts of rusting willow trees in the distance. We resembled neighbors who deeply respected and admired each other but knew not to talk religion or politics.

With numerous river crossings, bogs, and sinkholes, it pays to accept wet feet in Gates.

Soaring granite walls fill the lonely Arrigetch Creek valley.

In a relatively short distance, one can inhale everything that makes up the Arctic at its most epic (save the ocean): spruce-filled taiga, boreal forest, swampy muskeg, glacier-scooped valleys, rock walls and towers, braided rivers, kaleidoscopic yet barren tundra. Moose, musk oxen, wolverines, Dall sheep, black bears, the revered beaver, and the largest caribou herd in the world (300,000 strong) join the big bad brown bruins—though you will see fewer animals than you might expect, spread as they are over the vastness. Here, where the Rockies dead-end dramatically against the Arctic in the imposing Brooks Range, you can point to a forbidding ridge, scramble it, and find a colossal lake hidden behind, glowing blue like a robin's egg. Few of the 7,000-foot peaks you see hunched over it have names.

You can hike past midnight under a hallucinogenic midnight sun, or (much less commonly) tempt frostbite or worse in the -50 degrees cold terror of polar night. If you are lucky, the aurora borealis might come out to melt your mind with curtains, seams, and sparking drips of colored light. Science has explanations, people take pictures; all are rendered inadequate. Departed ancestors, lost children at play, shining Valkyrian armor: You instantly believe all the mythical explanations from early cultures and can't help but come up with your own.

People like the Nunamiut Iñupiat and Koyukon Athabascans have been here for over 13,000 years, and Gates allows you to see it in the same state as their ancestors did. Many other parks and wildlands feel like refuges from the built world, precious snow globes where civilization finds the cracks to trickle in nonetheless. In its overpowering wildness, Gates reduces us to little more than another fragile species on the landscape, one whose tenuous survival relies on the bounties and fortunes it bestows and the humility and hard-won knowledge to understand and feel our correct place within it.

An ancient Koyukon tradition taught by elders holds that when one kills an animal (especially a beaver) for meat or hide, one must place its bones back in the river and whisper to its spirit, *Tonon litseeyh* ("be made again in the water"). While in part meant to ensure that the reborn animal returns to your trap, this gesture also confers a respect for the restorative, transformative power

Three large glacial lakes fill the Aquarius valley.

of such an overwhelming landscape—a power that can be felt by anyone.

I have proof. Four of my closest friends joined me on our 10-day expedition to Gates of the Arctic. They came from varied places (Washington, DC, Vermont, Seattle), walks of life (opera singer, engineer, trombonist, drummer), and backcountry experience (extensive, moderate, essentially none). They all returned changed, and to end this chapter, I'd like to cede the floor and let them explain how in their own words.

I think about Gates a lot, certainly at least three to four days a week. I remember the feeling of a remoteness that blurred and maybe erased the line that usually separates people from the nature and environment that my ancient ancestors experienced. We all get a taste of that with any backpacking trip, but the consequences and rewards built into the terrain of Gates elevated the experience and deeply touched me. You can't train for tussocks, but the reward is worth the risk and challenge. There is no way to describe the scope and scale. To some degree, you will be uncomfortable.

But if you go, you might not be able to stop thinking about it when you must come back. —Travis D., Stowe, VT

I had this thought on the first day we set out, and it lingers: If you wanted, Gates would be a great place to give up. The muskeg would absorb you in no time. When you are so far away from your own life, in a place that absolutely does not care if you exist and will absorb you if you give up, you are forced to be completely present in every single moment. Each careful footfall, each cool breeze on your neck, each view around the next patch of alders, requires your full attention. It takes a while to even realize that you are in such an acute state of being present, so alert to and immersed as you are in your surroundings. —Elissa A., Washington, DC

The first thing that pops into my memory is watching the float plane fly away and the sudden and stark realization that the exit just flew away, and the only way out is through. I had that pit-in-the-stomach feeling for about 30 seconds before I was thrust into the one thing that could distract me: hard work trudging through the mud with a 65-pound pack on my back. That 30 seconds was real. Gates is one of the few places left in the world where you can feel you've stepped into a time machine. Want to know what a place looked like before they put up a Starbucks? Gates is a great place to find out. But it's the kind of place that could turn any average human into a conservationist. It's an experience that should be shared and protected. —Jonathan P., Seattle, WA

You never quite knew what you were in for each time you took a step: twisting an ankle on a tussock, losing a shoe in the mud, going thigh deep into water—all possible within ten to fifteen steps of each other. Nothing I did while training for this trip prepared me for that, and I'm not sure what would have. But it's hands-down the most beautiful place I've ever been, and it put me in one of the best headspaces I've ever been in, too. To share it with friends was great, but also to have moments where you felt completely solitary, like you were the only person out there. I'll never forget it. —Rob S., Seattle, WA

HIDDEN GEM

Given its status as a trailless, roadless, facility-free wilderness bigger than the state of Maryland, Gates of the Arctic in its entirety is the totemic hidden gem of the national parks system. Otherworldly granite monuments, wildlife in numbers and diversity to rival anywhere else in the world, best-ever views, and crushing solitude—those gems are scattered everywhere here in a scale found in few other places in the world, along with a particular Arctic magic found nowhere else. But boy, are they hidden: Treacherous terrain, daunting logistics, a vanishingly short practical season, and other assorted type-2 booby traps loom ready to thwart any aspirations to its grandeur. Looking at a map of this 200-mile-long, 130-mile-wide most northerly park might be enough to make you plan a beach vacation.

That said, if Gates has a milk-run trip, it's the **Arrigetch Peaks,** a cluster of sheer scarps, fins, and pinnacles that burst out of the tundra. (Arrigetch roughly means "fingers of the outstretched hand.") At least eleven cirque glaciers still cling to its granite knuckles, and it's possible to stare straight up 3,000- to 4,000-foot rock faces from the valley bottom. From a basecamp at the edge of tree line, you can spend days exploring at least three different valleys filled with unique wonders: Aquarius shelters a series of large aquamarine lakes; several towers known as the Maidens lord over their namesake drainage; and Arrigetch Creek winds through flat-bottomed meadows to find its headwaters at the base of fantastical peaks like Xanadu and the Melting Tower.

The route to the Arrigetch isn't defined: Spidering user and game trails crisscross the tundra bench to the left of Circle Lake, a cutoff oxbow bend of the Alatna River that serves as a shallow-water landing strip. Following portions of a small tributary paralleling the Alatna makes for sandy, easier going in some years. You'll need to hump it on a big climb through the muskeg, taiga, and tundra paralleling tumbling Arrigetch Creek to reach basecamp. The

The Maidens (named for the three spires seen at the entrance) are just one valley to explore in the Arrigetch Peaks.

best way to return is by water: Stowing pack rafts at the beginning of the trip enables you to hop on the mostly mellow Alatna River and camp at a series of beautiful stony beaches. Rivers act like highways, offering your best chance to spot wildlife.

Gates is a mind-bogglingly intimidating and complex place to plan an adventure, and Arrigetch is no exception. All but the most experienced wilderness travelers should consider hiring a guide service. In addition to knowing that year's best route (it often changes), they can help secure bush flights, plan meals, provide specialized gear, and reserve lodging to bookend the trip. (Typically starting from Fairbanks 200 miles south, getting to Gates usually requires no less than two bush plane flights, and hunters often take priority.) Even with a guide, all parts of the park demand a high degree of self-sufficiency and preparation.

And yet the trip requires no technical skills, which means anyone with a solid fitness level and high tolerance for Arctic suffering can access this ultimate hidden gem.

Architect Eero Saarinen designed the iconic Gateway Arch.

Gateway Arch National Park

Missouri | nps.gov/jeff | Visitation: 2,422,836

Gateway Arch is an outlier in the National Park Service. It's an urban park celebrating moments of US history with a centerpiece monument built by human hands, visible from I-70 as you pull into St. Louis.

The Arch, a 630-foot masterpiece conceived by Finnish American architect Eero Saarinen, is the tallest man-made monument in the Western Hemisphere and a beacon that has captivated millions since its completion in 1965.

The park sits near the historic site of St. Louis's founding in 1764 and the westward expansion of the nineteenth century that began with explorers Lewis and Clark. Their expedition, commissioned by President Thomas Jefferson, aimed to chart a course to the Pacific Ocean, opening vast new territories. Their daring journey is chronicled in the Museum at the Gateway Arch, situated beneath the Arch. The grounds also feature an old courthouse, statues, and plaques that give testament to Dred Scott's place in the debate over slavery in the United States

You can also venture inside the Arch itself. Enclosed trams whisk visitors up to the top, where sixteen tiny windows on each side offer a bird's-eye view of St. Louis and the Mississippi. On a clear day, you can see up to 30 miles in each direction.

Glacier Bay National Park

Alaska | nps.gov/glba | Visitation: 703,659

How is it that Glacier Bay, an immense 3.3-million-acre park with no roads in or out, is the most visited national park in Alaska? Or more popular than several in the Lower 48?

The answer lies in its location along the storied Inside Passage to the Frontier State. Most sightseers never set foot inside the park: They view its eye-popping fjords, breaching humpback whales, and calving tidewater glaciers from the deck of one of the many cruise ships that make it a stop on a 1,000-mile journey. A smaller portion see it on smaller local boats or flightseeing tours.

But hardier travelers who stay longer for a closer look—either by kayak or by embarking into the landscape via the park's short but sweet trail network—will be humbled by the skyscraping Fairweather Range peaks and up-close views of toothpaste-blue icebergs that break off glaciers in office-building-size chunks.

ZONES OF INTEREST

Glacier Bay National Park is a world-class destination for kayakers, offering a rich tapestry of marine wildlife, calving tidewater glaciers, and jaw-dropping scenery. Solitude and serenity abound in the spaces between cruise traffic, but all but the most experienced and self-sufficient paddlers should contact outfitters for guided tours.

West Arm

The premier West Arm route gets you up close and personal with the park's eponymous glaciers. Paddle from Bartlett Cove to Tarr Inlet, home of the famous Margerie and Grand Pacific Glaciers. Camp at Blue Mouse Cove on the first night, then paddle to Reid Inlet for the second. Be aware, this is a multiday trip and will require a drop-off/pickup by a tour boat service. The glaciers rule, but you're also likely to spot humpback whales, sea otters, harbor seals, and a variety of bird species. You'll also share the route with the bulk of cruise and boat tour traffic.

East Arm

A less-crowded option, the East Arm of Glacier Bay is larded with fjords and inlets. Begin your journey in Bartlett Cove and paddle toward the Muir Inlet. Depending on your timeline and skill level, you could explore McBride or Riggs Glacier. Campsites include Garforth Island and the Geikie Inlet area. You'll have the opportunity to spot moose, wolves, and brown bears along the shorelines in addition to abundant marine wildlife.

Glacier Bay offers intimate views of tidewater glaciers and marine wildlife.

Sunset over the Fairweather Range in Bartlett Cove.

Bartlett Cove

If you're short on time or less experienced on the water, a day-trip paddle around Bartlett Cove can be ideal. You can still paddle amid the icebergs that have calved from glaciers deeper into the inlets, and spy sea otters, harbor seals, and various seabirds.

HIKES

With its intricate waterways, vast glaciers, and remote landscapes, Glacier Bay is often seen more from the deck of a boat or a kayak than by foot. But there are a few fantastic and empty hiking trails for those who make landfall.

Bartlett River Trail

This trail is 4 miles round-trip and leads you through the lush rain forest, colorful meadows, and to the mouth of the Bartlett River. You'll likely spot bald eagles, river otters, or brown bears fishing in the river, especially during the salmon run.

Bartlett Lake Trail

At 8 miles round-trip, this trail is more strenuous and less traveled than the River Trail. It winds through dense forest and wetlands before opening to vistas of Bartlett Lake. Keep an eye out for signs of moose and bring insect repellent for the ravenous mosquitoes that plague the area in summer.

Mount Wright/Tall Trees Trail

This challenging trail steeply climbs 8 miles through the dense temperate rain forest up Mount Wright. Topping out brings smack-you-in-the-face views of the Fairweather Range's 15,000-foot peaks.

While glaciers are receding within the park, they've indelibly shaped the landscape.

Glacier National Park

Montana | nps.gov/glac | Visitation: 2,933,616

Glacier National Park looms larger in my mind than almost any other park. It began when I arrived well past midnight on a post-college road trip after a long slog through Wyoming and the entirety of Montana. As we pulled into the unstaffed entrance, blinking red stoplights illuminated a yellow sign stamped with the frowning visage of a grizzly bear and three ominous words: BEARS IN AREA.

When we proceeded, we saw ursine movement in every dimly lit branch juddering in the wind, in every ripple across Lake McDonald, painted slate in the dim early-morning light. Clouds hovered above us, dirty gray cotton we could touch through the sunroof of our matching Nissan Altima. We rounded a bend and became enclosed in thick fog as we climbed up the road.

Then, without warning, bright sun burst through, blinding us. Our eyes adjusted and dread turned to delight as we saw arcing fins, spiny arêtes, and shark-fin peaks painted in greens, blacks, and purples scudding through the clouds like massive ghost ships. Waterfalls poured off them like diamonds into a white abyss below. We floated above it all, high on discovering a mountain paradise more enchanting than any we'd ever seen. We hadn't slept that night, and we wouldn't for another 24 hours.

Going-to-the-Sun Road threads through Glacier National Park, offering one of the finest drives in certainly the Rockies and perhaps the whole of the park system. It provides easy access to much of the park's million-acre wilderness—and remains popular because of this. Though many of my recommendations will take you away from it, the 50-mile road is wholly worth a drive or, better, a ride on one of the antique-car shuttles operated by the park.

Though technically part of the American landscape, Glacier's extreme topography and overwhelming beauty bears more in common with the Canadian Rockies than anything in the Lower 48. (It runs continuously into Canada's Waterton Lakes National Park, forming the world's first International Peace Park.) Like much of the Rockies, ancient tectonic forces heaved and buckled the earth here, lifting great slabs of rock and tilting them heavenward many times over. Glaciers came and went, carving their way through these lofty peaks. A million years of erosion and the ceaseless march of ice chewed at the surface, revealing breathtaking U-shaped valleys, turquoise lakes and tarns, and hanging cirques cupping remnant glaciers. Lewis and Clark Schist, a metamorphic rock formed from sandstone and shale altered by heat, pressure, and chemical processes, dominates the terrain. Look for its dark color, fine-grained texture, and the presence of minerals such as muscovite, biotite, and garnet everywhere you step.

Roughly 300 grizzly bears live within Glacier National Park.

Early park booster George Bird Grinnell called the area that would become Glacier "The Crown of the Continent," and it looks and acts the part. Located at the convergence of several mountain ranges, the park contains the headwaters of the Columbia, Missouri, and Saskatchewan River systems. This rare "triple divide" drains into the Pacific, Gulf of Mexico, and Hudson Bay, respectively, making it a critical ecological and hydrological hub for all North America.

All that water feeds wildly diverse landscapes: verdant alpine meadows that burst with wildflowers; forests of subalpine fir and fragrant Engelmann spruce; steep-sided valleys filled with lakes made from the pristine waters of melted glaciers and fed and drained by big rivers. Glacier contains one of the few "intact ecosystems" in the Lower 48; essentially, all the species that were present pre-settlement remain. This includes the densest population of grizzly bears in the Lower 48; nimble and sure-footed mountain goats traversing dizzying cliffs; bald eagles, mountain lions, bighorns, bobcats, moose, elk, deer, coyotes, and so much more. You will likely see many of them, even on busier trails.

Native American tribes—the Blackfeet, Shoshone, Flathead, and Kootenai—have long held these lands sacred. They have hunted and sheltered seasonally here, and their stories and beliefs are woven into the fabric of the landscape. The Blackfeet called Glacier the "Backbone of the World"; the Kootenai spoke of Yawunik, a giant water serpent that yelled at the bottom of Lake McDonald. And in the twilight of the nineteenth century, explorers and conservationists, awed by the splendor of the park, set forth to ensure its protection for generations to come.

The namesake rivers of ice that have shaped and defined this landscape for millennia are fast disappearing, as rising temperatures have caused the glaciers to retreat at an alarming rate. In the mid-nineteenth century, 150 glaciers clung to the park's peaks and valleys. By 1966, the number dropped to around 50; as of 2021, only 26 glaciers remained. Some of those have lost as much as 80 percent of their surface area over the past century. Some studies indicate that under a moderate emissions scenario, most glaciers could disappear by the 2030s. Beyond invalidating the park's name, it would have far-reaching ecological consequences, as the glaciers play a critical role in regulating the region's water supply and supporting the park's unique biodiversity.

Like so many other parks threatened by climate change, venturing into Glacier comes with the bittersweet knowledge of how humans possess the power to make these enduring wild spaces impermanent, within the span of our own lifetimes. If you are fortunate enough to admire this crown jewel of a park before its defining features disappear, take those lessons with you, let them inform your choices, and consider becoming an advocate for responsible change wherever you can.

ZONES OF INTEREST

North Fork Area

Located in the remote northwest section of the park, the park service calls the North Fork "an area of reduced visitation." A bumpy, potholed, all-day drive via a gravel road goes a long way in keeping

Western larch turn gold in fall on the shores of Kintla Lake.

visitors out—as does the lack of services. The tiny town of Polebridge has a single mercantile store for last-second supplies (and tasty baked treats), but otherwise services are limited and there's no cell service should you blow a tire (a common occurrence out here). The rewards, though: Featuring two serene and picturesque lakes (Bowman and Kintla) surrounded by towering mountains, this region offers pristine solitude among mixed forests recovering from fires over the last thirty years.

Sample it on the Numa Ridge Lookout Trail, a stunning and moderately challenging 10.4-mile round-trip trail that takes hikers through a diverse array of landscapes. It culminates at the historic Numa Ridge Lookout, which offers panoramic views of the extremely dramatic mountains and valleys that characterize Glacier.

The trail begins at the Bowman Lake Campground. From the trailhead, the path meanders along the western shoreline of the lake, offering glimpses of shimmering water through the trees. The gentle terrain provides a leisurely start to the hike, allowing hikers to warm up and acclimate.

After 1.5 miles, the trail diverges from the lakeshore and begins a steady ascent into the mountains, snaking past thick conifer forest interspersed with occasional wildflower-pocked meadows during the summer months. Deer, elk, and mountain goats can be seen here as you climb.

At the 4-mile mark, the trail steepens, and switchbacks lead you up the final stretch toward the lookout. The trees wane and give way to increasingly expansive views of the surrounding peaks and valleys along a rockier and more rugged ridge trail until you reach the sweeping views at Numa Ridge Lookout, perched at an elevation of 6,960 feet. Built in 1935, it still stands as a testament to the park's complicated relationship with fire management. From this vantage point, drink in the jagged peaks, yawning U-shaped valleys, and glittering waters of Bowman Lake far below. On a clear day, the views extend to the Livingston Range, the Whitefish Range, and into the heart of the park. After savoring the scenery, hikers can retrace their steps back down the trail.

Two Medicine

Two Medicine is in the southeastern part of the park, accessible from the town of East Glacier Park. This area was once a primary destination for visitors before the construction of the Going-to-the-Sun Road. Today, it offers a quieter, less-crowded experience.

The remarkable Scenic Point Trail is a strenuous 7.4-mile round-trip jammer that lets you lord over Two Medicine Valley, as well as the plains stretching eastward toward the Blackfeet Reservation. Beginning at the Scenic Point parking area, the trail follows Appistoki Creek and climbs steadily through forests and wildflower-strewn meadows before reaching a series of switchbacks leading to the ridge. From the ridge, hikers are treated to a breathtaking panorama of peaks guarding the Continental Divide, including views of Two Medicine Lake far below. It tops out at a lung-busting 7,522 feet.

For those seeking a more challenging adventure, you can extend your trip by following the ridge northward toward Mount Henry, or by connecting to the East Glacier Trail, which descends to the Two Medicine Campground.

Cut Bank

Cut Bank, situated on the park's eastern boundary, is a quiet section of the park far from the madding crowds of Going-to-the-Sun Road, accessed by a gravel road branching off US 89. It's well maintained and most cars should be able to make it, but there are no services at the end of it—just a shaded, primitive campground.

But beyond the campground lies a unique, life-list destination: For the low, low price of 15 miles round-trip, hikers can stand astride a continental divide where water drains into the Pacific, Atlantic, and Arctic Oceans. The trail departs from the campground to initially follow soothing Cut Bank Creek and pass through vibrant alpine meadows and tall-treed forests. (This creek empties into the Atlantic, thousands of miles away.) Bad Marriage, Medicine Grizzly, and Razoredge peaks own the horizon, and they only get bigger as you approach.

Cut Bank leads to Triple Divide—a place where water drains into three oceans.

Seven miles into the hike, the trail reaches the junction with the Pitamakan Pass Trail. From here, hikers will continue to the west, following the path up the final ascent to Triple Divide Pass. No sugarcoating, it's grueling: That final section climbs 2,000 feet in a little less than 2.5 miles, but the view helps. When you reach Triple Divide Pass, at an elevation of 7,397 feet, the giant pyramid of Triple Divide Peak looms large above. If you poured your water bottle out on top of it, its contents could end up in the Atlantic, Pacific, or Arctic Oceans, a claim no other peak in the world can make. Experienced scramblers can attempt to summit via a Class 3 gully, but be careful: As with much of Glacier, the rock is loose and crumbly.

HIKES

Huckleberry Lookout

In summer, get ready to stain your hands purple from all the juicy namesake berries found on this 12-mile out-and-back hike. Bring your bear spray and make plenty of noise, too: Bears of all kinds love to gorge on the plentiful fruit as much as you do.

The trailhead for the Huckleberry Lookout hike is located along the Camas Road, a short drive from the popular Lake McDonald area. This family-friendly hike is usually quiet, though. Embark by cruising through towering stands of cedar, hemlock, and spruce casting shadows on a flat, easy trail crisscrossed with wooden bridges. Ferns and wildflowers carpet the underbrush, and the berries attract flocks of trilling songbirds, too.

As the trail progresses, it begins to climb steadily past stands of aspen and lodgepole pine. In the late summer and early autumn, this is a great place to look for tart-sweet wild huckleberries growing along the trail. Pick a few for a burst of energy or save them for the summit.

Traverse a mosaic of open meadows and rocky outcroppings, where marmots, pikas, and a variety of birds make their home among the boulders and grasses. Deer or elk can be seen grazing in meadows or seeking shade beneath the trees.

The trail reaches Huckleberry Lookout, a historic fire lookout perched at an elevation of 6,593 feet. Beyond offering a reminder of the days when these remote outposts served as the first line of

The current two-story structure was built in 1933 to replace the original built 10 years before.

defense against wildfire, this lofty vantage point gives you great views of the trademark steep-sided, pointy peaks of Glacier National Park stretching out in every direction.

Cobalt Lake

The views on this 11.2-mile round-trip hike begin right away, with Lone Walker, Sinopah, Painted Teepee, and Mount Helen cutting into the sky and reflecting in Lower Two Medicine Lake. Accessible from East Glacier via the Two Medicine Road, journey along the south shore of Two Medicine Lake's placid waters. At 0.5 mile, look for moose lounging and browsing in a string of beaver ponds. A series of turnoffs to view waterfalls comes soon after.

The trail soon diverges from the lakeshore, climbing gently into stands of lodgepole pine and subalpine fir, their branches draped with moss and lichen. Between miles 1.1 and 3.5, the trail leads hikers past a series of cascading waterfalls: Rockwell Falls is a double waterfall, but you'll have to bushwhack to see the second falls behind it.

Beyond here, the path traverses a set of switchbacks, guiding hikers up a U-shaped valley between Sinopah and Painted Teepee to the hanging valley that cradles Cobalt Lake. Soon you'll wander into a tundra-like subalpine zone full of flower meadows and stunted trees. At 5.5 miles the trail tops out and a short stretch leads to the shore of Cobalt Lake, a mesmerizing body of water cradled within a cirque of jagged peaks. With a permit, you can camp at one of two sites at Cobalt Lake.

Brown/Boulder Pass Loop

The Brown/Boulder Pass Loop is a difficult but unforgettable 38-mile horseshoe-shaped backpacking route into the remote northwest corner of Glacier National Park, far from the well-trodden paths of the park's more popular areas.

The journey begins at the Bowman or Kintla Lake trailheads, both accessible from the small community of Polebridge via a rough dirt road. (Both are great, but we'll start from Bowman Lake.) The trail initially follows the serene shoreline of Bowman Lake. The first campground, at the head of Bowman Lake, lies along the trail, offering an opportunity for an overnight stop before venturing deeper into the wilderness.

As the trail progresses, it veers away from the lake, climbing into the forests of the Livingston Range, toward the first pass of the journey, Brown Pass, at 6,230 feet. Snowcapped, imposing Boulder Mountain and Thunderbird Peak are an eye-popping sight from here on, as is the cascading Hole-in-the-Wall waterfall.

Just before Brown Pass, you'll encounter the Brown Pass campground (famous for its mosquitoes). Crossing Brown Pass, the trail offers two more miles of nonstop sights before it begins its descent, following the course of Boulder Creek as it tumbles through the valley below, its crystal-clear waters providing a vital source of hydration for both hikers and abundant wildlife.

As the trail continues its journey, it passes a few small sapphire tarns before dropping down a series of steep switchbacks—about 3,000 feet in a little more than 3 miles. Soaring views of Kintla and Kinnerly peaks goad you on and distract you from your aching knees.

The final leg of the loop follows the course of the remote and pristine Upper Kintla Lake (where you'll camp for a final night). After following the shoreline of Kintla Lake, exit at the Kintla Lake trailhead. The catch: Bowman and Kintla trailheads are separated by 20 dirt road miles, so you'll need to have stashed a car or bike or arranged a shuttle to get back to your starting point at Bowman. Most outfitters won't go to Kintla, so it'll take some wrangling. We think that's a small price to pay for one of the greatest routes in the whole of the Lower 48.

HIDDEN GEM

The **Coal Creek Cross-Country Zone** in the park's southern region delivers a true solitary wilderness experience in some of the wildest, most seldom visited terrain you can find in a national park. This is a true test piece for any backpacker, and it demands research, preparation, self-sufficiency, and a dollop of bravery.

Access to the Coal Creek area begins at the Walton Ranger Station, located along US 2 east of Essex. From here, hikers can inquire with rangers about an extremely difficult 43-mile loop sometimes called the Coal Creek-Nyack route. Expect plenty of bushwhacking, difficult route finding, and bridge-less, waist-high water crossings—including an intimidating ford of the Middle Fork Flathead River at the start of your trip. The safest place to cross

Visiting the Coal Creek Cross-Country Zone requires off-trail navigation and deep self-sufficiency.

often changes depending on river flow and current conditions, so it's vital to check in with rangers before attempting it (ask about the Nyack Crossing, between mile markers 164 and 165 on US 2).

That's a start. In fact, think of this as a homework assignment—the rangers will thank you. Break out the topo map and string together these places that form the rough route: Nyack Crossing, Boundary Trail, Lower and Upper Nyack Campgrounds, Cutbank Pass, Surprise Pass, Martha's Basin, Coal Creek Valley and Campground, and back to Nyack Crossing. If you aren't willing and ready to complete this assignment, then you aren't ready for the trek. If you are: Prepare for soul-quieting solitude, frequent sightings of charismatic megafauna, lonely lakes, and neck-craning views of some of the park's tallest peaks.

Grand Canyon National Park

Arizona | nps.gov/grca | Visitation: 4,733,705

A hole. A very, very large hole.

Easy place to commit murder. Just push the dude over the cliff and no body find out. Such a creeper.

Whoopity do, Grand Canyon. You are a giant hole in the ground. You were caused be erosion. You don't have roller coasters or dippin' dots. Jeeesh. Can you say 'overrated?'

It's to big. I almost fell like 20 miles away from it by my car but I could still see it. Also my wife decided to divorce me while we were there. It's also to big. I was expecting smaller.

I would really love help understandin what is so grand about a canyon.

—one-star Yelp reviews of the Grand Canyon

The Grand Canyon isn't a hole in the ground—it is *the world's premier hole in the ground*, the hole in the ground by which all other holes are judged and found severely wanting. On sight, no other place on earth presents such a visually shocking, mind-boggling geological story of the world in its infancy, its epic growth into maturity, and its decline into old age. If you can't understand what's grand about that, heaven help you. (Sorry for the divorce, though.)

Let's tell the story first in numbers: 277 miles long, up to 18 miles wide, over a mile deep, 2 billion years old at the bottom, 8,000 feet high on the North Rim, 7,000 on the South. The Colorado River took 6 million years patiently gnawing through sedimentary layers, eating into the heart of the continent and slicing through time to reveal 2-billion-year-old rock at the bottom, some of the oldest on earth.

Many national parks feature geologic features that enable us to travel deep into the past. But few have such a complete view of epochs and eons, of creatures long extinct, of seas rising and falling, of mountains that grew and crumbled and rose again. If those other parks are intriguing books, the Grand Canyon is the whole damn library.

Cape Royal lies on the Grand Canyon's quieter North Rim.

Though it rules our lives, the precise dimensions of time can be difficult for people to grasp. We come up with complex equations and aphorisms to help us grok it. But walking into the canyon, or up from it, turns time into something you can see, touch, feel, and taste, even if we can't quite find the words to describe it. You stand at the edge or look up from the bottom, your life a mere blink in the vast cosmic calendar, dwarfed by the immensity of space and time itself. In two footsteps it renders human time scales an absurd joke.

There's no better way to feel simultaneously tiny and enormous—a speck and a god in the same breath.

That's how I felt touching the Vishnu Schist, somber gray-green stone at the bottom of the canyon. It twinkled a little as I passed, and I could swear it made a noise beyond my hearing, like it was breathing. Named for the Hindu god, this set of metamorphic rocks found in the inner gorge of the Grand Canyon represents the oldest known rock formations within the park, the "basement rocks" resting at its deepest and most inaccessible depths.

This ancient rock formed 1.8 billion years ago during the Proterozoic era. Earth was a different world, with an atmosphere devoid of oxygen, with only the simplest life forms beginning to emerge. It began life as sediment and volcanic lava deposited in an ancient ocean. Over time, under intense heat and pressure, these deposits metamorphosed into schist and gneiss, creating the complex, swirling patterns we see today. High quantities of mica, feldspar, and quartz give it a shiny, flaky appearance, with a distinctive dark color that stands in stark contrast to the layers of lighter sedimentary rock above it. Another basement rock, called Zoroaster Granite, intruded into the Vishnu Schist around 1.7 billion years ago and appears as light-colored streaks and patches within the darker schist. This is but one of a staggering forty layers of rock within the canyon, each with a tale better told in books much longer than this one.

The park's ecology is as diverse as the strata it exposes. From the desert scrub of the canyon floor, the ecosystem ascends through a series of life zones, equivalent to traveling from Mexico to Canada. In the depths of the canyon, where the clear and cold Colorado River flows, the climate is hot and arid, a desert ecosystem full of hardy cacti and sagebrush and coyotes. It's also frequently so hot the air feels like it's pressing into your ear holes.

As you ascend the canyon, you pass through a riparian zone, a thin ribbon of green cast against the red and brown cliff walls. The Colorado River nurtures cottonwood trees and a variety of shrubs, which shelter mule deer, ringtail cats, and a variety of birds, including the rare and colorful southwestern willow flycatcher.

Climb higher and the ecosystem changes again. The pinyon pines and junipers of the transition zone give way to a forest of fragrant ponderosa pines and white fir. In this montane environment, you might spot elk and mule deer or the rare Abert's squirrel. Mountain lions hunt them all, though you probably won't see them. Over 1,500 plant, 355 bird, 89 mammalian, 47 reptile, 9 amphibian, and 17 fish species call the layers of the park home.

The "basement rocks" at the bottom of the canyon are some of the oldest on earth.

That includes people. The canyon has been home to various Indigenous cultures for 12,000 years. The Ancestral Puebloans, the Cohonina, and the Paiutes all built dwellings, hunted game, farmed land nearby, and held ceremonies in the shadow of its cliffs. The Hopi people believe their ancestors emerged from a sipapu, a portal between the spiritual and physical worlds, located deep within the Grand Canyon, which counts as their spiritual home. Today, the Havasupai tribe, known as the "People of the Blue-Green Water," still live within the canyon, in the village of Supai, surrounded by thundering waterfalls cascading into travertine pools of electric turquoise. The village, one of the most remote in the United States, is accessible only by foot, mule, or helicopter.

Spanish explorers, led by Garcia Lopez de Cardenas, were the first Europeans to gaze upon the Grand Canyon in 1540, arriving in search of mythical cities of gold. They left as bummed as those Yelp reviewers, finding neither gold nor a navigable river. They saw only an obstacle to their dreams of conquest, so they departed and left the canyon in relative isolation.

American exploration began in earnest with the expedition of Major John Wesley Powell in 1869. A one-armed Civil War veteran, Powell led a team of nine men on an audacious journey down the

Colorado River. Despite hardships, mutinies, and the loss of three men, Powell's expedition unveiled the wonders of the Grand Canyon to the wider world. Powell's vivid accounts of the journey captured the public's imagination with descriptions of roaring rapids, impossible cliffs, and ancient ruins.

In the early twentieth century, the Santa Fe Railroad brought the first wave of tourists, transforming the Grand Canyon into a national spectacle. In 1908, President Teddy Roosevelt declared the Grand Canyon a national monument and left a 5-star review, saying, "Leave it as it is. You cannot improve on it. The ages have been at work on it, and man can only mar it."

Plenty of people try. Despite its relatively remote location, this second-most visited park endures swarms of people crowding the South Rim, sometimes littering or otherwise disrespecting this fragile place. (I once passed David Beckham and Posh Spice with kids and security detail in tow as I approached the lip of the rim on the Bright Angel Trail. They seemed polite and awed.) Unprepared hikers hell-bent on descending to the river or tackling routes beyond their ability tax park rangers and search-and-rescue operations every year. Some of them die. I encountered a man in a full business suit with a briefcase and dress shoes halfway down the South Kaibab Trail, staring into the mouth of his empty 16-ounce Dasani bottle. I refilled it from my Nalgene and urged him to go back, but he kept on.

With care and preparation (and lots of sun protection, water, and salty snacks), you can easily avoid joining the ranks of the dumb or deceased. But hear me when I say this: Neither the prospect of death nor disrespect can diminish the overwhelming power of the canyon. It will outlast us and all our shenanigans, and you will feel it—especially if you find your empty spot in it, which is not that difficult in a place so, well, grand.

Five stars. No notes.

ZONE OF INTEREST

The North Rim

Since it sees only 10 percent of all park visitors and lies a 4.5-hour drive from the South Rim, the North Rim of the Grand Canyon provides a quieter, more remote experience than its southern counterpart. At an elevation of 8,000 feet, the North Rim is significantly higher than the South Rim, and its cooler climate supports a distinctly different set of flora and fauna. A thick forest of ponderosa pines, aspens, and spruce trees covers the area, providing a stark contrast to the desert environment found below the rim.

Another barrier to entry is seasonal. The North Rim is typically open from mid-May through mid-October, with the exact dates dependent on weather conditions. The centerpiece of the North Rim is the historic Grand Canyon Lodge, a charming structure offering lodging, dining, and great canyon views.

Get an intimate encounter with the canyon's shifting moods on the North Kaibab Trail, the least-visited but arguably the most unique of the Grand Canyon's three major maintained trails. The

Sunset from Toroweap Point on the North Rim.

North Kaibab Trail is the only maintained trail into the canyon from the North Rim. Here, the canyon is greener, narrower, and more secluded.

This journey begins at the North Kaibab trailhead, located 2 miles north of the North Rim's Grand Canyon Lodge. From an altitude of 8,241 feet, you'll start your descent surrounded by an aspen and spruce-fir forest, evidence of the cooler climate of the North Rim. The first leg of the trail winds down Roaring Springs Canyon on a series of steep and relentless switchbacks.

Roughly 5 miles and 3,000 vertical feet into your journey, you'll arrive at the lush oasis of Roaring Springs. The spring gushes from a cliffside, cascading down rock faces before coalescing into Bright Angel Creek. This spring is the primary water source for the Grand Canyon's south and north rims, making it a crucial point in the canyon's ecosystem.

At this point, there's a spur trail that leads to Roaring Springs day-use area, a worthwhile side trip for a picnic and rest break (no camping allowed, though).

Beyond Roaring Springs, you'll find Cottonwood Campground, a small, quiet, tree-shaded respite located 6.8 miles from the trailhead. It's here you'll find a composting toilet, tap water (seasonally available), and picnic tables.

Past Cottonwood, the trail continues to descend, meandering through the striking narrow walls of the "Box," a section of the trail where the canyon squeezes to less than a quarter mile wide. This area is notoriously hot and arid, a marked contrast to the cooler, forested trailhead above.

You'll then reach the oasis of Ribbon Falls, another worthy side trip. This unique waterfall flows over a mineral-encrusted spire, creating a surreal, glowing spectacle.

After 14 miles of descent, you'll reach Bright Angel Campground and Phantom Ranch, located on the canyon floor near the Colorado River. Here, the elevation is 2,480 feet. Phantom Ranch has dormitory spaces and cabins that require reservations well in advance, while the Bright Angel Campground offers tent sites.

Ribbon Falls on the North Kaibab Trail shelters a green oasis.

Keep in mind that hiking the Grand Canyon is a serious undertaking, and the North Kaibab Trail is no exception. The trail is steep, long, and depending on the time of year, can be incredibly hot. Hiking from the North Rim to the Colorado River and back in a single day is strongly discouraged.

As with any backcountry trip in the Grand Canyon, it's essential to check in with the Backcountry Information Center for the latest conditions and to obtain a permit if you plan on camping. Still, it's a chance to witness the entirety of the Grand Canyon in a way few others do.

HIKES

Tanner Trail

Tanner Trail, leading from Lipan Point, offers breathtaking views and solitude that are unmatched on the more popular trails of the South Rim. The trail descends over 5,000 feet in 9 miles, making it a very strenuous hike into the eastern section of the canyon. However, here views at the base of the tall walls on both sides down the canyon are wide and unimpeded—a rarity anywhere in the park. As in much of the canyon, it's in some ways best navigated not by mileage but by familiarity with the canyon's layers of stone.

Begin at Lipan Point, and follow an eroded, narrow trail as it descends steeply through the Kaibab and Toroweap Formations. You'll pass through a tunnel of Coconino Sandstone (rockfalls have obscured the trail in spots and will require route finding and care over insecure terrain). Soon you'll reach the Redwall Limestone; excellent views from the top transition into a loose, gravel-coated steep descent. Take your time as the trail narrows and the switchbacks increase in number.

Once past the Redwall, you enter the Muav Limestone, where the trail becomes less steep and you're rewarded with stunning views of the Colorado River and the eastern Grand Canyon. The trail continues through the Tapeats Formation before narrowing to a foot wide in the Dox Formation and steeply dropping you at Tanner Beach, a quiet and secluded spot on the banks of the Colorado River with lots of sun exposure and those promised epic views.

The difficulty level of this route requires that hikers prepare well and be very experienced. There is no water along the route, and it's notable for being exceptionally sun-exposed and hot (it's often nicknamed "Furnace Flats") at the river. Avoid it in hot weather and check in with rangers before attempting.

The steep, exposed Tanner Trail has fantastic views for its entirety.

Grandview-Tonto Trail Loop

The Grandview-Tonto Trail Loop is a challenging and rewarding hike in the Grand Canyon. This 13-mile loop offers breathtaking views and a taste of the solitude and vastness of the canyon. Here, we'll take you through the steps and give you a sense of the experience.

Start at the Grandview Point. Take a moment to absorb the stunning view before embarking on your journey. The first 3 miles of the trail are steep as it descends through layers of Coconino Sandstone and Hermit Shale, dropping roughly 2,500 feet. Along this section, you'll come across remnants of mining history: old tramway cables and a miner's cabin.

After the miner's cabin, the trail continues to Horseshoe Mesa, once the site of Pete Berry's Last Chance Copper Mine in the late nineteenth century. You can explore the ruins of old mining buildings and the mine itself, but remember not to disturb or take any artifacts. This area also offers a good spot for camping if you wish to break up your hike.

From Horseshoe Mesa, the trail connects to the Tonto Trail. This section is flatter and easier as it winds along the Tonto Platform. The trail offers an ever-changing panorama of the inner canyon, and you may spot some bighorn sheep.

Continuing along the Tonto Trail, you'll find the established Cottonwood Creek and Grapevine Creek campsites. Both have reliable water sources, but remember to treat any water before drinking.

After Grapevine Creek, you'll ascend back up the rim via the South Kaibab Trail, which offers some of the most spectacular views in the park. The South Kaibab is steep and has little shade, so start early to avoid the midday heat.

Don't take this hike lightly. It's long, steep, and has limited water sources. Make sure you're well prepared with plenty of water, food, sun protection, and a detailed map. Also, always check in with the Backcountry Information Center for a permit if you plan to camp, and for the latest trail conditions.

Traverse the canyon midway down on the Tonto Platform.

Uncle Jim Trail

The Uncle Jim Trail is a delightful, less-trafficked lollipop loop trail located on the North Rim of the Grand Canyon. This trail is named for "Uncle" Jim Owens, a game warden who worked to control the cougar population in the early 1900s by reportedly killing 500 of them.

The trail starts at the North Kaibab Trail parking area, accessible via a paved road from the North Rim visitor center. From the parking area, the trail heads northeast, sharing the initial stretch with the Ken Patrick Trail.

After 0.6 mile, the Uncle Jim Trail branches off to the right, looping around and cutting through a dense stand of ponderosa pines and aspens. This portion of the trail is relatively flat, and you're likely to encounter wildlife including the unique Kaibab squirrel, mule deer, and a variety of bird species.

As the trail progresses, it turns back toward the rim of the canyon, reaching Uncle Jim Point at the 2.5-mile mark. Here, you'll be rewarded with sweeping views of the canyon, including the dramatic North Kaibab Trail switchbacks and Roaring Springs Canyon. There are no guardrails here, so tread carefully.

"Uncle Jim" Owens supposedly killed 500 mountain lions within the park.

Widforss Point on Grand Canyon's North Rim.

After you take in the views, the trail loops back toward the starting point, offering different perspectives of the forest and occasional peeks at the canyon through the trees. The trail is well marked and generally well maintained, though it can be a bit rocky in places.

The total length of the loop is 5 miles, and the hike is considered moderate with limited elevation change. It's an excellent choice for those seeking a relatively easy, peaceful hike with a touch of grandeur at the viewpoint.

Remember to carry plenty of water, as sources are not available along the trail. Its higher elevation makes the North Rim cooler than the South Rim and subject to rapid weather changes, so check the forecast and dress in layers.

HIDDEN GEM

Overnight backpackers should aim for the unique **North Bass Trail,** also known as the Shinumo Wash Route, a historic, rugged, and seldom-visited route that descends from the North Rim to the Colorado River via one of the Grand Canyon's most remote and challenging trails. The Swamp Point trailhead is accessed by a long, rough 20-mile road from the main North Rim developed area, and the trail itself is unmaintained and difficult, requiring steady footing and comfort with sketchy exposure. However, the solitude and wildness of the North Bass experience are unmatched, and you'll wander through hoodoos, past waterfalls, and over Shinumo Creek, and you'll encounter an orchard near the bottom of the Grand that still offers the prospect of munching on a juicy peach after a demanding, rocky, 13.5-mile one-way hike.

This less-traveled path was established by William Wallace Bass in the late nineteenth century as part of his ambitious tourist operation on the North Rim. Today, the trail serves as an adventurous route into the depths of the canyon for experienced backpackers who are well prepared to navigate its challenging terrain and isolation.

The trailhead is located at Swamp Point on the North Rim. To reach it, you'll need a high-clearance vehicle to navigate the rutted and rocky forest service roads. The trail begins at an elevation of 7,600 feet, winding through a forest of ponderosa pines, aspens, and spruce. Enjoy the views of Powell Plateau and the surrounding landscape before you start your descent.

The trail descends steeply, dropping a staggering 1,400 feet within the first mile and a half. The path is rugged and unmaintained, and you'll need to navigate around loose rocks and steep cliffs. As you continue to descend, you'll be treated to panoramic views of the canyon and the distant Colorado River.

At 4 miles, you'll reach White Creek, a tributary of Shinumo Creek. This is a good place to set up camp. White Creek typically has water year-round, but it's crucial to purify any water you collect.

Following the trail past White Creek, you'll continue your descent into Shinumo Amphitheater, where you're flanked with towering red and white sandstone cliffs. The trail can be challenging

Shinumo Creek offers a reliable water source year-round.

to follow here, and you'll need to rely on cairns and your navigational skills.

You'll reach Shinumo Creek, a perennial water source with several suitable camping spots. The trail continues downstream, following the creek toward the Colorado River. As you approach the river, the trail becomes a route, requiring scrambling and careful navigation.

After 14 miles, you'll reach the Colorado River. The river marks the end of the North Bass Trail. Some deeply experienced people raft across the river to connect with the South Bass Trail for a unique rim-to-rim option, but we wouldn't recommend it unless you're John Wesley Powell himself.

Arrowleaf balsamroot bloom on the Jackson Hole valley floor in June.

Grand Teton National Park

Wyoming | nps.gov/grte | Visitation: 3,417,106

Imagine seeing the Grand Tetons for the first time: A row of impossibly sheer spires jutting as much as 7,000 feet heavenward, like the fanged lower jaw of some beast taking a bite out of the clouds. You can forgive the lonely French trappers and beardy mountain men of the 1800s who famously gave it the most majestic name they could think of, a name that would delight middle-school kids for centuries—*les trois tetons*, or "three breasts." Har-har.

(Nomadic Shoshone tribes who followed game to spend summers in the valley for at least 10,000 years gave it an older name that favored functional accuracy: Teewinot, or "many pinnacles.")

Juvenile jokes aside, the granite shards that comprise the Grand Tetons' striking profile are undeniably the most iconic peaks in the Rockies and arguably the whole of North America. And while the region and 310,000-acre park also feature a broad and level 55-mile-long, 6- to 18-mile-wide valley (Jackson Hole), a string of jewel-like lakes, and the looping Snake River S-ing its way throughout, the 40-mile mountain chain defies belief, no matter how many times we've seen it in pictures and postcards. The 13,776-foot-tall Grand Teton hovers above all the rest, but barely: Nine other peaks jut higher than 12,000 feet.

This fresh range first formed 6 to 10 million years ago, though the geological processes that informed it prior to exposure began millions and millions of years before that. It's a familiar story of lava cooling into granite underground, faults, and uplift. But glaciers did most of the work of shaping the points, cirques, moraines, and steep walls over the last 700 years. A few remain, but probably not for long.

It's all coated in a gradation of ecosystems, each with unique flora and fauna. At the lower elevations, lush riparian zones support willows and cottonwoods in places like the banks of the Snake River, providing shelter for beavers, otters, and loads of birds. Farther up, the conifer forests dominate slopes, home to mule deer, moose, and elusive cougars. At the highest elevations, we find windswept alpine meadows where pikas and bighorn sheep cling to the cliffsides. Highest up, naked granite remains the province of circling eagles and brave climbers.

As part of the Greater Yellowstone Ecosystem, Grand Teton National Park shares that park's charismatic megafauna: grizzly bears, wolves, and bison share the spotlight with lesser-known but equally enchanting species like trumpeter swans and western tanagers. With its relatively small size, solid infrastructure, and proximity to the chic town of Jackson, you're never far from hearing an iconic elk bugle or a haunting wolf howl.

The area was originally inhabited by several Native American tribes, including the Shoshone, Crow, and Blackfeet. These tribes relied on the abundant wildlife and natural resources of the area for their survival, and their presence has left a lasting impact on the landscape and ecology of the region. After ancient Native American tribes, fur trappers and homesteaders left their mark on the landscape in the form of historic cabins that once housed grizzled pioneers.

In the late nineteenth century, white settlers began to move into the area, drawn by the potential for mining and other natural resources. The town of Jackson, Wyoming, was established in 1894, and the area quickly attracted tourists drawn to the natural beauty of the Teton Range. In 1929, Grand Teton National Park was established, protecting the area from further development and ensuring its preservation. It expanded to its present size in 1950.

Whether you're a seasoned backpacker or a casual day hiker, the park's 270 miles of trail offer a chance to immerse yourself in both the rugged and the sublime. The mountains themselves are surprisingly narrow: The western side of the range is characterized by steep fault scarps, while the eastern side is gentler. And while you might feel frustration while caught in a buffalo or bear jam on the way to a crowded trailhead parking lot, crowds drop off considerably as you ascend into the spine of the range.

HIKES

Avalanche Divide

The Avalanche Divide hike in Grand Teton National Park is a premier best-kept secret. This section is only 1.8 miles long, but there's a catch: It's perched between popular Cascade Canyon and the more obscure and unmarked Avalanche Canyon. This hike in total covers around 8 miles one-way, with an elevation gain of around 1,800 feet.

To reach the trailhead, drive north from Jackson, Wyoming, on US 191 for 5.5 miles, then turn left onto the Gros Ventre

Hurricane Pass connects to Avalanche Divide.

Road. Continue on Gros Ventre Road for 9.5 miles, then turn left onto Antelope Flats Road. Follow Antelope Flats Road for 4.2 miles, then turn right onto the road leading to the Taggart Lake trailhead.

The hike starts at the Taggart Lake trailhead and follows the trail to Bradley Lake. After 2 miles, you'll reach a fork in the trail. Turn left (west) onto the unmarked trail leading to Avalanche Divide (it's sometimes blocked by sticks). From here, the trail gradually ascends a ridge between Taggart and Bradley Lakes, climbing through steep talus marked with cairns, opening to sweeping views of the surrounding valleys and mountains as you make your way to Lake Taminah. From here, navigate cross-country up the canyon to reach 10,680-foot Avalanche Divide, 4 miles from the trailhead. You'll get incredible shots from a scenic viewpoint of the Teton Range, including the Grand Teton, Middle Teton, and South Teton. The views from the top are breathtaking and well worth the effort.

You can extend your hike into a monster 17-mile day hike by connecting with Cascade Canyon back to Jenny Lake, or go back the way you came. This is a hard, unofficial hike with a lot of route finding and potential bushwhacking, but such is the price of solitude in a popular park.

Granite Canyon to Marion Lake

Located in the southern region of the park, Granite Canyon is a quieter area that begins at the Granite Canyon trailhead off Moose-Wilson Road. (An alternate version of this hike begins from the top of the Jackson Hole Ski Resort tram.)

Start at the Granite Canyon trailhead, moving through a coniferous forest with occasional streams; the canyon narrows, and the surrounding peaks become more prominent. At around 5 miles, take a fork leading away from the main Granite Canyon route, heading

With a permit, you can camp high up above Granite Canyon.

toward the western side of Housetop Mountain. Ascend a series of switchbacks to reach the robin's-egg-blue Marion Lake nestled at 8,500 feet. Circle the lake and take a break if needed before heading southeast from Marion Lake, descending back toward the Granite Canyon path. Rejoin the main Granite Canyon Trail, retracing your steps to return to the trailhead, roughly 18 miles round-trip.

Consider nabbing a permit for Granite Canyon Camping Zone to fully immerse yourself in the Teton Range. There are no designated campsites in the five camping zones, but several suitable locations can be found along the trail. Be sure to obtain a backcountry camping permit from the park's visitor center prior to heading out.

For hikers looking to extend their adventure, the Granite Canyon Trail connects to several other trails, including the Open Canyon Trail and the Teton Crest Trail.

Two Ocean Lake

Two Ocean Lake straddles the Continental Divide, which is the imaginary geographic line that separates the watersheds that drain into the Pacific Ocean and those that drain into the Atlantic Ocean.

Springing from Two Ocean, Pacific Creek flows westward, reaching the Pacific Ocean via the Snake River and the Columbia River, while Atlantic Creek flows eastward, reaching the Atlantic Ocean via the Yellowstone River and the Missouri River.

The trailhead can be reached by driving north from Jackson on US 89/191/287 and turning right onto Pacific Creek Road. After 4.7 miles, turn left onto Two Ocean Lake Road and follow it for 2 miles to the trailhead.

The moderate 6.4-mile loop circumnavigates the lake, offering fantastic views of the Teton Range and the chance to spot various wildlife species, including moose, bears, and waterfowl. The trail meanders through lodgepole pine forests, aspen groves, and meadows filled with wildflowers.

For those seeking a longer hike with more elevation gain, a side trip to Grand View Point can be added. The trail junction to Grand View Point is located on the western side of the lake. This spur trail

Two Ocean is so named because its waters drain into both the Atlantic and Pacific Oceans.

The 3- to 5-day trek requires significant planning, preparation, and experience. Steep ascents and descents, high elevation, and exposure to the elements feature throughout. The highest point on the trail is Paintbrush Divide, which reaches an elevation of 10,700 feet.

The trail is typically hiked from south to north, starting at the Phillips Pass trailhead and ending at the String Lake trailhead. Hikers can obtain backcountry permits from the park service and stay the night at marquee locations including Marion Lake, Death Canyon Shelf, and Alaska Basin.

climbs 1.8 miles and 840 feet in elevation, offering panoramic views of Two Ocean Lake, Emma Matilda Lake, and the broader Teton Range.

HIDDEN GEM

To get the biggest bite of the Tetons and the grandest stretches of solitude, the **Teton Crest Trail** traces the spine of the entire Teton Range over 40 miles. The trail starts at Phillips Pass near Teton Pass, Wyoming, and ends at String Lake near Jenny Lake. The Teton Crest Trail is one of the premier backpacking routes in the United States and offers stunning views of the Teton Range, glacial lakes, alpine meadows, and diverse ecosystems.

Cross the entire Teton Range over 40 miles on the Teton Crest Trail.

Great Basin National Park

Nevada | nps.gov/grba | Visitation: 143,265

Getting to Great Basin is half the battle: Spread across 77,180 acres, the park lies 290 miles north of Las Vegas and about 240 miles west of Salt Lake City on the literal "Loneliest Highway" in the empty heart of Nevada. The closest town of any size is Ely, 70 miles to the west. The tiny town of Baker, situated 5 miles from the park, serves as the park's gateway, but it offers only minimal services.

There are no major airports within an easy drive of the park, and no train or bus services come close. Forget cell service.

This is among the most uncrowded parks in the whole system, and it combines some of the best aspects of both the Rockies and the Sierras, despite being separated from each by hundreds of miles of desolation. Thirteen-thousand-foot peaks, ancient trees, weird caves, and some of the darkest night skies anywhere greet visitors who make the long journey.

The park takes its name from the entire region between the Rockies and the Sierras. Beneath the wide Nevada sky, the earth's crust has pulled apart, creating a system of mountain ranges and valleys that ripple across the landscape like a stone-skipped pond, known as the "Basin and Range." This location of odd geology resists the concept of continental divides; instead, any water that falls within the Basin and Range fails to drain to any ocean. Instead, it pools in isolated lakes and marshes, where it collects underground or evaporates into thin air.

In the shadow of Wheeler Peak, the second-highest mountain in Nevada, vast pinyon-juniper woodlands fill the lower elevations. Higher up, subalpine forests and alpine tundra thrive in short growing seasons' rarefied air.

In these ecological strata, life clings tenaciously to the land. The most fascinating are bristlecone pines: Their unique ability to withstand harsh conditions and poor soils means they grow at high altitudes where few other organisms can survive. Their gnarled and twisted forms are a testament to the extreme conditions they endure, marked by cold temperatures, high winds, and a short growing season.

The slow growth rate of bristlecone pines, coupled with the dense, resinous wood, makes them resistant to disease, insects, and other environmental stressors and contributes to their remarkable lifespan, with many bristlecone pines living for several thousand years.

The oldest known bristlecone pine in Great Basin National Park was named Prometheus, also the oldest tree ever recorded. Unfortunately, we learned of its exact age in 1964, when a researcher

At 13,065 feet, Great Basin's Wheeler Peak is the second-tallest in Nevada.

who didn't realize the tree's extraordinary age cut it down. Prometheus died at 5,000 years old.

Today, the exact ages and locations of the oldest living bristlecone pines are kept secret to protect the trees. However, in the park's Wheeler Peak grove, where the Prometheus tree once stood, many bristlecone pines reach ages above 3,000 years.

Beneath the surface, water carved the Lehman Caves, an intricate subterranean labyrinth of limestone adorned with delicate draperies of flowstone and towering stalagmites. The Lehman Caves can only be explored through guided tours led by trained National Park Service rangers; tours vary in length and depth. The Lodge Room Tour is shorter and more accessible, perfect for families or those with limited mobility. The longer, strenuous Grand Palace Tour takes visitors deeper into the cave system, where they can see the famous "Parachute Shield" formation.

Despite all these wonders, Great Basin National Park remains a gem largely unexplored. Its remoteness is both a blessing and a curse; it stands untouched by the tourism that floods other parks, but it demands effort to get here. If you seek solitude in the Lower 48, go here.

Explore Lehman Caves on ranger-guided tours.

Two glittering lakes lie on this 13-mile loop.

HIKES

Baker Lake and Johnson Lake Loop

The Baker Lake and Johnson Lake Loop is a challenging, 13-mile trail that wanders into remote folds of the South Snake Range and serves up two gorgeous, sparkling lakes.

From the trailhead at the end of Baker Creek Road, follow a moderately steep path through quaking aspen groves and aromatic stands of pine and fir.

At 2.5 miles in, the trail forks. Veer left to continue toward Baker Lake through thinning vegetation to a panoramic view of the Snake Valley and the wider Great Basin.

Baker Lake itself is a sapphire pool nestled at the base of Baker Peak in a glacial cirque. Its surface mirrors the wide Nevada sky, and on a clear day, the reflection of the surrounding peaks shimmers in the gentle ripples of the water.

From Baker Lake, the trail turns from a modest uphill walk into a steep, heart-pounding climb toward the saddle connecting Baker and Johnson Lakes. The saddle itself offers a moment of respite and more great views of the South Snake Range.

Descending from the saddle, you enter the Johnson Lake basin. Johnson Lake, like its sister Baker, is a glacial cirque, with blue waters cast against the barren, rocky slopes surrounding it.

From Johnson Lake, the trail loops back toward the junction with the Baker Lake Trail. This segment of the hike offers a different perspective on the landscape you've traversed.

Lexington Arch Trail

The Lexington Arch Trail is a moderate, 3.4-mile out-and-back journey that lets you explore one of the park's more unique geological features.

The trailhead for Lexington Arch is located off the Snake Valley Road, 20 miles south of Baker. The last 7 miles are on an unpaved, rough road that is not suitable for low-clearance vehicles or during inclement weather.

The trail starts on a relatively flat, sandy path that meanders through a sparse forest of pinyon pine and juniper. As the trail continues, it winds up the rocky slopes on a loose and uneven path. After 1.5 miles, the trail rounds a bend, and Lexington Arch comes into view. Standing at 70 feet tall and 50 feet wide, this natural limestone arch is one of the few known examples in the world found in the West (most are sandstone), a possible remnant of a whittled-down limestone cave system.

Bristlecone and Glacier Trail

Catch two of the most fascinating features inherent to this remote corner of Nevada on a moderate hike stretching over 4.6 miles round-trip that immerses you in the park's alpine world and geological past.

From the Bristlecone Parking Area at the end of the Wheeler Peak Scenic Drive, ascend through a mixed forest of Engelmann spruce and limber pine on a well-maintained trail over rocky but easy terrain.

After a mile or so, you'll reach a grove of ancient bristlecone pine trees. These gnarled, weather-worn trees are among the oldest living organisms on earth, with some in this grove exceeding 3,000 years in age. Their twisted forms reflect the countless seasons that have passed over this land.

The trail continues from the bristlecone grove toward the only glacier in Nevada, nestled in a cirque on the eastern flank of

Hardy bristlecone pines can live for thousands of years.

On a clear night, you can see over 7,500 stars in Great Basin.

Wheeler Peak. Don't mistake the patches of snow for the glacier itself: This slow-moving river of ice and stone is a rock glacier—a grotty blend of commingled ice and rock that nevertheless moves and grinds the mountainside the same as blue-ice glaciers found elsewhere. If you look closely, you can see the lobes of the gray glacier that sport the same striations as an icy glacier.

HIDDEN GEM

As one of the least-visited parks in the system, the whole of Great Basin is essentially a hidden gem. But if you're looking for extra pizzazz, wait until the sun sets and look up: On clear, moonless nights, the night sky vibrates with a **diamond array of stars.**

Recognized as an International Dark Sky Park, it's one of the best places in the United States to stargaze, owing to its remote location, high elevation, and arid climate. To provide some context, in most urban areas, you would be lucky to see a few dozen stars. Under ideal conditions at Great Basin National Park, you can see over 7,500 stars, the creamy smear of the Milky Way, various planets, and many other celestial objects. Star clusters, nebulae, and distant galaxies become visible with the use of a telescope.

During the summer months, rangers lead night-sky programs that include telescope viewing, identification of celestial bodies, and programs about the importance of preserving dark skies.

Great Sand Dunes National Park and Preserve

Colorado | nps.gov/grsa | 512,219

Some national parks feel like experiencing the best version of our planet. But some feel like we've jumped through a wormhole to set foot on a different world in some galaxy far, far away.

Few parks embody this otherworldliness like Great Sand Dunes. The heart of the park is a 30-square-mile ocean of sand where wind-whipped dunes top out at 750 feet—the tallest in North America. Snowcapped peaks ring an undulating maze of beige; venturing into it triggers "singing sand" that vibrates and hums underfoot, hinting at unseen alien beasties hiding in the park's gritty depths. Yell as loud as you can, and instead of hearing your voice boom and echo across the endless San Luis Valley, you'll find it dies inches from your face. Sand, it turns out, offers spectacular sound insulation: Out here, no one can hear you scream.

Put your blaster away. While this seeming "wasteland" hosts a surprisingly diverse array of wildlife (elk, kangaroo rats, tiger salamanders), none of them are bloodthirsty sand worms.

How did this surreal dune field plop itself in between snowcapped peaks? It begins with the San Juan and Sangre de Cristo Mountains—twin 14,000-foot mountain ranges that flank the Connecticut-size San Luis Valley. Over eons, water and wind reduced their granite and gneiss summits to grains of sand that washed down into an ancient lake fed by long-gone glaciers. The lake carved through the southern mountain barrier, drained, and reduced into the Rio Grande, but the sandy lakebed remained.

The valley's powerful winds pushed the piles of sand eastward across the valley, where the high passes of the Sangre de Cristos blocked their passage and storm winds coming off the peaks kept them tucked in a stony bend in the mountains. Surrounded on three sides, the dunes began to rise vertically, grain by grain, under the pressure of opposing winds over 400,000 years until they reached their dramatic height. Streams running off the surrounding peaks and the steady supply of raw material blowing in from the ancient lakebed create a stable sand recycling system: The dune field isn't growing, but it isn't shrinking, either.

Great Sand Dunes' highest dune soars to 741 feet.

Great Sand Dunes' main dune field encompasses 30 square miles.

Humans followed mammoths and bison to these shifting sands at least 11,000 years ago, but fossilized human footprints farther south in White Sands dating to 22,000 years ago indicate people came much earlier. More than eighteen affiliated Native American tribes, including the Pueblo, Ute, Apache, and later the Navajo all claim stewardship of the dunes in their memories and stories. Imposing Blanca Peak, the seventh-tallest mountain in the United States, looms behind the dunes and marks the eastern border of the Dinetah, or the traditional Navajo homeland.

Europeans came later, explorers and settlers homesteading and making their way west on the Old Spanish Trail. The first Spanish colonists arrived 400 years ago, some staying to eke a living out of this hard land. The high valley's natural position as a crossroads between mountains where the Southwest and the Rockies meet makes it a nexus for the exploits of early US explorers who drove westward expansion: John C. Fremont, Kit Carson, Zebulon Pike, and John Gunnison all lived out portions of their drama-filled lives here.

The dunes make up a relatively small portion of the park. Aspen and evergreen forests, wetlands, grasslands, wildflower meadows, and alpine tundra shelter mule deer, beavers, bighorn sheep, pronghorns, bison, black bears, squirrels, marmots, pikas, grouse, coyotes, turkeys, and numerous songbirds and birds of prey. The Ord's kangaroo rat is the only mammal to bounce into the dune field and live off the sparse vegetation.

Most visitors congregate around the shallow, intermittent Medano Creek, which serves as a refreshing border between dune field and visitor center. Some will slog their way up the first ridge of dunes or attempt to summit the visible High Dune (not the highest) beyond; some ski or sled their way down. Disappearing farther into the trailless dune field ensures solitude and quiet, but the trails that lead deeper into the mountains offer high views of the dune fields and the chance to spot wildlife in the park's diverse life zones.

In summer, the surface temps of the dunes can reach an egg-frying 150 degrees Fahrenheit; dig below the surface a little, however, and they're always cool and damp. Winter brings frigid temps but also the surreal spectacle of seeing the dunes blanketed in white after fresh snowfall (the snow usually melts quickly into the dark sand).

The surest way to feel like an alien that fell to Earth is to get a permit and camp in the dunes. Squint hard enough, and you might imagine twin suns setting behind the La Garita Mountains across the valley.

HIKES

Music Pass to Upper Sand Creek Lake

Beginning outside the borders of the park, hiking to Music Pass offers an alternative to popular Mosca Pass with similar montane-to-alpine transitional terrain, high-perspective views of the dunes, and the option to continue and camp or fish at a trout-filled lake. Extending your journey from Music Pass, this trail is a total round-trip of a little more than 8 miles.

Reach the trailhead via Music Pass Road, accessible after driving south on CO 150 from Westcliffe. In 4 miles, turn right onto a rocky road. Be forewarned: It's a demanding 6-mile stretch of off-road driving best done in a high-clearance, 4WD vehicle.

At the trailhead, ascend through ponderosa and spruce forests and intermittent alpine meadows until you reach Music Pass after a mile. Standing over 11,000 feet, the vistas encompass the sprawling Sand Creek Basin and the park's namesake dunes in the distance. Marmots and elk can be seen throughout the basin.

Beyond the pass, the trail winds downward into the basin. At the base of your descent, turn right at the junction onto Upper Sand Creek Trail, following signs and the creek. Keep right at junctions to attain Upper Sand Creek Lake. Nestled at around 11,700 feet, this pristine lake reflects Tijeras Peak, Music Mountain, and Milwaukee Peak.

Medano Lake and Mount Herard

The trail to Medano Lake and onward to Mount Herard takes you on an exciting off-road adventure toward a glittering alpine lake and bird's-eye views of the dune field from the top of a 13,000-foot peak.

The road leading up to Medano Pass trailhead.

Your journey begins on the Medano Pass Primitive Road. A regular car won't suffice for this route; you'll need a high-clearance 4WD vehicle to get through creek crossings, deep sand, and rocky conditions. Starting from the park's main entrance, drive northeast toward the dunes but veer right at the road's fork, following signs for Medano Pass. The trailhead is located 6 miles in.

After parking, you'll embark on a moderately strenuous 3.5-mile hike that winds through dense forests of spruce and aspen. The babble of Medano Creek accompanies you for a portion of the route. As you climb, glimpses of the vast San Luis Valley start to appear between the trees. Upon reaching Medano Lake, nestled in a high-alpine cirque, you're greeted by serene waters that mirror the surrounding peaks. The lake is a perfect spot to rest, snack, and camp (stay at least 200 feet from the lake).

For those wishing to venture farther, a challenging path ascends from the lake up Mount Herard. This portion is 2 miles one-way but involves steep and rugged terrain. As you climb, alpine meadows awash in wildflowers give way to rockier landscapes and alpine tundra. The trail becomes less defined, so careful navigation is crucial.

At 13,297 feet, from the summit of Mount Herard, you'll see the entirety of the Great Sand Dunes sprawling out golden against the green valley beyond. The surrounding Sangre de Cristo Mountains ripple off into the horizon.

HIDDEN GEM

While the heights of the dunes are relatively stable, slight fluctuations mean that the tallest all hover near 740 feet; as of 2020, remote and aptly named **Hidden Dune** tied the much closer Star Dune to become the tallest at 741 feet. It can't be seen from the visitor center or the high first ridge of dunes, and a false summit blots it out for much of the 7-mile, 6-hour round-trip trek to its top. Beginning from the main Great Sand Dunes parking lot, you'll need to plot your own north-northwest course on a GPS to find it. Here are those magical coordinates: N37 46.555 / W105 31.915.

Great Smoky Mountains National Park

North Carolina, Tennessee | nps.gov/grsm | Visitation: 13,297,647

The Smokies handily win the park popularity contest. It isn't even close: This grand wilderness of the East hosts three times the visitors as the second-place Grand Canyon each year—5 million more than the population of New York City. You would think that would make Great Smoky Mountains as packed as a Tokyo subway car. But despite the numbers, countless people lose themselves on over 800 miles of trail stretching over half a million acres of misty peaks, high ridges, ancient forests, deep valleys, and clear, rushing streams. Ask anyone who's been, and their eyes go as misty as morning in the park. Crowds rarely come up.

Straddling North Carolina and Tennessee, the Appalachian peaks that make up the Smokies represent some of the oldest. Over a billion years ago, the forces of plate tectonics birthed these mountains, thrusting up the earth's crust to form the towering peaks. Millennia of weathering and erosion sculpted them into their current form 200 million years ago, creating a landscape that is both majestic and gentle, rugged and serene.

Among the park's most impressive features is Clingmans Dome; at 6,643 feet it's the highest point in the Smokies in Tennessee, and the third highest east of the Mississippi. From its observation tower, one can behold a panoramic view of ridge upon ridge of forest, their tops wreathed in the misty "smoke" that gives the Smokies their name.

The Smokies are also famous for their "balds"—essentially open areas mostly free of trees found atop the peaks of the Southern Appalachians. These open expanses are characterized by grasses, sedges, and shrubs, and the exact origins remain a topic of scientific debate and research. Indigenous peoples may have cleared these areas for agriculture or other activities, and natural processes prevented trees from reclaiming these spots. Other theories suggest that grazing by large herbivores or unique microclimates or soil conditions could have created conditions unfavorable for tree growth but supportive of grasses and shrubs. Hiking trails leading to their summits often provide glorious, unobstructed 360-degree views.

The mountains here are also geologically stable, escaping the tumult of volcanism or glaciers that affects many mountains in North America. This means all forms of life here evolved and multiplied over long periods without catastrophic interruption or severe weather. By far the most

The black-lipped salamander is one of many species found in the Smokies.

Aspirating plants contribute to the Smokies' famous haze.

biologically diverse national park in our system, it's one of the most diverse regions on earth outside the tropics. The park is recognized as an International Biosphere Reserve; scientists have documented more than 19,000 species, and they believe an estimated 80,000 to 100,000 more species may live here.

Great Smoky Mountains draw their evocative name from the natural fog or smoke-like haze emitted by the profusion of plant life that grows here. It often envelops these mountains, giving them a blue-gray tinge that's especially visible at a distance.

The expansive biodiversity colors the view. That includes everything from big-racked elk roaming the lush valleys to the synchronous fireflies casting glowing patterns on summer nights. The sheer scale is better told by numbers than individual species: Old-growth forests of more than 100 species of trees make homes for more than 200 species of birds. Beneath them, a carpet of wild-flowers unfurls in the warmer months, just a few examples of 1,600 species of flowering plants (the most iconic of which is the great white trillium, a delicate three-petaled flower that carpets the forest floor from April to June). Forty kinds of reptiles, 50 types of fish, 60 mammals, and 1,500 individual black bears roam this massive wild habitat.

And then there is the slimy salamander, the emblem and mascot of the Smokies' rich biodiversity. This "Salamander Capital of the World" shelters a greater variety of these creatures than anywhere else on the planet. More than thirty different species representing five families live here, thriving in the temperate climate, moist forests, abundant water sources, and rocky crevices that provide the perfect environment for salamanders at each stage of their life cycle.

The human history of the Smokies is as rich and varied as its natural one. The Cherokee first inhabited these lands; they hunted and gathered and formed a sophisticated society through a network of villages. When Spanish explorers saw this sprawling civilization as early as the late 1500s, it was already hundreds of years old.

But when European settlers later expanded into the region, it sparked the Indian Removal Act of 1830—one of the more shameful and tragic episodes in our country's history. The US Army drove more than 15,000 Cherokee forcibly from here to Oklahoma on the infamous Trail of Tears (a third of them died). Some of their descendants resisted and disappeared into the mountains. Today, their legacy lives alongside the preserved log cabins, churches, and abandoned mills of the settlers who forced them out.

Many of these settlers would be removed themselves upon the foundation of the park in 1934. Ghost towns found throughout the park exist in varying stages of natural reclamation, as Great Smoky Mountains' unstoppable green tendrils envelop and dismantle them brick by brick, grain by grain.

ZONE OF INTEREST

Manways

Manways in Great Smoky Mountains National Park refer to unofficial trails that are not maintained by the National Park Service. Originally created for purposes such as firefighting, park operations, or historical use, these paths are not officially recognized or maintained for recreational use. As such, they can be more difficult to navigate than official trails, often involving tricky terrain, lack of clear signage, and more natural hazards. However, for experienced hikers seeking solitude and a more rugged, off-the-beaten-path experience, manways can provide an enticing challenge.

One of the more well-known manways in the park is the Greenbrier Pinnacle manway. This trail is considered moderately difficult, ascending steeply to offer fantastic views of the Greenbrier area and Mount LeConte. However, it's important to note that this manway is not marked and can be difficult to follow, particularly in the fall when the trail is covered with leaves.

Before venturing onto any manway in the park, it's crucial to remember that these paths are not maintained or marked. This means that navigation can be challenging and the risk of getting lost is higher. Always carry a good map and compass, bring the 10 Essentials, wear appropriate hiking gear, and ensure that you're prepared for a more challenging and potentially hazardous hiking experience. Always tell someone where you're going and when you plan to return, and, if possible, hike with a partner. It's worth being prepared to spend a night out (tent, bag, pad, bivy sack, etc.)

The Old Settlers Trail, while technically an official trail, also offers a more secluded hiking experience. It's a long, meandering path of 15.9 miles that follows rocky routes through old homesites, offering a dive into Smokies history. It doesn't feature substantial elevation changes, which can make it more approachable for hikers of varying fitness levels. Hikers can opt to explore shorter sections if they aren't up for committing to its entirety.

Starting at the trailhead near Cosby, Tennessee, the Old Settlers Trail winds its way through lush forests, crossing sparkling streams, and passes by old stone walls, chimneys, and foundations—reminders of the settlers who once made their homes in these mountains. Look out for an abundance of stone fences. As early European settlers cleared the land for their crops, they used the stones they unearthed to mark their property.

The trail itself is believed to follow the path that these early settlers would have used to travel between settlements and to access the now-gone Webb Creek and Birds Creek schools. One can imagine the ghosts of the past on their walks to and from these long-disappeared communities.

HIKES

Mount Cammerer Fire Tower

The Mount Cammerer Fire Tower Trail is one of the more challenging hikes in the park, but it rewards hikers with spectacular views and the chance to explore a unique piece of the park's history. The round-trip is 11.1 miles, making it a substantial day hike.

A steep climb leads to Mount Cammerer's 365-degree views.

From the Cosby Campground near the town of Cosby, Tennessee, you'll start on the Lower Mount Cammerer Trail, which winds through a lush hardwood forest. After 0.4 mile, you'll reach a junction. Here, you'll turn right onto the Low Gap Trail.

The Low Gap Trail is a steep climb, gaining 2,000 feet in elevation over a short 2.5 miles. It's a challenging stretch, but the pressing forest and the sounds of trickling streams helps distract from the effort. At the top of Low Gap, you'll intersect the Appalachian Trail (AT). Turn right onto the AT.

Now on the AT, you'll hike another 2.1 miles, taking you across the slopes of Mount Cammerer. The trail here is less steep than the Low Gap Trail and offers great views of the surrounding mountains.

You'll reach a spur trail that leads to the fire tower. This final, steep 0.5-mile stretch runs until the fire tower, where the 360-degree views of surrounding peaks and valleys rule all, particularly in the fall.

The fire tower itself is a piece of history. Built by the Civilian Conservation Corps in the 1930s, it was part of a network of lookouts used to spot wildfires in the park. Unlike many fire towers, which are simple metal structures, the Mount Cammerer Fire Tower is a unique, octagonal structure built from hand-cut stone, restored and maintained in its present form.

After taking in the views and exploring the fire tower, you'll return the way you came, back down the spur trail, along the AT, down the Low Gap Trail, and along the Lower Mount Cammerer Trail to the Cosby Campground.

Maddron Bald

The Smokies' balds attract hikers like flies, but Maddron Bald remains a bit less popular without sacrificing any of the others' alluring landscapes, from lush old-growth forests to sweeping mountain vistas. Though challenging, this 12-mile round-trip trail offers a bounty of natural beauty and a satisfying sense of accomplishment for those who undertake it.

Flowering rhododendron covers the lower slopes of Smokies' balds.

Near the town of Cosby, Tennessee, follow US 321 to Baxter Road, continuing to its end to find the trailhead. Begin with a pleasant walk along an old roadbed, passing through hemlock and rhododendron stands. After a little over a mile, you'll come across the Baxter Cabin, a well-preserved historic homestead dating back to the 1880s.

The route steepens as it transitions from the old roadbed to a traditional hiking trail. At 2.5 miles in, you'll reach the junction with the Gabes Mountain Trail. Stay right to continue on Maddron Bald Trail.

As you ascend farther, you'll enter an area of old-growth forest, where you'll be surrounded by massive, towering trees—a reminder of what the entire park once looked like before logging in the early twentieth century.

Around 4 miles in, you'll reach the Albright Grove Loop Trail. This 0.7-mile detour leads you through one of the most impressive old-growth forests in the park, where you'll encounter tulip trees, hemlocks, and silverbells.

Back on the Maddron Bald Trail, the path becomes increasingly steep, but your effort is rewarded by the stunning views from Maddron Bald, a grassy high-elevation meadow. The Bald offers wonderful views of the surrounding mountains, a perfect place for a rest and a picnic before you begin your journey back down the trail.

Hen Wallow Falls

The Hen Wallow Falls Trail, more formally known as the Gabes Mountain Trail to Hen Wallow Falls, offers a moderate challenging route to a secluded cascade. The hike provides a rewarding mixture of verdant greenery, a diverse array of plant and animal life, and the peaceful sounds of cascading water in a short 4.4 miles.

To find the trailhead, you'll start at the Cosby Picnic Area near the town of Cosby, Tennessee. The trail begins at the back of the picnic area.

Start on the Gabes Mountain Trail, winding through a verdant, hemlock-dominated forest. You'll wander among these tall trees, the path muffled by a thick layer of decomposing leaves and pine needles.

Hen Wallow Falls freezes into massive icicles in winter.

The trail features a moderate incline and gentle ascent, passing under rhododendrons and through tunnels of mountain laurel, which grow particularly beautiful in late spring when they are in bloom.

At 2.1 miles in, you'll reach a signed side trail to Hen Wallow Falls. This side trail is steep and descends 0.1 mile to the base of the falls.

Hen Wallow Falls is one of the larger waterfalls in the park, dropping 90 feet from top to bottom. The waterfall narrows in its middle section, then fans out at the bottom, creating a beautiful, multi-tiered cascade. In winter, the falls can partially freeze, creating an entirely different sculpture of ice and snow.

Once you've enjoyed the falls, you'll ascend back to the Gabes Mountain Trail and retrace your steps to the Cosby Picnic Area.

Spruce Flats Trail

While the trail is not officially recognized on most park maps, Spruce Flats Trail is well maintained and leads to a wonderful waterfall away from crowds on a 2-mile out-and-back hike.

Historic homesteads can be found through the Smokies.

The trail begins at the Great Smoky Mountains Institute at Tremont in the western part of the park. To find the trailhead, walk behind the main building and look for the sign pointing the way to the "Lumber Ridge Trail."

From the trailhead, you'll start uphill on the Lumber Ridge Trail. After 0.4 mile, you'll see a sign for the Spruce Flats Falls Trail branching off to the right.

The trail meanders through a mixed forest of hemlock, yellow birch, and tulip trees. There are several undulating ascents and descents as you navigate the terrain, but these are manageable with careful footing.

As you near the falls, the trail descends sharply. Hidden until now, Spruce Flats Falls reveals itself out of the dense forest. This multi-tiered cascade tumbles 30 feet over mossy rocks into a small pool below.

You can enjoy the view from several large rocks at the base of the falls, perfect for a break or a picnic. In the warmer months, the space around the falls is cool and refreshing, while in the fall, the surrounding foliage lights up in a display of colors.

After you've taken in the beauty of the falls, retrace your steps to return to the trailhead.

Spruce Flats Falls pours more than 30 feet into a placid pool.

Little Cattaloochee Trail

The Little Cataloochee Trail winds through the heart of the Smokies, and it's steeped in history. It's a roughly 12-mile out-and-back trip, but for a shorter hike, you can arrange a shuttle and do the trail as a 6-mile point-to-point.

To reach the trailhead, take Cove Creek Road to Cataloochee Road and continue to the campground.

The trail begins by crossing a footbridge over Cataloochee Creek, then quickly diverges from the main road and begins a steady climb through a hardwood forest. Listen for mountain warblers serenading you as you ascend the path lined with rhododendrons and mountain laurel.

After 1.5 miles, you'll arrive at the Little Cataloochee Baptist Church, an old white building dating back to 1889 and complete with a cemetery where many original settlers of the area are buried.

Beyond the church, the trail winds through the forest, with the occasional clearing providing stunning views of the surrounding mountains. Keep an eye out for wild turkeys, white-tailed deer, and the park's famous elk herd, which often graze in these meadows.

Three miles into the hike, you'll reach the Hannah Cabin, a log cabin built in the 1860s by early settler John Jackson Hannah. The trail concludes at the well-preserved Caldwell House, another historic homestead that dates to the late nineteenth century. Return the way you came.

HIDDEN GEM

Just because it's known as the **"Salamander Capital of the World"** doesn't mean these fascinating amphibians are easy to find. But if you're lucky enough to do so, they astonish with their bright colors and alien shapes.

The Smokies' salamander population is so diverse because the park's wide range of elevations and moist, temperate climate offers ideal habitats for these creatures. There are two main types of salamanders in the park: lungless salamanders and hellbenders.

The hellbender is the largest salamander in North America.

Lungless salamanders breathe through their skin and the linings of their mouths. This family includes the largest diversity of salamanders in the park, with species such as the Jordan's salamander, the red-cheeked salamander, and the black-chinned red salamander. Many of these species are brightly colored, warning potential predators of their nasty taste.

The hellbender is the largest salamander in the park and can grow up to a terrifying 29 inches long. These amazing aquatic creatures wear wrinkled, brownish skin that helps them blend in with their riverbed habitats. They are nocturnal and spend most of their time hiding under large rocks in swift, clean streams.

While salamanders are generally secretive and can be hard to spot, your best chance of seeing one is by looking carefully near rocks and crevices in a stream or wet area. Never lift rocks or otherwise attempt to disrupt the salamander's habitat.

Salamanders are an important part of the park's ecosystem, serving as both predator and prey. They help control insect populations and, in turn, provide food for larger animals. Their presence is also a good indicator of a healthy, unpolluted environment.

As always, when observing wildlife in the park, it's important to do so responsibly. Never remove a salamander from the park or touch them, as the oils found on human skin can be harmful to them.

El Capitan and Guadalupe Peak rise thousands of feet above the Texas desert.

Guadalupe Mountains National Park

Texas | nps.gov/gumo | Visitation: 227,340

Texas doesn't inspire visions of high mountains. Yet snug against the border of New Mexico, the Lone Star State hides peaks 2,000 feet taller than anything east of the Mississippi. You must disappear into the barren, lonely western panhandle to find them.

The Guadalupe Mountains, austere and solitary, rise 3,000 feet from the Chihuahuan Desert. Here, alpine terrain lives on sky islands floating far above the arid desert floor. They are dramatic enough to host their own El Capitan—a 1,000-foot limestone cliff face that echoes the more famous one found farther west in California.

Three hundred million years ago, this rugged range was once the floor of an ancient sea, containing reefs teeming with life, corals and crinoids, and ammonites whose coiled forms lie fossilized in stone now. Over the millennia, the waters receded, and the land heaved the limestone bones of the reef toward the clouds.

The harsh beauty of this land belies a complex ecology. In Guadalupe the desert meets the mountains in a paradox of extremes. The lowland bajadas sizzle under the fierce desert sun, where creosote, cacti, yuccas, and agaves thrive. Pig-like javelinas forage under the watchful eyes of hawks, falcons, and eagles circling in the endless Texas blue. At night, the desert comes alive with the eerie glow of the kit fox's eyes and the rustle of the kangaroo rat in the underbrush.

Ascend the mountains and the world changes. The desert gives way to cool forests of ponderosa pines and Douglas firs, the air fragrant with resin and damp earth. In the shadowed coolness, mule deer graze and black bears rummage in the undergrowth. On the craggy cliffs, peregrine falcons make eyries and shriek into the sky.

Humans came first as hunter-gatherers, drawn to the springs and the abundant game. Later, the Mescalero Apache found refuge in these mountains, launching sorties and fading into the canyons in their conflict with the US Army until the 1880s. More recently, settlers, ranchers, and miners came and left weathered facades of old homesteads and rusted remnants of a once-thriving industry. The discovery of oil brought wildcatters. The donated and purchased lands of petroleum geologist Wallace Pratt and rancher J. C. Hunter formed the nucleus of what would become the 86,000-acre national park.

Guadalupe Mountains National Park is a place of contrast and continuity. From the soaring height of Guadalupe Peak, at 8,751 feet the highest point in Texas, to the subterranean depths of the park's numerous caves, from the arid desert lowlands to the verdant mountain forests, the park showcases biodiversity and resilience in a distant corner few park fans ever visit.

In the hush of a desert night, this is also a place where a blanket of stars descends in a dense curtain. There's something humbling and ominous about Guadalupe Mountains, a mystery that unravels step by step. You will share it with very few.

ZONE OF INTEREST

Dog Canyon

Tucked away in the northern part of Guadalupe Mountains National Park, Dog Canyon offers refuge from the more crowded areas of the park like Guadalupe Peak and McKittrick Canyon (though crowds are still low in those parts by most park standards). This low-key gem is appreciated for its lower temperatures, unique flora and fauna, and the pristine beauty of the canyon itself.

Fall colors explode in Guadalupe's remote canyons.

Dog Canyon is surrounded by walls of limestone, offering shade and cooler temperatures. The lush canyon floor, particularly in comparison to the surrounding Chihuahuan Desert, is filled with trees like Texas madrone and bigtooth maple. As you climb the trails, you'll transition through pinyon pine, juniper, and oak woodlands. Bird-watchers will appreciate the varied avian species, and if you're lucky, you might spot a mule deer or elk.

Fall is an especially beautiful time in Dog Canyon, when the bigtooth maples blaze red and yellow across the desert landscape. Springtime's mild temperatures and blooming flowers are also ideal; summer can scorch to the point of being lethal, so it's essential to start and finish hikes early in the morning. In winter, the canyon can receive snowfall, which adds a serene beauty, but be prepared for chilly temperatures and potentially icy trails.

Some key hiking trails to tackle off Dog Canyon include the family-friendly Indian Meadow Nature Trail (0.6 mile), panoramic Lost Peak (6.4 miles), forested Marcus Overlook (4.6 miles), and über-burly Bush Mountain (11 miles), the second-tallest peak in the park.

HIKES

Permian Reef Trail

The Permian Reef Trail is a geological wonder tucked within the rugged beauty of Guadalupe Mountains National Park on a strenuous 8.4-mile round-trip that explores the ancient remnants of a 265-million-year-old marine fossil reef.

The journey begins at the McKittrick Canyon Contact Station. To get there, you'll travel along US 62/180 and turn onto the road to McKittrick Canyon. The trailhead is by the visitor contact station, which is 7 miles from the highway. Be sure to pick up the trail guide available at the station, as it will provide valuable information corresponding to numbered posts along the trail.

Your trek begins by crossing a footbridge over the usually dry McKittrick Creek bed. The path then meanders through the desert

Unique chainlink cactus can be seen along the Permian Reef Trail.

Like White Sands in neighboring New Mexico, Salt Basin's dunes are made of gypsum.

scrubland, populated by agave, yucca, and sotol. It ascends steadily, granting you sweeping views of McKittrick Canyon's vibrant foliage against the barren desert backdrop. (In fall, it can glow red.)

A mile or so in, the trail steepens, and the vegetation changes. Junipers and pinyon pines appear as the desert gives way to mountainous terrain. The trail stays rocky and rugged.

Climb to Wilderness Ridge, where you'll find a small shelter and views that stretch across the sea of rock and scrub splayed under the vast Texas sky. Here, at 7,200 feet, you stand on the edge of an ancient reef, once full of the weird creatures that inhabited a Permian sea. The exposed cliff faces along the trail showcase an array of fossilized organisms: sponges, bryozoans, brachiopods, and more.

The return journey retraces your steps down the mountain. As you descend, watch how the light changes across the land, the shadows lengthen, and the colors deepen.

Salt Basin Dunes

In the western reaches of Guadalupe Mountains National Park lies Salt Basin Dunes, a dazzling expanse of white gypsum dunes that rise and fall like the waves of a frozen ocean. The Salt Basin Dunes Trail takes you through it on a round-trip journey of 3 to 4 miles, depending on where and how far you amble over the dunes.

Start at the Salt Basin Dunes parking lot, located off US 180, 50 miles west of the park headquarters. A small sign marks the turnoff from the highway, and from there, a rough gravel road takes you to the parking lot.

The trail starts at the western end of the parking lot. A flat, well-marked path cuts through desert scrub, creosote bushes, and yucca. Roadrunners or lizards might dart out of the underbrush across your path.

Soon, the desert gives way to the dunes. The sand underfoot is cool and fine, made of ivory gypsum washed down from the surrounding mountains and whipped by the wind into sinuous curves and sharp ridges. On the south end of the dune field, the shortest dunes stand 3 feet tall and are spiked with vegetation; near the north end, vegetation ceases and the dunes rise to 60 feet.

At the end of the trail, a small hill offers a panoramic view of the dunes and the surrounding landscape. To the east, the Guadalupe Mountains float mirage-like above the desert floor.

The Salt Basin Dunes are a fragile ecosystem, home to several species of plants and animals that have adapted to this harsh environment. As you walk, tread lightly and respect the natural environment. Especially take care not to walk on the black cryptogamic crust; this living mix of fungus, lichen, and soil helps prevent erosion and lock in nitrogen so vegetation can take root. Stick to trails or non-vegetated dunes.

Haleakalā is the site of many Native Hawaiian creation stories.

Haleakalā National Park

Hawaii | nps.gov/hale | Visitation: 791,292

In the middle of the Pacific Ocean, Hawaii, with its tropical allure, beckons travelers of all kinds: surfers, divers, snorkelers, sunbathers, sunburners. But this mountainous island chain is also paradise for hikers, who can traverse everything from rocky moonscapes to drenched rain forests and empty beaches.

Haleakalā National Park is named for the ancient Hawaiian demigod Maui's audacious feat of lassoing the sun from its summit to make the day last longer. Spread across Maui's eastern expanse, Haleakalā National Park offers the chance to explore barren volcanic landscapes in the summit area as well as lush, waterfall-laden forests in the Kipahulu District. The park is home to more endangered species than any other national park in the United States, including the nēnē, or Hawaiian goose, which you'll probably see puttering around, oblivious to the precarity of its survival.

Geologically speaking, Haleakalā is a 10,000-foot shield volcano built up by successive layers of lava flows from hot spots in the ocean floor where the Pacific Plate moves northwest 4 inches per year, exposing magma from the inner earth to the deep sea. Only 5 percent of the mountain's volume is above the sea. Though it tops out at 10,023 feet above sea level, measured from the seafloor it's well over 28,000, which would make it the third-tallest mountain on earth. Its vast summit crater—2,600 feet deep in places—is a valley shaped by erosion and filled in with cinder cones and flows. The most recent eruption was probably in the seventeenth century.

Multicolored cinder cones of red, brown, and gray dot Haleakalā's crater—a landscape so harsh and alien that Apollo astronauts trained here for their lunar missions. It hosts the endemic, shimmering silversword plant, which can live up to ninety years but flowers only once in a spectacular bloom before dying.

The first Polynesians landed around 1,500 years ago, arriving in outrigger canoes larded with literal seeds required to start a flourishing civilization. These early seafarers left their mark in the form of rock walls, terraces, and petroglyphs. This culture flourished until and through European colonization in the 1700s. Many Hawaiian mo'olelo—stories that help explain the world—developed here. More recent history includes ranching and destructive introduced species like the mongoose and grasses that exacerbated the devastating Lahaina wildfire.

For now, Haleakalā remains a portal to Hawaii as it was. Descending from the summit to the Kipahulu District, the Mars-like landscape gives way to rain forests, waterfalls, and freshwater pools.

Countless native species call this tropical Eden home. Some, like the 'Ihi'ihi-laua'e-fern, are found only in this part of Maui. Here, you can hike the Pipiwai Trail through a bamboo forest to the incredible 400-foot Waimoku Falls.

Haleakalā National Park is a place where you can watch the sunrise above the clouds, then hike through alien landscapes and lush rain forests, all in one day. You'll wish Maui could lasso the sun again to give you more time to take it all in.

HIKES

Halemau'u Trail

A less-crowded alternative to the popular Sliding Sands Trail, the Halemau'u Trail offers stunning views of Haleakalā's crater and the opportunity to explore the park's unique ecosystems. The trail starts at the Halemau'u trailhead, located along Crater Road. Descending from the trailhead, you'll traverse shrubland, home to native plants like the Haleakalā silversword, and pass by several impressive cinder cones.

Four miles in, you'll reach the floor of the crater and the surreal, Mars-like landscape of Pele's Paint Pot, known for its vivid reds and oranges. The trail then winds past silversword meadows and lava flows toward Holua Cabin, your turnaround point for this 8.2-mile round-trip hike.

Starting at the Halemau'u trailhead along Crater Road, the trail descends through native shrubland, home to plants like the 'āhinahina, or Haleakalā silversword, a plant found nowhere else in the world. As you switchback down the crater rim, take a moment to marvel at the panoramic views of the Ko'olau Gap and the vast crater floor below.

At 1.1 miles in, you'll reach a lookout point that offers a jaw-dropping view of the crater. Here, the trail becomes a footpath etched into the cliff face. Don't let the seeming precipitous drop intimidate you, though; the trail is well built and safe, but do watch your step.

Volcanic activity stains the soil brilliant colors.

After the cliff section, the trail descends farther into the crater, reaching the crater floor 4 miles in. The landscape here is other-worldly, with cinder cones, lava flows, and the vivid colors of Pele's Paint Pot.

Once on the crater floor, you'll find the trail meandering through the surreal landscape toward the Holua Cabin. Here, amid a field of 'āhinahina and the looming cliffs of the crater rim, is your turnaround point.

The Holua area also houses a wilderness campsite for those seeking an overnight adventure. If you plan to camp, ensure you have a wilderness permit from the park.

The return trip is mostly uphill, so make sure to pace yourself and stay hydrated. As you ascend, take in the changing views of the crater and the silversword meadows, and watch as the panoramic vista of the crater floor gradually transforms back into the view of the Ko'olau Gap and the ocean beyond.

Supply Trail

The Supply Trail is a 3.9-mile one-way trail that takes you from Hosmer Grove Campground to the Halemau'u trailhead, passing through cloud forest and shrubland. You'll start at the upper end of the Hosmer Grove Campground loop and make your way through a grove of eucalyptus and pine, listening to the chorus of native honeycreepers.

The journey starts at the upper end of the Hosmer Grove loop, where you'll find the trailhead. The initial stretch of the trail weaves through a cloud forest, a unique ecosystem characterized by constant, low-level cloud cover. As you tread softly through this emerald cathedral, the cool, misty air carries the songs of native honeycreepers, a family of birds unique to the Hawaiian Islands.

As you ascend, the dense cloud forest gradually gives way to a shrubland dominated by hardy native plants adapted to the harsh, high-elevation conditions. You'll likely spot 'ahinahina, or Haleakalā silversword, a rare plant found only on the slopes of Haleakalā.

The trail continues to climb, offering increasingly spectacular views. To the west, the West Maui Mountains and the central isthmus of Maui are laid out like a verdant patchwork quilt. To the east, the stark beauty of Haleakalā's crater rim looms, a breathtaking contrast to the lush vegetation you've been traversing.

You'll reach the trail's end at the Halemau'u trailhead, located along Crater Road. From here, you can arrange a pickup or turn around and hike back down, or, for a more extended trek, connect to the Halemau'u Trail and venture into the heart of Haleakalā's crater.

Remember, the Supply Trail's elevation gain can make it a moderately challenging hike, so it's crucial to pace yourself and stay hydrated. Also, the weather on Haleakalā can be unpredictable, with rapid changes in temperature and precipitation. Always check the weather forecast and park advisories before setting out, and bring layers to adjust to changing conditions.

HIDDEN GEM

The **Haleakalā silversword,** or 'ahinahina in Hawaiian, is a striking plant endemic to the volcanic slopes of Haleakalā. Its name translates to "very gray," while "silversword" refers to the plant's rosette of narrow, silvery leaves that glint in the sunlight like wrought silver.

A member of the sunflower family (Asteraceae), it grows in the form of a round rosette, with leaves that can be up to a foot long. Covered in silver hairs, the leaves help the plant reflect sunlight and conserve water—essential adaptations to the harsh, high-altitude environment of the Haleakalā crater.

An individual silversword plant can live beyond fifty years. It spends most of its life in this rosette form, slowly growing and storing energy. Then, in a final dramatic burst of life, it sends up a tall flowering stalk—sometimes up to 6 feet high—covered in hundreds of small, purple, sunflower-like blooms. After flowering, the plant produces seeds and then dies.

This symbol of Haleakalā National Park remains vulnerable to climate change, invasive species, and human impact. The National Park Service has undertaken efforts to protect and restore silversword populations, but visitors must respect these unique plants by not touching or disturbing them and staying on marked trails.

A silversword blooms within the Haleakalā crater.

Visitors can see the islands being made with active lava flows.

Hawai'i Volcanoes National Park

Hawaii | nps.gov/havo | Visitation: 1,620,294

In a park system full of awe-inspiring geology, none are more grand, chaotic, or terrifyingly *alive* than the two explosive peaks of Hawai'i Volcanoes National Park. Here we come face to face with the overwhelming forces at work in the roiling, superheated guts of the planet. It's also a storybook tracing the steps of ancient Polynesians and informing the culture of present-day Hawaiians. It's an ark of rare and endangered species, and (if you're lucky) a Disneyland for anyone who gets mesmerized by molten lava.

Picture a landmass under the ocean, created by the earth's inner churning, spewing forth in hot molten lava that erupts, subsides, and repeats until the landmass breaks the surface. This is how Kīlauea and Mauna Loa, two of the world's most active volcanoes and the star attractions of the park, formed the Big Island of Hawaii. The ornery star here is Kīlauea, a temperamental diva of a volcano that erupted continuously from 1983 until 2018, painting the landscape with new layers of earth and altering the geography of the island in real time. The dramatic summit collapse of 2018 was thought to stop eruptions for perhaps a generation, but eruptions returned periodically in 2020 before pausing again in June 2023.

The lava fields may look desolate, but they are home to astonishingly resilient creatures like the happy-face spider—a tiny arachnid with markings on its back that resemble a smiley face.

On the other end of the scale are massive 'ōhi'a trees with bright red lehua flowers, standing tall and defiant in the volcanic soil. They're among the first plants to colonize a fresh lava field. The park also protects the habitat of the endangered nēnē, or Hawaiian goose, a bird that was so near extinction that at one point in the 1950s, only thirty of them remained. Now they're back in the hundreds, thanks to long-standing conservation efforts.

The park is a significant site for Native Hawaiians, who have lived on these lands for a millennium. It is a place where their oral histories come alive, where Pele, the goddess of volcanoes, resides, and where ancient petroglyphs document these stories.

Famous sites like the Thurston Lava Tube (Nāhuku), an illuminated cave formed by flowing lava, or the Kīlauea Iki Trail, which takes you through rain forest and across a solidified lava lake, or

Lit pathways guide hikers into dark lava tubes.

the Chain of Craters Road that leads to where lava flows have met the sea, deliver a sense of wonder and insignificance.

In Hawai'i Volcanoes National Park, the earth rumbles, steams, and occasionally spews forth new land, reminding us that our planet is still under construction. As much as the park is a place of science, it is first a place of deep Native Hawaiian culture. Take care to immerse yourself in both.

ZONE OF INTEREST

Mauna Loa and Kīlauea

The Hawaii Volcanoes National Park hosts two of the world's most active volcanoes: Kīlauea and Mauna Loa. Both volcanoes are part of the Hawaiian-Emperor seamount chain, a series of volcanoes created by the movement of the Pacific Plate over a stationary hot spot deep within the earth's mantle.

Kīlauea is one of the most active volcanoes on earth. Since 1952, it has erupted thirty-four times. Its most recent eruption began on September 10, 2023, in the summit caldera but ceased after six days. The eruptions of Kīlauea are usually effusive, characterized by the steady outflow of lava rather than explosive eruptions. However,

explosive eruptions can occur, often triggered by the interaction of groundwater with the magma.

Mauna Loa, on the other hand, is the largest shield volcano on earth, covering an area of 2,035 square miles. It last erupted in 1984, and while it has been less active than Kīlauea in recent years, scientists closely monitor it because of its potential for large-scale eruptions.

Seeing an eruption in Hawai'i Volcanoes National Park requires luck and timing, and the experience of a volcanic eruption at the park can vary greatly. During effusive eruptions, visitors might see the vibrant glow of lava lakes, or the slow, mesmerizing crawl of lava as it eats its way down the volcano's slopes toward the sea. In contrast, explosive eruptions might be accompanied by plumes of ash and steam, as well as impressive lava fountains. The park updates the website frequently to keep visitors as informed as possible, but given Pele's fickle nature, it's always possible to hop a plane to see an eruption only to land and find it over.

A past eruption on Mauna Loa.

It's important to remember that these are volcanoes. They fascinate but pose lethal hazards, including volcanic gases, falling ash, and fast-moving lava flows. The park has safety measures in place and may close certain areas during periods of increased volcanic activity to protect visitors.

The US Geological Survey's Hawaiian Volcano Observatory conducts continuous monitoring of these volcanoes. They use various tools and techniques, including seismometers, gas detectors, GPS, and satellite imagery, to track the volcanoes' activity and provide early warnings of potential eruptions. The threat to nearby communities and visitors is very real, but for Native Hawaiians it's also a part of life, woven into belief and reality as a constant reminder of the destruction, chaos, and renewal that defines what it means to live on this planet.

HIKES

Pu'u Huluhulu Trail

The Pu'u Huluhulu Trail guides you on an expedition into the strange, surreal, and alien experience of walking among cooled lava. Starting from Mauna Ulu's parking area off the Chain of Craters Road, this trail's 3 miles round-trip traverses a seemingly barren landscape that's as fascinating as it is desolate.

Begin your journey walking on a hardened lava field, with rugged, uneven terrain underfoot and a vast open sky above that evokes the surface of the moon. A closer look reveals hardy plants sprouting through the blackened earth.

Your destination, the cinder cone Pu'u Huluhulu or "Hairy Hill," rises from the lava landscape like an island oasis. It's a lush little green haven sprouting from the surrounding lava fields.

The trail ascends the pu'u, weaving through a thicket of native Hawaiian plants. You'll be flanked by 'ōhi'a lehua trees with their fiery red flowers, ferns unfurling their fronds, and the spongy trunks of the hapu'u pulu.

Reaching the summit, you're treated to panoramic views of Mauna Ulu, the volcano responsible for the lava field you crossed, now slumbering. On a clear day during eruptions, you can sometimes spot the plume of steam where lava from Kīlauea pours into the sea miles away.

Footprints Trail

The Footprints Trail leads to a series of footprints originally pressed into layers of volcanic ash, a chilling snapshot of a dramatic day in the late 1700s when residents fled Pele's awesome fury. They may not have escaped.

Your journey begins near the Ka'u Desert trailhead off the Chain of Craters Road. The trail stretches 3.5 miles round-trip and takes you through an arid, seemingly inhospitable landscape of the Ka'u Desert, a stretch of land smothered in volcanic ash and pumice, punctuated by scrubby vegetation.

The trail leads to imprints left behind by Native Hawaiians caught in a devastating eruption of the Kīlauea Volcano. These footprints have been preserved for centuries in the hardened ash layer, a physical relic of the panic that arose on a day when the sky turned dark and rained fire.

Along the trail, interpretive signs attempt to reconstruct the scene. It is believed that the people who left these footprints belonged to traveling warriors and families, caught unawares by sudden eruption.

Kīpukapuaulu Trail

The Kīpukapuaulu Trail, also known as the Bird Park, exists in vibrant contrast to the omnipresent volcanic landscape. This 1.2-mile loop trail will introduce you to an oasis of life thriving amid the surrounding lava fields—an island of green known as a kīpuka.

The term *kīpuka* in Hawaiian refers to an older, elevated area of land surrounded by more recent lava flows. Over time, these kīpukas become havens for plants and animals, pockets of life amid the seemingly desolate landscape.

The ʻōhiʻa lehua tree figures prominently in Hawaiian folklore.

Your journey begins at the Kīpukapuaulu parking area off Mauna Loa Road. As you step onto the trail, you're stepping into a veritable glass case of native Hawaiian plants and birds. Interpretive signs along the way guide you with tales of the flora and fauna that call this place home.

Stroll under the canopy of towering koa and ʻōhiʻa lehua trees, their bark gnarled and twisted over decades. Ferns and flowering plants form the undergrowth, painting the ground in various shades of green, dotted with bursts of flowers.

Above, a symphony of birdsong echoes through the foliage. Keep an eye out for native Hawaiian birds like the ʻapapane, ʻamakihi, and the elusive ʻiʻiwi with its curved beak and brilliant red feathers. If you're lucky, you might spot one of the many endemic Hawaiian honeycreepers flitting in the trees. The biological diversity is mirrored by the Hawaiian concept of ʻohana (family), where every living thing plays a crucial role in the grand, interconnected scheme of life.

HIDDEN GEM

If you catch an ocean view from a high point or coastal trail in Hawaii Volcanoes National Park, train your eyes southeast toward a patch of blue Pacific 21 miles offshore. There, hidden some 3,100 feet below the surface lies the 10,000-foot **Kamaʻehuakanaloa seamount** (formerly known as Lōʻihi): This is the newest volcano in the Hawaiian-Emperor chain, a tagalong baby brother to Mauna Loa waiting to break through the surface and become the next Hawaiian island. It already features a flat top with a summit crater known as Pele's Pit, with hydrothermal vents spewing water as hot as 390 degrees Fahrenheit. Observations of fresh pillow lava and regular eruptions indicate that it's growing steadily skyward. Don't plan a visit yet: It won't break the surface for another 10,000 to 100,000 years.

Hot Springs National Park

Arkansas | nps.gov/hosp | Visitation: 2,502,967

Hot Springs National Park is a bit of an anomaly in the park system. Its preservation predates the concept of national parks. For thousands of years, Native American tribes regarded the springs as sacred ground, a place of healing and peace. European settlers pushing westward stumbled upon the springs. Recognizing the potential for a good thing when they saw it, they built a bustling resort town where people could "take the waters" and enjoy the sulfurous springs' supposed curative properties for ailments like rheumatism. Set aside as a federal reserve in 1832, it developed into a resort well before it earned national park status in 1921.

Natural hot springs have drawn people to this area since prehistory.

Despite centuries of human development, you can spy white-tailed deer, armadillos, and over a hundred species of birds among the hickories and oaks that occupy the park's forested fringes.

Most visitors dunk themselves in the comforting waters and visit the stately Gilded Age structures of Bathhouse Row and the Grand Promenade. Hot Springs National Park doesn't have the reputation of being a hiker's park compared to its more wilderness-focused siblings, but it does offer a network of trails that can provide a pleasant escape from the busy bathhouses and historic sites.

ZONE OF INTEREST

Sunset Trail

At 10 miles, the Sunset Trail is the longest trail in Hot Springs National Park. It traverses the varied landscapes of the park, offering expansive views, pleasant woodland walks, and a glimpse into the park's history. The ability to dip in and out of the trail at various points depending on interest or time is what makes it unique and fun.

You can access the Sunset Trail from various points within the park, but a common starting point is the Gulpha Gorge Campground near the Gulpha Gorge trailhead.

The trail is divided into three sections. The West Mountain section is 2.8 miles long and takes you around West Mountain with several overlooks providing views of the city of Hot Springs and the Ouachita Mountains. The ascent can be a bit steep, but the rewarding views are worth the effort. The 3.8-mile Sugarloaf Mountain

The Goat Rock Trail is a highlight spur on the Sunset Trail.

section meanders through the forested slopes of Sugarloaf Mountain. A highlight is Balanced Rock, a large sandstone boulder precariously perched on a pedestal.

The final Stonebridge Road section is 3.4 miles long and winds through rolling woodland. Watch for remnants of old stone walls, a reminder of the original settlers who once called this place home. You can choose to do sections individually or combine them for a longer hike.

Indiana Dunes National Park

Indiana | nps.gov/indu | Visitation: 2,765,892

Nestled on the southernmost tip of Lake Michigan, Indiana Dunes attained national park status in 2019. Like many recent additions, it represents our evolving concept of what constitutes a park, where borders between the built and natural worlds grow porous and overlap.

That's apparent upon approach: To the west, the stark factory skyline of Gary, Indiana, looms, a rusting monument to industrial ambition. To the east you'll find the more genteel university town of Michigan City. And 50 miles across the lake, the skyscrapers of Chicago spike the horizon. In between, we find a 15,000-acre oasis of sand, water, greenery, and prairie that predates civilization.

During the last ice age, glaciers plowed down from the north, grinding the earth and rocks beneath them into a fine powder. As the climate warmed, the glaciers retreated, leaving behind a vast plain of glacial flour. Westerly winds picked up this material and carried it eastward, depositing it along the shores of the newly formed Lake Michigan. Over millennia, these particles accumulated, forming the dunes we see today. There's more: The park includes wetlands, quiet forests, and sprawling prairies and savannas.

Within each of these habitats, you can spot more than 350 species of birds, from the majestic sandhill crane to the diminutive ruby-throated hummingbird. Numerous mammals live here, from white-tailed deer to little brown bats. Reptiles, amphibians, and insects abound, many of them rare and endangered. Over 1,100 species of plants—some found nowhere else in the world—sprout from dune to forest and back.

Native Americans lived here for thousands of years, hunting, fishing, and farming. European explorers arrived in the seventeenth century, followed by fur traders, settlers, and industrialists. In the twentieth century, the dunes became a battleground between conservationists who sought to protect their natural beauty, and industrialists who saw in them a source of raw materials and a site for development. The creation of the national park in 2019 marked a victory for conservationists.

But don't let this fool you into thinking that Indiana Dunes is some pristine wilderness. You're still a stone's throw from Chicago, as likely to stumble upon a rare orchid as an abandoned car. And the birdsong competes with the distant rumble of freight trains and the hushed thrum of wind turbines.

Indiana Dunes is one of the newest national parks.

Still, the sheer resilience of nature in Indiana Dunes amazes. Tucked amid the factories and the freeways, life finds ways to thrive. It's a reminder that nature isn't something "out there," separate and apart from us, but something that threads its way into our lives, no matter what we build, tear down, and build again.

HIKES

Cowles Bog Trail

If you're up for a bit of a challenge, this 4.7-mile loop trail traverses a variety of habitats, including dunes, wetlands, and forests. The trailhead is located off North Mineral Springs Road. Be prepared for

Boardwalks help hikers descend the tallest dunes.

A path leads over dunes bordering the southern shore of Lake Michigan.

some hilly terrain and a few potentially muddy spots. The end lands you on a secluded beach with views of the Chicago skyline on a clear day. This trail is named for Henry Cowles, a botanist from the University of Chicago, who studied plant succession in the dunes.

Tolleston Dunes Trail

Named for a geological era, this 3-mile loop trail offers a moderate hike with plenty of biodiversity. Starting from the trailhead off US 12, you'll traverse various dune habitats that offer sightings of different plant species depending on the season. The trail has interpretive signs describing the changing habitats and the succession of dune development. Ascend the dune ridges for panoramic views of the surrounding woods and wetlands, an artist's palette of greens in the summer and a fiery spectacle in the fall.

Little Calumet River Trail

This relatively flat, 3.4-mile trail is tucked away near US 12 and County Line Road. The trail follows the Little Calumet River through mature forests. You'll cross several bridges and boardwalks and connect to the Bailly Homestead and Chellberg Farm, sites that offer a glimpse into the region's history, from the fur trading era to Swedish immigration.

HIDDEN GEM

Watchful hikers can find a strange desert orphan among the dunes: The **prickly pear cactus** thrives here, often in the border zones where prairie meets sand. Its purple fruits are edible, and the spiny plant sprouts bright yellow flowers in June and July.

Improbably, prickly pear cactus grows in Indiana Dunes, hundreds of miles from the desert.

Rock Harbor in remote Isle Royale National Park.

Isle Royale National Park

Michigan | nps.gov/isro | Visitation: 28,965

In the northwestern corner of the inland freshwater sea of Lake Superior, a stone's throw from the Canadian border, lies Isle Royale National Park—the least-visited park in the Lower 48. This unpeopled wilderness archipelago is perhaps the only park that provides abject remoteness and pure solitude found in the more remote Alaska parks. That extends to the park's logistics: You get here only by ferry or seaplane, and the only ways to move around once you arrive are by foot or by boat. The season is short—April to October—and in another nod to the Last Frontier, legendary clouds of blackflies and mosquitoes often plague the peak summer months. But the rewards can be sublime. When the boat or plane disappears on the horizon, a rugged but accessible wilderness splays out before you to explore.

Basaltic lava flows formed the island's bedrock over a billion years ago; faults flipped those layers and immense glaciers scoured what would become the islands. Glaciers then retreated and melted around 10,000 years ago to form the world's largest lake by surface area. They left behind a mixture of rocky ridges, marshy bogs, and dense forests poking above the water's surface; stunted pines cling to rocky outcroppings and hardy lichens paint the stones in subtle hues of red, yellow, and green. It's all crisscrossed by a network of hiking trails to thrill the most seasoned wilderness enthusiasts. At 45 miles long and 10 miles wide, Isle Royale is large enough to get lost in, but the park also encompasses another 450 or so smaller islands surrounding it.

Isolation and a harsh climate fostered a unique and resilient ecosystem. Wolves and moose are famous residents and subjects of the longest predator-prey study in the world—an ongoing saga of survival that has fascinated scientists for over sixty years. The moose arrived only around the turn of the twentieth century, while wolves crossed an ice bridge over the frozen Lake Superior sometime in 1948. Since then, the wolf population has fluctuated from a high of fifty in 1980 to a low of two in 2018. Beavers, foxes, snowshoe hares, and loons round out the wildlife haunting the mixed forests of pine, fir, spruce, aspen, oak, and maple.

Humans have also left their mark on the island, from ancient copper miners over 4,500 years ago to the commercial fishers in the nineteenth century. While no permanent settlements have been found, Native tribes returned seasonally to dig pits and extract copper for trading. The island is scattered with remnants of its past inhabitants: abandoned mines, old fishery cabins, trash middens, abandoned equipment from the timber industry, and more.

Paddling in Isle Royale requires experience: Lake Superior often behaves more like a cold inland ocean.

With visitor numbers capped to preserve the island's delicate ecosystems, you're more likely to encounter a red fox or a snowshoe hare than another person. It's a rare opportunity to disconnect, to swap the ringing of cell phones for the call of loons, the glow of screens for the glitter of the Milky Way.

Any adventure in Isle Royale begins with planning. The most popular ferry, the *Ranger III*, departs from Houghton, Michigan, and takes 6 hours. *The Isle Royale Queen IV* operates from Copper Harbor, Michigan, for a 3.5-hour sail. *Voyageur II* and *Sea Hunter III* leave from Grand Portage, Minnesota. The *Voyageur II* travels around the entire island, making multiple stops, while the *Sea Hunter III* makes a direct trip to Windigo (these trips can take between 1.5 and 3 hours). Seaplanes are faster but much more expensive. Isle Royale Seaplanes operates from Houghton County Memorial Airport in Michigan and the Grand Marais/Cook County Airport in Minnesota. Flights last 35 minutes from Houghton and 45 minutes from Grand Marais.

ZONES OF INTEREST

As with most drowned parks, taking to the water allows for efficient and exciting adventures. Special care must be taken when kayaking or canoeing at Isle Royale, however. Lake Superior behaves more like a sea, with sudden fog, squalls, large waves, and cold water all presenting significant risks. (Beginners can keep to the main island's inland lakes for more manageable adventures.) Still, this is a paddling paradise where wilderness character, diverse wildlife, and clear waters abound.

Rock Harbor to Chippewa Harbor (Intermediate)

This route provides a great introduction to the rugged shoreline of Isle Royale, passing several islands and allowing you to spot moose, wolves, and many bird species. Start at Rock Harbor and head southwest along the coastline. This trip will likely take two days to cover the 10 miles it takes to get to Chippewa Harbor. Consider camping overnight at one of the many campsites along the way.

McCargoe Cove to Belle Isle (Advanced)

Paddle through the heart of Isle Royale's wilderness on a demanding route with potential for large waves and challenging weather. McCargoe Cove is known for its fjord-like natural beauty, while Belle Isle offers great camping. Begin at McCargoe Cove and paddle along the north coastline toward the east until you reach Belle Isle. The 20-mile paddle is best managed over two or three days, depending on conditions. Camping is available at both McCargoe Cove and Belle Isle.

Listen for loon calls at dusk in Isle Royale.

Windigo to Washington Harbor (Beginner)

Even young paddlers with some experience can attempt this trip's calm waters and look out for plentiful wildlife viewing opportunities. Start at Windigo and paddle southwest to Washington Harbor for 5 miles. Complete the route in one day, or camp at Washington Harbor.

Rock Harbor to Lane Cove (Intermediate)

A journey along the northern shoreline gives broad views of the island and the opportunity to explore multiple coves and inlets. From Rock Harbor, paddle northeast along the shoreline for 7 miles until you reach Lane Cove. It can be completed in a day, although many choose to camp at Lane Cove and return the next day.

Tobin Harbor Day Trip (Beginner)

A serene day trip, Tobin Harbor offers a flat-water paddle with an abundance of wildlife as you leave from Rock Harbor and paddle through Tobin Harbor, exploring the shoreline as you go, for 6 miles round-trip.

Before you head out, always check in with the National Park Service for the latest information on camping permits, weather,

The view of Canada from Mount Franklin.

and other requirements. Always have a map and compass handy. Bring your own gear, or you can rent canoes or sea kayaks from the Rock Harbor Lodge or Windigo Store.

HIKES

Mount Franklin to Lane Cove

Head north to top out on Mount Franklin, an understated peak that rewards travelers with intimate encounters with the island's varied terrain and isolated coves over 6.9 miles.

The first leg of the journey takes you through a dense forest of spruce and birch, where the air is heavy with the scent of earth and greenery. The trail then descends sharply toward Lane Cove, a secluded spot on the northern coastline. Watch for moose, otters, and foxes, and listen for the hoot of owls.

Windigo to Huginnin Cove

Starting from the Windigo Visitor Center, this 8.4-mile round-trip trail travels through old-growth forest and wetlands before reaching the untouched shoreline of Huginnin Cove with views of the Canada shoreline across the water.

As you navigate the trail, watch for the wildflowers that dot the landscape in the spring and summer, and keep an eye out for the park's iconic wildlife, including foxes, snowshoe hares, and the island's resident moose and wolf populations.

East Chickenbone Lake to McCargoe Cove

This 3-mile trek weaves its way from the campsite at East Chickenbone Lake to the secluded waters of McCargoe Cove. The trail can be a bit of a challenge, with some steep sections, but as you traverse this path, you'll pass through a rich mosaic of ecosystems, from dense boreal forests to shimmering wetlands. The trail culminates at McCargoe Cove, a hidden inlet on the island's northern shore. Here, you'll find a peaceful, rocky cove where the only sounds are the gentle lapping of waves against the shore and keening loon calls in the evening.

Scientists have studied moose-wolf interactions on Isle Royale for decades.

Joshua Tree National Park

California | nps.gov/jotr | Visitation: 3,270,404

Joshua Tree National Park sprawls across 800,000 acres of Southern California, overlapping the Mojave and Colorado Deserts. The park got its name from the Joshua trees, a peculiar type of yucca that Mormon pioneers thought resembled the biblical Joshua, arms outstretched in supplication. It's a fitting symbol for a place that thrums with a spiritual grandeur in between the sand and piles of desolate rock.

In recent years, Joshua Tree National Park has experienced some of the fastest rates of growth in visitation in the national park system. Attendance has more than doubled in the last seven years, and it's easy to understand why. A mere 130 miles from Los Angeles, it's a quick hop for throngs of people to visit a topsy-turvy wonderland of compelling rock formations and only-here vegetation. Nearby Coachella and its taste-making music and culture festival bear some responsibility: Droves of hipsters now seek out balanced boulders and trees resembling stick figures on vintage Pearl Jam posters for the 'gram.

Joshua Tree National Park's geological wonderland of rugged rock formations plunked on stark desert landscapes took more than 100 million years to make. The higher-elevation, western Mojave portion of the park is a land of boulder piles and bare rock, sculpted by the elements and draining groundwater into a maze of monzogranite monoliths—a type of cooled-lava granite characterized by the way it breaks into rectangular blocks. Erosion weathered away weaker rock and stone to leave andesite, pegmatite, and aplite intrusions as terraced walls between the softened edges of these rectangular boulders.

The park's famous tree, *Yucca brevifolia*, thrives in the Mojave's cooler climates at 2,000 to 5,000 feet. These distinctive trees, with their spiky leaves and twisted, bristled branches, provide shelter and food for numerous species. The Little San Bernardino Mountains dominate the park's southwestern edge, offering higher-elevation vistas and cooler temperatures.

The Colorado Desert half (a subset of the gigantic Sonoran Desert) is warmer than the Mojave and characterized by open vistas and its own suite of flora and fauna. You'll find stands of creosote bush, palo verde, smoke trees, adorable teddy bear cholla cactus, and ocotillo plants, whose tall, whiplike branches often burst into a fiery display of red blooms after rainfall.

The tenacious crew of animal survivors includes kangaroo rats, coyotes, and golden eagles. Nine species of lizards skitter over boulders, and bighorn sheep scale rocky heights. Jackrabbits, ground squirrels, foxes, and at least seven species of rattlesnakes leave varied tracks though the hot sands.

A Joshua tree stretches skyward in the Black Rock section of Joshua Tree National Park.

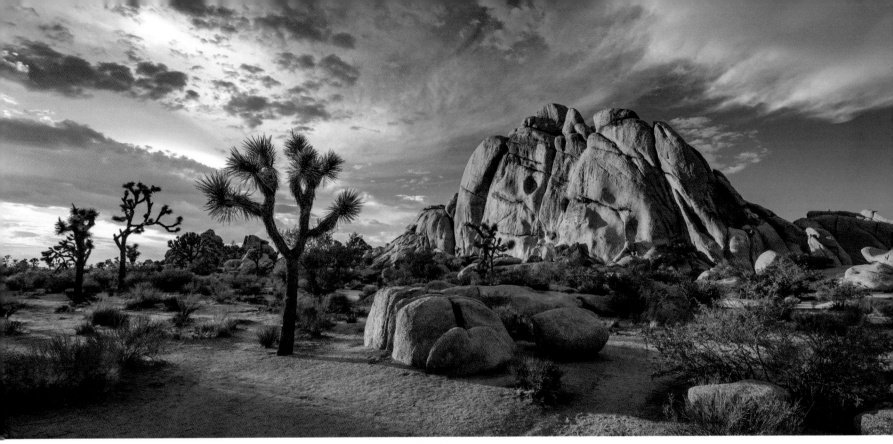

Old Woman Rock, a famous rock formation within Joshua Tree National Park.

Ancient petroglyphs etched into the stone tell stories of the Serrano, Chemehuevi, and Cahuilla tribes who once called this land home. In more recent times, cattle rustlers and gold seekers left their own marks on the landscape. Mine ruins, ranching implements, and other artifacts both prehistoric and modern litter the landscape.

The varied and extensive mazes of rock present in Joshua Tree make it a mecca for climbers of all abilities. But visitors tend to cluster at trailheads and entrances, and given the park's size, opportunities for hikers to disappear into quieter reaches abound. Don't get too lost: It's a big wilderness, and even experienced hikers can get caught in the heat or lost in a boulder maze. Maps, skill, and water, water, water are required for any extended excursions within J-Tree.

ZONE OF INTEREST

Black Rock Canyon

The Black Rock Canyon area, located at the northwest corner of Joshua Tree National Park, has a separate entrance and offers a quieter and more remote experience. The park's more famous spots, such as Hidden Valley, Keys View, Barker Dam, and the Joshua Tree forests in the main section, tend to overshadow this area—which leaves plenty of room to roam for those willing to add a few miles to their drive. It has its own dense Joshua Tree forest, which provides a serene setting for hikes.

The Black Rock Canyon Trail, 7.5 miles round-trip, takes you deep into its namesake canyon, offering panoramic views in exchange for moderately difficult hiking over a few steep sections.

Panorama Loop's 6.6-mile run offers stunning vistas, especially during sunrise and sunset. The trail takes you through a dense Joshua Tree forest and across a few sandy washes.

The quieter West Side Loop covers 3.8 miles over a loop that offers a good overview of the varied landscapes of Joshua Tree, from cacti-studded flats to boulder-strewn vistas. For families, there are several shorter trails in this zone, perfect for an easy stroll or for those with limited time, including the Hi-View Nature Trail (1.3 miles).

HIKES

Eureka Peak

Nestled within the serene and less-traveled corners of Joshua Tree National Park, the hike to Eureka Peak promises an intimate escape and a high view in a quiet portion of the park.

Begin your journey at the Black Rock Canyon Campground, located on the northwest side of the park. The drive into the Black Rock area is distinct from the main park entrances and is lined with the iconic, spiky silhouettes of Joshua trees. When you enter the park, the road will lead you straight into the heart of the campground. To access the Eureka Peak trailhead, navigate to the western end of the campground. Parking is available, but during peak season, it's advised to arrive early to ensure a spot.

Setting out from the trailhead, the route stretches roughly 11 miles roundtrip to the peak. Initially, the trail is flat, winding through dense clusters of Joshua trees. The landscape here is characteristic of the Mojave Desert, with the trees interspersed with cacti, yucca, and other desert flora.

As you move deeper into the trail, gentle inclines begin weaving you in and out of small canyons and arroyos punctuated by ancient granite boulders. These rocky landmarks provide ample opportunities for brief climbing detours or photo ops.

Halfway up, the trail steepens and demands a bit more effort. Turn around: The vast expanse of Joshua Tree National Park unfolds behind you in a mosaic of rock formations, valleys, and sprawling Joshua tree forests.

When you reach the summit of Eureka Peak, views of the park stretch to the east. To the west, the San Gorgonio Mountains rise from the horizon. On exceptionally clear days, you might glimpse the distant sparkle of the Salton Sea.

For photographers, the sunrise or sunset views from Eureka Peak are unparalleled. The sun's rays reliably paint the desert landscape in hues of gold, pink, and orange.

Boy Scout Trail

Stretching between two of the park's most visited areas, the Boy Scout Trail offers a unique blend of the park's most iconic features, an intimate desert experience, and a walk through geological time.

The Boy Scout Trail can be accessed from two primary trailheads: The northern trailhead begins near the Indian Cove Campground. To get there, take CA 62 and turn south on Indian Cove Road, following signs to the campground. The southern trailhead is located off Park Boulevard, a short distance west of the intersection with Keys View Road.

The trail itself stretches 8 miles one-way, making it a perfect choice for a long day hike or an overnight backpacking trip.

Start your trek by hiking past giant monoliths interspersed with sections of flat desert strewn with cacti, yucca, and Joshua trees. Cross narrow valleys and over modest ridges. Soon you'll enter the Wonderland of Rocks, a maze-like area with intricate rock formations and hidden nooks and crannies that beckon explorers and photographers.

The trail hosts an array of desert flora, from the iconic Joshua trees to blooming cacti and wildflowers in the spring. Wildlife, too, makes its presence known. You might catch sight of a roadrunner darting across the trail or hear the distant call of coyotes at dusk.

Halfway along the trail, backcountry boards mark areas where overnight campers can set up for the evening. Remember, camping

Piles of boulders create a maze on the Boy Scout Trail.

is only allowed 500 feet away from the trail and water sources to protect the environment.

Given its length and desert environment, it's imperative to come prepared. Carry ample water, sun protection, and a first-aid kit. Always inform someone of your plans, and if possible, hike with a companion.

While the trail is generally well marked, carrying a map or GPS device is always wise, particularly if you plan to explore off-trail regions like the Wonderland of Rocks.

Munsen Canyon/Summit Springs Oasis

Joshua Tree is unique among desert parks for its oases: These groundwater springs support a profusion of plant and animal life in an otherwise barren desert, and in some places shelter stands of fan palms—the only palm tree native to California. And while Lost Palms, 49 Palms, and other oases rank high on hikers' hit lists, exceptionally hardy and resilient hikers can make for hidden oases located in the deep reaches of Munsen Canyon. ***Caution:*** This route is only for exceptionally competent and prepared hikers. Food, water, navigation, and self-rescue skills should be dialed before attempting this route. Bouldering, scrambling, and route finding will be required to access these hidden oases.

Eleven and a half miles of trail and 2,500 feet of elevation gain await from your start at the Cottonwood Spring trailhead. The trail begins by passing under the swaying fan palms of Cottonwood Spring Oasis before entering a succession of maze-like canyons and washes. Bypass the Mastodon Peak split at 0.7 mile to drop into a wash at 2.45 miles and start climbing an ocotillo-lined ridge with views of the Salton Sea at 2.8 miles.

Joshua Tree's oases host groves of fan palms.

Pass through green Lost Palms Oasis at 3.7 miles before bouldering toward Victory Palms Oasis. Find a cholla cactus garden and then begin a challenging section of tough bouldering at mile 4 until it relaxes a bit in 0.5 mile. Look for bighorn sheep as you approach Victory Palms at mile 5, with its underwhelming but refreshing twin palms.

At around 0.3 mile beyond Victory Palms, spy for a break left toward the entrance to Munsen Canyon (GPS: N33 42.378 / W115 44.877). After an arduous 0.5-mile, 400-foot scramble, you'll reach two oases filled with palms and lush greenery. And you will have them to yourself.

HIDDEN GEM

Owing to its distance from major cities and comparative lack of amenities, 1.6-million-acre **Mojave National Preserve** (MNP) draws a fraction of the crowds compared to J-Tree while retaining all the pluses: mind-bending rock formations, wildlife-rich oases, and massive groves of splayed-out Joshua trees. It's a vast sanctuary for those seeking a rawer desert experience.

It rivals Joshua Tree at its namesake game: Cima Dome is a geologic formation that houses one of the largest and densest Joshua tree forests. (Unfortunately, many burned in a 2020 fire). It also features Kelso Dunes, singing sand dunes covering 45 square miles and rising 600 feet. You can hike the Mojave Lava Tubes near the cinder cone area where lava once flowed, and Teutonia Peak, located in the Cima Dome region, is filled with rich history and offers spectacular vistas at the end of a 3.4-mile hike to its summit. Located in the Hole-in-the-Wall area, the Rings Loop Trail's 1.5 miles requires hikers to use metal rings to ascend through narrow canyons, offering a mix of adventure and assisted canyoneering.

With fewer amenities and more remote areas, it's crucial to prepare with sufficient water, food, and navigation tools. There's no lodging, restaurants, or supplies within stabbing distance of the park. Cell coverage is sporadic, and the visitor centers are often closed. Inform someone of your plans before heading out.

Castle Peaks in Mojave National Preserve

Katmai hosts one of the densest populations of brown bears in North America.

Katmai National Park and Preserve

Alaska | nps.gov/katm | Visitation: 33,763

Despite being an under-visited park, Katmai hoovers up international attention and viral fame every fall thanks to Fat Bear Week. Since 2014, park rangers have created a weeklong bracket-style competition wherein the public votes for their favorite chonky grizzly. And do they get chonky: The bears in Katmai can gain hundreds of pounds over the summer season, with some males reaching weights over 1,000 pounds (2022 champ 747 crushed the estimated scales at 1,400 pounds).

Katmai National Park remains one of the premier locations in the world to observe brown bears. An estimated 2,200 brown bears live here, one of the highest densities on earth. Rich salmon runs in the park's rivers support their numbers with a reliable and high-quality food source.

The bears of Katmai have been a focus of scientific study and observation for decades. One of the most accessible locations for bear viewing is at Brooks Falls, where platforms allow visitors to safely watch bears fishing and competing for salmon, often catching the fish in their jaws midair. It's not uncommon to see other animals like wolves or eagles joining the action.

The contest emphasizes the fact that fat bears are healthy bears. Brown bears in Katmai must eat a year's worth of food in fewer than six months to survive hibernation, during which they lose up to one-third of their body weight.

But Katmai's 4 million acres contain more than celebrity ursids. Skyscraping peaks, glacial valleys, thick rain forests, and a vast, undisturbed coastline skin a region that first came to our attention because of its roiling, violent depths. The land still bears the scars of the 1912 Novarupta eruption, one of the most powerful volcanic events of the twentieth century. Over a century later, the park's otherworldly Valley of Ten Thousand Smokes preserves the ghost of that eruption in a 40-square-mile valley of barren ash framed by high mountains. Lake Naknek, located in the interior, is the largest lake held wholly within national park borders.

On the coast, sea otters frolic in the surf while harbor seals keep a watchful eye for orcas, which prowl for them as well as salmon and halibut. Offshore, the Shelikof Strait serves as a marine highway for whales as they journey to and from their feeding grounds.

The Valley of Ten Thousand Smokes is the remnant of one of the largest volcanic eruptions in history.

Truly a wilderness park, Katmai National Park offers more of an open-country hiking experience than traditional well-marked trails. However, some established routes and destinations can be accessed by intermediate hikers.

ZONE OF INTEREST

Valley of Ten Thousand Smokes

The Valley of Ten Thousand Smokes in Katmai National Park is a geological marvel, a testament to the cataclysmic eruption of the Novarupta Volcano in 1912. This 40-square-mile, 100- to 700-foot-deep pyroclastic flow deposit still bears the scars of the eruption. It's named for the numerous fumaroles that once vented steam from the still-hot ash and pumice.

To explore this surreal landscape, a manageable route is going to Ukak Falls via Windy Creek (8 miles round-trip). You start at the Robert F. Griggs Visitor Center, which is accessible via a 25-mile bus tour from Brooks Camp. Please note that this is a challenging back-country hike with no established trail; navigation skills are required.

From the visitor center, descend steeply into the valley on a well-maintained trail. Once you're in the valley, you'll hike along the Lethe River toward Windy Creek. Loose, slippery volcanic ash and pumice make the terrain here difficult, so sturdy hiking boots are essential.

Upon reaching Windy Creek, follow it upstream until it converges with Knife Creek. This area provides an excellent vantage point of Ukak Falls, where Knife Creek cascades over a series of waterfalls. This is often the turnaround point for many hikers, although those with sufficient backcountry experience may wish to explore further.

This is a remote wilderness, with rapidly changing weather conditions and no amenities or services available. It's essential to carry sufficient water, food, clothing, navigation tools, and emergency supplies. Take special care (or avoid) crossing the hard-to-gauge Lethe and Knife Creek Rivers, which often conceal sinkholes hidden by suspended ash.

HIKE

Dumpling Mountain

While most visitors don't make it past the mesmerizing bears at the falls seen from the viewing platforms at Brooks Camp, you can get a true taste of wild Alaska by venturing beyond on this 8-mile round-trip trek, but beware: The lack of a defined trail can make it feel longer.

Starting from the Brooks Camp, head east, slowly gaining elevation as you cross through a mix of low-lying vegetation and forested sections. The trail gets steeper and more challenging as you approach the top. But from the summit you'll earn views overlooking the wide expanse of Naknek Lake and the Brooks River far below.

While there are no designated campsites along this route, backcountry camping is permitted (though appropriate sites can be hard to find). And while you're not far from the bear watchers on the Brooks, take all proper precautions—this is still raw Alaska.

HIDDEN GEM

Accessible only by plane or boat, **Hallo Bay**'s sedge meadows and long sandy beaches give visitors the once-in-a-lifetime chance to see bears playing, sleeping, digging for clams, courting, and fighting from a safe distance. It's all framed by astounding glaciated peaks. Once you arrive, there are no set trails, but you can wander the coastline and meadows, always keeping a respectful space between you and the bears. Soft sand and tidal changes can make coastal walking difficult, but the wildlife viewing is unparalleled; you will probably see more bear prints than boot prints. Booking guided tours is recommended.

Hallo Bay can be reached only by boat or floatplane.

Spire Bay in Kenai Fjords.

Kenai Fjords
National Park

Alaska | nps.gov/kefj | Visitation: 387,525

More than half of Kenai Fjords is covered in ice—the heart of which is the Harding Icefield, an expansive sheet of ice that feeds forty glaciers flowing down into fjords. These fjords, steep-walled valleys carved by glacial activity, extend like fingers into the Gulf of Alaska.

But this 700,000-acre park (small for Alaska, big for anywhere else) is a 2.5-hour stone's throw from Anchorage. Trails are limited, and the park is best seen paddling along 545 miles of wilderness coastline. But the trails that do exist are standouts. Some of the best will give you an eye-popping vista of our country's biggest ice cube tray.

The Harding Icefield's 700-square-mile world of white and blue is the largest in the United States and a relic of the last ice age. It's mostly frozen still, but patience can bring thrilling action. Glaciers break off into the sea through a process known as tidewater calving, bringing a roar that echoes through the fjords and waves that jostle frightened kayakers and boaters who've wandered too close.

The often-turbulent Gulf of Alaska batters the coast while housing a wide variety of marine life. Sea otters bob in the waves, while harbor seals haul out on ice floes to rest and sun themselves. Sea lions bark from their rocky haul-outs, and in the sky above, bald eagles and goofy puffins wheel and dive. The seabirds here are too numerous to count, and many of them spend more time swimming than flying. Dolphins and porpoises leap out of dark teal ocean swells. But the undisputed kings of this marine world are the whales—orca, humpback, and fin whales—that can be seen breaching and spouting throughout the park's waters.

On land, black and brown bears roam the forests and meadows, while mountain goats navigate the steep cliffs of the fjords. The Harding Icefield and its glaciers are home to a unique community of organisms, including ice worms and pinkish snow algae (also called watermelon snow).

The Alutiiq people have lived in this region for thousands of years, relying on bounties from the sea and the land. European explorers first arrived in the late eighteenth century, followed by prospectors and settlers in the nineteenth and twentieth centuries. Today, the park is a popular-but-not-too-popular destination for visitors seeking its unique blend of natural beauty, wildlife, and adventure. The charming fishing town of Seward abuts the park, offering an easy staging ground for

Mountain goats graze near the Harding Icefield.

adventures, as well as cold pints and freshest-in-class seafood upon your return.

The Exit Glacier area is the most popular hiking zone, but that doesn't mean it's crowded. And it shouldn't be missed: A small network of trails leads to the outwash plain of the glacier, and an 8-mile out-and-back hike climbs a little over 3,000 feet to an expansive view of the Harding Icefield itself, a sea of blinding white studded with nunataks (ice-enclosed peaks) that break the skin of the glacier like black shark fins on the horizon. I've never seen more than fifteen people on the trail in three times hiking it.

HIKES

While Kenai Fjords National Park is mostly water (frozen and liquid varieties) and doesn't offer an extensive network of hiking trails, there are a few lesser-known trails where you can find solitude and explore the wild landscape.

Tonsina Creek Trail

This 4-mile round-trip trail begins near Lowell Point, a few miles south of Seward. The trail meanders through coastal forest and leads to a secluded cove at Tonsina Point. This area can feel remote, despite being close to town. To reach the trailhead, drive south from Seward on Lowell Point Road for 2 miles. The trailhead is near Lowell Point State Recreation Site.

The trail offers a serene beach walk, opportunities to spot wildlife (including sea otters and bald eagles), and beautiful views of Resurrection Bay.

Derby Cove Cabin Trail

A 5.4-mile one-way journey leads to a public-use cabin nestled between the forest and beach on Resurrection Bay's western side. The trail starts from the Exit Glacier paved path, before the Exit Glacier Nature Center. The first section is also the start of the Harding Icefield Trail, so follow signs for North Arm/Thumb Cove.

Wind through dense forests and along a rocky beach, with excellent chances to spot marine and birdlife. The cabin at the end of the trail can be rented for overnight stays.

Lost Lake Trail

While not a "secret" trail, the length and challenge—15 miles one-way—keeps people at bay. The trail starts on the outskirts of Seward and climbs steeply through lush rain forest before emerging above the tree line to give hikers wide purview over the surrounding mountains and Resurrection Bay.

Alpine meadows, the lake itself, and wildlife such as black bears and mountain goats make it well worth the distance.

ZONE OF INTEREST

Touring **Aialik Bay by kayak** gives visitors one of the best and most accessible day kayaking trips in Kenai Fjords National Park. Located near the heart of the park, Aialik Bay is home to a number of tidewater glaciers, including Aialik and Holgate Glaciers, which makes it an ideal destination for a day trip.

Most Aialik Bay kayaking tours start with a boat ride from Seward to Aialik Bay. On this scenic journey you'll have the opportunity to view marine wildlife such as sea otters, seals, puffins, and whales along the way.

Lost Lake Trail is steep, rugged, lonely—and gorgeous.

Once you reach Aialik Bay, launch your kayak into iceberg-dotted waters. You can paddle within a safe distance of the Aialik or Holgate Glaciers, watching and listening to the crackling ice. Being on water level to witness these ancient rivers of ice creaking and calving into the bay creates an eerie, humbling scene.

Typical itineraries include more coastline paddling, exploring the smaller bays and inlets, watching for wildlife, and stopping for a lunch break on a secluded beach.

Keep in mind, conditions in Aialik Bay can change rapidly, with cold temperatures, strong winds, and rough waters. For safety, it's recommended to go with a guide if you're not an experienced sea kayaker. Several outfitters in Seward offer guided day trips to Aialik Bay that include boat transport, equipment, a guide, and sometimes lunch.

HIDDEN GEM

You'll need a water taxi or advanced paddling skills to cross the 12 miles of ocean to get there, but **Bear Glacier Lagoon** lets you see and paddle among building-size icebergs floating in a lagoon pinned between the calving Bear Glacier and a long strip of sandy beach that opens to the Gulf of Alaska. From a landing west of Callisto Head, a 3-mile paddle upstream gains access to the lake and a few rocky islands to camp on. While the deep-blue whorls and arches carved into the bergs can be enticing, keep your distance: They can break, roll, or otherwise swamp you without warning.

Icebergs often calve and float into Aialik Bay.

Kings Canyon's majestic high country is often quieter than its Sierra brethren.

Kings Canyon National Park

California | nps.gov/seki | Visitation: 643,065

Though they are managed together and run together over a single massive 900,000-acre swath of the southern Sierras, Sequoia and Kings Canyon are officially different parks. Kings Canyon sees a little more than half the traffic of Sequoia—so though both offer a brilliant alternative to their more celebrated sibling Yosemite, Kings Canyon remains a bit more secretive, known mostly to wilderness seekers confident enough to wander on the long backcountry trails that lead to its most splendid features.

Even without Half Dome and El Capitan, Kings Canyon offers top-shelf granite mountain grandeur. Volcanic activity birthed its deep gorges and towering cliffs hundreds of millions of years ago, and ancient glaciers cut granite domes and walls reminiscent of Yosemite. The peaks here are higher—especially the toothy Palisades group, which houses no less than four mountains above 14,000 feet. The South and Middle Forks of the Kings River have carved an impressive namesake gorge, with canyon walls reaching heights of up to 8,200 feet. It regularly duels with Idaho's Hell's Canyon for the title of deepest in the United States. (The controversy largely has to do with discrepancies in measurement and the imprecise definition of "canyon." Its steep-sided peaks and mountain valleys don't appear "canyonesque" the way Hell's or the Grand do, and it lacks a discernible rim from which to measure.)

Regardless, the park showcases an astonishing 10,000 feet of vertical relief, harboring a potential year's worth of seasons in one day across these varied elevations. This gives rise to rich biodiversity: Black bears and mule deer roam the valleys while golden eagles and peregrine falcons patrol the skies. High-altitude talus fields and tundra act as a stronghold for the American pika, an adorably teeny relative of the rabbit that is increasingly threatened by climate change.

The lower elevations feature a mix of chaparral and oak woodlands, while higher elevations blend subalpine forests and alpine tundra. And then there are the sequoias: Kings Canyon, along with neighboring Sequoia National Park, protects some of the largest trees on earth. The General Grant Tree, the world's second-largest sequoia, lives here.

Human history in Kings Canyon intertwines with the broader history of the American West. Native Americans, including the Monache and Yokuts, lived in the area for thousands of years before

The General Grant Grove contains the second-largest known sequoia.

In the 1930s, President Franklin D. Roosevelt established Kings Canyon as a national park, in part to protect the giant sequoias from logging. But the park came into its own during World War II. With coastal areas vulnerable to attack, the military encouraged inland travel, and Kings Canyon saw an increase in visitors. After the war, visitation declined, and Kings Canyon receded into relative obscurity compared to its famous neighbors.

The less-crowded trails and campgrounds of Kings Canyon offer a solitude of increasing rarity, especially in California. Park trails range from gentle meanders in the Yosemite Valley–aping Zumwalt Meadow to challenging alpine ascents of peaks like the Palisades or Mount Brewer. The park's remoteness and ruggedness are precisely what make it the least visited of the Sierra parks.

Fame is not a reliable measure of worth. Think of Kings Canyon as the quiet, introverted sibling who becomes far more interesting than their more popular counterpart once you get to know them. For those who visit, it provides a unique Sierra Nevada experience—unspoiled, undisturbed, unforgettable.

ZONE OF INTEREST

Monarch Divide

Within Kings Canyon, Monarch Divide lies farther away from the highest peaks and basins in the park—which means you can get excellent views of those peaks and basins while tooling through exceptional high-country tundra, lakes, and peaks in the 12,000-foot range. There are multiple options in this region, but you'll get the biggest helping on the Monarch Divide Loop, an ambitious, multiday backpacking trip. This monster lollipop route measures around 40 miles in length and includes significant elevation change, making it a strenuous hike best suited for experienced hikers.

The journey starts at the Roads End Permit Station in Cedar Grove. From there, head east on the Bubbs Creek Trail. The first day is a steady climb through mixed conifer forest, with the South Fork Kings River churning below. Plan to camp the first night

the arrival of European settlers. Spanish explorers gave the river its original name, Rio de los Santos Reyes (River of the Holy Kings). Both Ansel Adams and John Muir spent time here as well, with Muir occasionally proclaiming Kings Canyon superior to Yosemite, depending on the day. Logging and grazing operations came later, and one can see remnants of these activities in some areas as ruins or rusting artifacts.

The High Sierra at dawn

around Sphinx Creek (approximately 5 miles from the start), where you'll find good campsites and water.

The second day, continue on the Bubbs Creek Trail 6 miles to Junction Meadow, where the trail forks. Take the East Lake Trail heading north. You'll cross Bubbs Creek, which can be challenging early in the season. The trail continues to climb steadily to reach East Lake after 5 miles, where you can camp for the night.

From East Lake, the trail continues to Lake Reflection. These 4 miles end at a serene alpine lake surrounded by towering peaks. From Lake Reflection, the trail becomes faint, and you'll need to use your navigation skills to continue up to Harrison Pass.

Harrison Pass (12,640 feet) offers sweeping views of the Great Western Divide. This challenging section is steep and rocky, so take your time. It's 2 miles, but the elevation and difficult terrain can make it feel much longer. From here, descend over 6 miles to find good camping at Vidette Meadow.

From Vidette Meadow, rejoin the Bubbs Creek Trail and follow it back down to the trailhead at Roads End. Your final stretch is 12 miles, but the majority is downhill or flat.

Along this route, you'll see a variety of Sierra Nevada ecosystems, from mixed conifer forest to alpine tundra. You may spot wildlife like mule deer, black bears, and a variety of bird species. In the high country, look for marmots and pikas among the rocks.

This is a strenuous hike with significant elevation gain and loss, and it includes sections of off-trail navigation. Be sure to check with park rangers for current trail conditions, obtain a wilderness permit for overnight stays, and practice Leave No Trace principles.

HIKES

Granite Basin

In exchange for a brutal 5,000-foot climb, hiking Granite Basin offers solitude, stunning alpine vistas, and a taste of the Sierra's wild backcountry. The round-trip journey covers around 9 miles, requiring solid endurance to reach the basin itself.

You'll start at the Copper Creek trailhead, at "Road's End," 5 miles beyond Cedar Grove. There's a parking area and restrooms here at an elevation of 5,000 feet.

The first section of the trail is well defined and ascends steadily through mixed conifer forest. You'll have occasional glimpses of the canyon's deep gorge as you steadily climb, with an overlook 1 mile in looking down the length of the canyon. After 3 miles, the Granite Basin turnoff is not clearly marked, and you'll need to rely on your navigation skills. At 4 miles in, you can find Tent Meadow, which is the best and maybe only place to camp on the way to the basin.

At this point, the journey becomes more challenging as you climb northwest through patches of thick alpine forest and occasional meadows. Rocks and boulders begin encroaching on your forested hike until you reach the lip at 10,360 feet, which rewards your perseverance with an overview of Granite Basin itself, a world of towering granite peaks, bubbling streams, and wildflower-dotted meadows. You can descend here into the basin and spend days exploring high-altitude lakes and bagging cross-country peaks. You might spot wildlife like mule deer, pikas, and marmots. There are no official campsites in the basin, so if you choose to stay overnight, ensure you follow Leave No Trace principles.

Mist Falls is one of the largest in Kings Canyon.

Retrace your steps to the trail and then to the Copper Creek trailhead. The descent can be as rough as the climb, especially on knees after a long day, so be careful.

This hike is best suited to experienced, fit hikers comfortable with cross-country navigation if you plan to descend and explore the basin.

Mist Falls

Clamber over an easy 8-mile round-trip hike to see a 100-foot cascade pouring over slabs of granite. Start at the Roads End Permit Station, where you'll find the trailhead. The first part of the hike is relatively easy, following the course of the South Fork of the Kings River through a canyon. It's 4 miles to Mist Falls with a moderate 600 feet of elevation gain.

The trail takes you through a forest of incense cedar and ponderosa pine, and you'll see a variety of plants along the river, like willows and wildflowers in the spring. Historically, the area was used by Native American tribes like the Monache and the Yokuts and later by settlers during the California Gold Rush.

The trail steepens as you get closer to the falls. Mist Falls is one of the largest waterfalls in the park, and its flow is especially impressive in the spring and early summer when the river is at its fullest.

After enjoying the falls, retrace your steps to the trailhead.

HIDDEN GEM

The **Brewer Loop,** sometimes referred to as the Brewer Traverse, is an exceptional backcountry route in Kings Canyon National Park not for the faint of heart. It takes you deep into the park's wilderness to experience some of the most beautiful and least-visited areas. Depending on the precise route taken and how many peaks you bag and secret basins you explore, this trip can grow up to 52 miles long and post elevation gains of 12,000 feet, so prepare for a Big-Gulp-size adventure.

The best method is to break out a map and plot a precise itinerary with a backcountry ranger, who can guide you to some of the best camping and side trips. But below is a rough itinerary to get you started.

Begin at Roads End Permit Station to start a big first day of 9 miles with a 3,000-foot elevation gain on the Bubbs Creek Trail. Hike along Bubbs Creek Trail for another 8 miles until you reach Junction Meadow. From there, take East Creek Trail, a faint and sometimes difficult-to-follow path that will lead you toward East Lake. Continue your hike up to Lake Reflection for 6 miles, reaching a beautiful alpine lake with smashing views of the Great Western Divide. The next section is off-trail, so good navigation skills are crucial. From Lake Reflection, you'll hike over Longley Pass to South Guard Lake, a distance of 5 miles with 2,200 feet of elevation gain. From South Guard Lake, you'll continue your off-trail journey, crossing over Thunder Ridge to reach Sphinx Creek, about 7 miles with 1,200 feet of elevation gain.

The final stretch will take you back to Roads End. This section is 15 miles with 1,000 feet of elevation loss.

The Brewer Loop climbs high into the stellar backcountry of Kings Canyon.

There are no designated campsites along this route but plenty of options for dispersed camping. Always remember to follow Leave No Trace principles when selecting a campsite.

The Brewer Loop offers breathtaking views of the Great Western Divide and the Kings-Kern Divide, as well as numerous alpine lakes and meadows. The off-trail sections provide a sense of solitude and wilderness that's hard to match.

Kobuk Valley's taiga forest is located high above the Arctic Circle.

Kobuk Valley National Park

Alaska | nps.gov/kova | Visitation: 17,616

Second farthest north and second least visited, Kobuk Valley exists on the fringes of the known world in an era when we think we've discovered everything. It doesn't show up on even experienced adventurers' itineraries: It's a place of desolate beauty, unreachable and untamed.

Kobuk Valley is located entirely above the Arctic Circle, 35 miles north of the Inupiaq village of Noatak and 200 miles north of the nearest road, Alaska's infamous Dalton Highway. To get there, you must embark on a pilgrimage by bush plane from frontier outposts Kotzebue or Bettles. Calling it "off the beaten path" is an understatement.

Great swaths of the park's territory contain a myriad of ecosystems that define the Arctic. Most famous is the Great Kobuk Sand Dunes—a 30-square-mile region of sand dunes, some reaching as high as 100 feet. During the summer, the dunes can heat up to 100 degrees Fahrenheit, a stark contrast to the extremely cold winters. This sandy Arctic desert seems airlifted from the Sahara and plopped in the tundra.

The Kobuk River is the park's lifeblood, meandering through 2 million acres of sedge lowlands, spruce forests, and the sand dunes. Its waters teem with sheefish and salmon, and adjoining tributaries and wetlands serve as nesting sites for ducks, geese, swans, and loons for the short summer. The river valley attracts large mammals including moose and brown bears, which come to feast on the salmon making their way upstream to spawn. Each year, half a million caribou from the Western Arctic Herd ford the river, their millions of hooves drumming.

Beyond the river and the dunes, the boreal forest's (or taiga) world of white spruce and paper birch trees gradually thins out into a tundra of dwarf shrubs, lichens, mosses, and sedges. In the high alpine, a world of lichen-covered rocks and permanent snowfields hides elusive musk oxen, a living relic of the last ice age.

People have been here since before the thaw. Archaeological sites scattered throughout the park date back 12,500 years. Inupiaq people continue to live on the park's borders, their lives entwined with the land. Fishing, hunting, berry picking, and other subsistence activities still play a big part in many people's lives.

With no facilities in the park itself, visiting Kobuk Valley is a lesson in patience and careful planning. Summer is the most popular time to visit, when July and August bring the great caribou migration and midnight sun. The winter brings 24-hour darkness but also the aurora borealis painting the sky in shimmering greens, purples, and reds.

ZONES OF INTEREST

In Kobuk Valley, you become keenly aware that you are a visitor not only in space but in time. It requires meticulous planning and prep, so building a visit around the days you can spare is the most practical way to plan a visit.

One Day

If you have only one day to spend in Kobuk Valley National Park, charter a flightseeing tour from one of the local air taxi operators based in Kotzebue or Bettles. You'll gain an overview of the park's landscape—flying over the Kobuk River, the striking Great Kobuk Sand Dunes, and the vast boreal forests and tundra. Keep your eyes peeled for caribou herds and other wildlife. The short timeframe makes landing to explore unlikely, but the aerial perspective is unforgettable.

One Weekend

In a couple of days, you can plan a brief overnight trip in the park. This typically involves a chartered flight into the park, with a landing near the Kobuk River or the Great Kobuk Sand Dunes. Once on the ground, you can spend a day hiking in the vicinity of the sand dunes or take a quick dip in the Kobuk River, which warms a little in the summer months from the constant daylight. Camp overnight (there are no designated campgrounds, so you can set up camp anywhere following Leave No Trace principles), and then catch a pickup flight the following day.

Braided rivers dominate Kobuk's interior.

One Week or More

With a week or more, you can disappear into abject wilderness. Again, you'll charter a flight in, but with more time, you can arrange for the plane to drop you off in one area and pick you up in another, enabling a backcountry hiking or river trip.

Consider a float trip down the Kobuk River, where you can fish for sheefish and Arctic grayling. You could also plan a long-distance hiking route, but with no trails crisscrossing the extremely rugged terrain, you'll need to have extensive experience in off-trail hiking and navigation. Movement here is exceptionally slow, except in the drier, rocky, high-altitude tundra.

Lake Clark National Park and Preserve

Alaska | nps.gov/lacl | Visitation: 16,728

On Alaska's coast 120 or so miles southwest of Anchorage lies wild, remote Lake Clark National Park. Established in 1980 and stretching over 4 million acres, it contains everything we think of as a natural hallmark of the state: giant glaciers, icy mountains, steaming volcanoes, vast tundra plains, big rivers choked with salmon runs, a profusion of wildlife, and of course, Lake Clark itself—the largest lake in the state.

Despite all this, Lake Clark National Park remains one of the least-visited national parks. The scenery would seduce any wilderness lover, but with no roads leading into the park, access is limited to small aircraft or boat only (usually pricey). But those who manage to brave the journey and land on a remote beach or lake often have a bucket-list adventure entirely to themselves.

In this tallest section of the Aleutian Range, the Chigmits punch the sky to elevations above 10,000 feet. They also represent the northeasternmost spur of the Pacific Ring of Fire: Twin volcanoes Iliamna and Redoubt lord over the landscape and burp smoke, ash, and lava every few decades (Redoubt, the park's tallest peak, last erupted in 2009), grounding planes and reminding us of the turmoil in the earth's belly.

Lake Clark boasts loads of wildlife: Moose meander through the forest, while Dall sheep daintily traverse the precarious rocky heights. Brown bears amble along the shores of the lake, fishing for sockeye salmon. In the skies, you'll spot majestic bald eagles, and if you're silent, patient, and unobtrusive, you could catch a glimpse of rare wolves or lynx.

Lake Clark has long been home to the Dena'ina people, the only Athabascan group to live on the coast year-round. They have fished, hunted, and gathered in this lush environment for millennia. European contact came relatively late, so the area remains a stronghold of Dena'ina culture. The watershed draining from Lake Clark supports one-third of the famous Bristol Bay sockeye salmon fishery.

Except for a few unmaintained trails leading out of teeny gateway town Port Alsworth, hiking Lake Clark requires expedition-grade skills and self-sufficiency, plus the resilience to handle Alaska's most chaotic maritime weather. With no designated trails, Lake Clark is a place for the confident and the compass-equipped. If that's you, then this untamed landscape presents boundless

Glaciers, volcanoes, epic salmon runs, and abundant wildlife cast Lake Clark as the essence of wild Alaska.

opportunities for exploration: Wander through vibrant wildflower meadows in the lowlands, scale a challenging mountainside, or stroll along a scenic coastline. This paddler's paradise features countless lakes, rivers, and miles of coastline for kayakers and rafters. Choose your own adventure, with both high stakes and rewards.

The height of summer—June, July, and August—is an ideal time to enjoy long days of constant daylight, milder temperatures, and less rain. Those who don't mind a little chill might prefer the shoulder seasons of May or September, which bring fewer visitors and the chance to see northern lights. Winter visits are only for the extremely adventurous and/or foolhardy. Be prepared to face sub-zero temperatures and limited daylight hours.

HIKES

Tanalian Peak

Set in the heart of Lake Clark National Park, the Tanalian Trail is an exceptional way to experience this raw Alaskan wilderness.

The trailhead to Tanalian Peak is located at the end of the Port Alsworth runway, making it one of the more accessible hikes within the park—though "accessible" remains a deeply relative term in such a remote locale.

The full round-trip to Tanalian Peak and back covers 8 miles and sees an elevation gain of around 3,400 feet. Expect this hike to take around 6 to 8 hours depending on your pace and how long you spend enjoying the unreal views.

From the trailhead, the trail starts out relatively flat, meandering through dense forests of spruce and birch. After a mile, the path starts to ascend more steeply. The canopy begins to thin, replaced by brush and alpine flora.

At 2.5 miles in, you'll reach the Lower Tanalian Falls, a stunning cascade that makes for an excellent resting point and photo opportunity. Beyond the falls, the trail gets steeper and the terrain rockier. You'll traverse a series of heart-pounding switchbacks and a final push to the peak over a steep grade and loose rocks. Take it

A grizzly sow stands up in Lake Clark's wild backcountry.

slow, tread carefully, and keep an eye on the trail—help and emergency services are far away. At the top, a 360-degree panorama greets you with views of vast Lake Clark, the rugged Alaska Range, and the countless rivers, lakes, and ponds dotting the landscape.

The return journey follows the same trail back down. Be careful as you descend: The loose rocks can be slippery, and the weather in Lake Clark can change rapidly, making the trail difficult to follow in poor visibility.

Telaquana Route

The Telaquana Route in Lake Clark National Park is an incredibly remote and rugged wilderness journey usually undertaken as an

Look for Dall sheep on the slopes of Tanalian Peak.

8- to 10-day backpacking trip, covering roughly 50 miles. The route is a trailless cross-country trek that requires experienced backcountry skills, navigation, fitness, and deep self-sufficiency. In the event of an emergency, help could be days away.

Beginning at Telaquana Lake and ending at Twin Lakes, this route passes through a varied landscape of tundra, spruce forests, and high-alpine passes with no sign of civilization in sight—save for Richard Proenneke's cabin at the end of the journey. Proenneke was a homesteader from Iowa who lived alone in the park for over thirty years in a hand-built cabin, which still stands.

Day 1–3: After being dropped off by floatplane at the southern end of Telaquana Lake, the first few days involve hiking northeast along the lake's edge and then turning northwest to ascend into the hills. The going is challenging, with no trails, numerous creek crossings, and tussocky tundra underfoot.

Day 4–5: The terrain steepens as you make your way toward Turquoise Lake. You'll reach a high pass with expansive views of the surrounding wilderness before descending toward the lake itself. Keep an eye out for caribou and bears, which are common in the area.

Day 6–7: From Turquoise Lake, the route continues westward, climbing over another pass before descending into the Twin Lakes basin. The terrain is a mix of tundra and spruce forest, and navigation can be tricky—keep your map and compass close at hand.

Day 8–10: Once in the Twin Lakes basin, the route passes between the two bodies of water before concluding at the northern end of Lower Twin Lake. Don't miss a visit to the historic Richard Proenneke's cabin, a hand-built log cabin that stands as a testament to human self-sufficiency in the wilderness.

Lassen Volcanic National Park

California | nps.gov/lavo | Visitation: 418,978

Lassen Volcanic National Park combines attributes found in bigger parks flung across the West and tucks them into a quiet corner of northeastern California. Yellowstone's geothermal spectacle, the Sierra's pine-scented woods, Crater Lake's blue alpine water, and a Rainier-style volcano—it's all here in miniature, packed into 100,000 acres connected by 150 miles of trail.

Lassen Peak, the park's titular feature and the southernmost volcano in the Cascade Range, last erupted in 1917. But evidence of its fiery innards breaks ground in many places today. The park is threaded with geothermal features: steaming fumaroles, boiling springs, hissing steam vents known as "solfataras," and mud pots gurgling with gases from deep within the earth. Lassen is the rare volcanic area to feature all four classes of volcano: cinder cone, shield, stratovolcano, and lava dome (at 10,457 feet, Lassen is the biggest lava dome on earth).

This geothermal activity creates a surreal lunar landscape that interrupts and blisters sections of mountain forest, meadow, and rock. In the shadow of the peak, red foxes weave their way through dense manzanita undergrowth, their flaming coats a splash of color against the earthy browns and greens. At higher elevations, hardy pikas eke out an existence in the rocks and snow, whistling loud in the thin mountain air.

Since the last major eruption happened in modern history, we have eyewitness accounts: People in towns 40 miles away saw clouds of ash and gas soar 30,000 feet into the sky, and daredevil observers close by saw flows of lava 20 feet tall pouring out of Lassen. Lahars and subsequent floods destroyed at least six houses, though residents escaped with minor injuries. Today, Lassen is classified as a high-threat volcano, though scientists are quick to point out that's more a factor of proximity to populated areas than a worry that it will erupt. Hundreds or thousands of years often pass between eruptions in active volcanoes like this one. But a future eruption is a matter of when, not if.

Indigenous tribes such as the Atsugewi, Yana, Yahi, and Maidu have lived on the flanks of Lassen for thousands of years, making pilgrimages to gather, hunt, and use areas near the peak as a summer meeting and trading spot. The promise of gold, timber, and open land drew settlers in recent centuries.

Lassen's last eruption occurred in 1917.

Despite its stark beauty and unique features, Lassen often plays second fiddle to other California parks. Yosemite, with its monumental granite cliffs and sequoia groves, draws millions each year, while Death Valley, in all its desolate, sun-scorched splendor, lures those with a taste for extremes. Lassen offers its own form of quiet allure. The crowds here are smaller, the sense of solitude and communion with nature stronger.

The key to visiting Lassen lies in understanding its moods. The park is often snowbound until mid-June. Come summer, the meadows explode with a colorful display of wildflowers, and trails invite you to wind through forests and around the many mirror-still lakes. Autumn brings a cool hush and aspens turning gold and chattery.

HIKES

Juniper Lake Loop

In the southeastern corner of Lassen Volcanic National Park, Juniper Lake's shimmering waters, bordered by dense forests and rocky outcrops, are enough of a destination. But many trails radiate from here, offering options to extend your hike by bagging peaks, visiting smaller lakes, or combining a few into an overnight or multiday backpack.

To access Juniper Lake, take CA 36 to the town of Chester. Follow Feather River Drive to Juniper Lake Road. It's a 13-mile journey from the park entrance to Juniper Lake, the last stretch being gravel. While the road is usually passable for regular vehicles, high-clearance models fare better.

The 6.8-mile trail encircling Juniper Lake is fairly flat, making it perfect for families or those looking for an introductory backpacking experience. It's mostly forested but offers occasional views of the lake and nearby peaks.

Starting from the Juniper Lake Campground, proceed clockwise around the lake. The western side provides dense woodlands and occasional meadows with wildflowers. On the northern edge, you'll pass Juniper Lake's inlet stream. On the eastern and southern edges, the trail offers the best lakeside views with opportunities for picnics and swimming.

A 3.8-mile one-way spur from the Juniper Lake Loop lets you climb 1,200 feet to the historic Mount Harkness Fire Lookout, where you can enjoy panoramic views of the park and beyond from a little over 8,000 feet. From the southeastern portion of Juniper Lake Loop, there's a junction to the Mount Harkness Trail. The trail ascends steadily through forests, meadows, and over volcanic rocks. Once you reach the top, on a clear day you can spot Mount Shasta to the north and Lassen Peak to the west.

For those desiring a longer journey, extend your hike by combining the Juniper Lake Loop with nearby trails. You can hop on the Pacific Crest Trail (PCT) for a few days, or link up with Snag, Butte, Jakey, or Feather Lakes. Most require detours of 5 miles or less, with minimal (under 1,000 feet) elevation gain.

Cinder Cone Trail

You can reenact Frodo and Samwise's trip up and into Mount Doom on this marvelous 4-mile hike up to and into a volcano. Luckily, the last eruption was in 1666, so there's no need to worry about wrestling with Gollum over a moat of lava. Cinder Cone is one of the youngest volcanoes in the park, and it gives hikers the chance to gawk at a variety of bizarre volcanic features. The Painted Dunes, seen from the top, are a surreal and beautiful product of hot volcanic ash falling onto the still-cooling Fantastic Lava Beds, where they oxidized into bright colors. The frozen lava flows known as Fantastic Lava Beds themselves altered the course of local creeks to create both Butte Lake and Snag Lake.

The trail begins at the Butte Lake parking area. Access to this area is from the northeastern park entrance via a rough, unpaved road.

As you set off, you'll skirt the southern edge of Butte Lake, with striking views of the Fantastic Lava Beds, which border the lake to the south. You'll begin to notice cinders from the Cinder Cone beneath your feet as the trail starts its gentle ascent.

Cinder Cone's moon-like landscape makes for an otherworldly hike.

After 1.5 miles, you will reach the base of the Cinder Cone itself. The trail up the cone is steep, gaining 846 feet in a little under a mile, and the loose, shifting cinder underfoot makes the climb at altitude a bit of a huff-and-puffer.

Once you reach the summit of Cinder Cone, you can look down into the crater of the volcano and marvel at this natural wonder. You can also descend 100 feet into the summit crater. If you choose to take the additional loop around the rim, you'll be rewarded with panoramic views of Lassen Peak, Snag Lake, the Fantastic Lava Beds, and the Painted Dunes. After enjoying the views, carefully make your way back down the Cinder Cone and follow the trail as it returns to the Butte Lake parking area. The descent is often easier and quicker, but the loose cinder still requires caution.

Boiling Springs Lake
With waters colored with brilliant hues and steaming from the earth's heated depths, Boiling Springs Lake offers a fascinating hydrothermal alternative to Bumpass Hell and Devil's Kitchen on an easy 3-mile round-trip path with minimal elevation gain.

Starting at the Warner Valley trailhead, the path gently descends into a bird-filled forest. As you progress, you'll notice smaller fumaroles—steam vents—hissing softly. Soon pockets of steaming ground and bubbling mud pots appear, and the smell of sulfur fills the air. As you approach the lake, you're greeted with its steaming teal waters, stained by an array of colorful mud and soil caused by commingling minerals and extremophile algae and bacteria colonies in shades of green, yellow, and brown. The center of the lake often roils and bubbles from geothermal emissions.

Terminal Geyser lies 0.6 mile farther from Boiling Springs Lake. It's not a true geyser; instead, it's a steam vent that has found its way up through a creek bed, making it appear as a geyser when steam forcefully erupts out of the creek.

Straying from the path can be dangerous—the ground near the lake and fumaroles can be scalding and unstable. Some might find the constant strong sulfur odor unpleasant, but it's harmless.

HIDDEN GEM

The area around Lassen is the homeland of a **man known as "Ishi"**—at one time perhaps the most famous Indigenous person on earth. Born in 1860 into a Yahi family, as a child he witnessed the massacre of most of his 400-strong tribe sometime between 1865 and 1871. He hid in the forest for the next forty-one years, likely with remnants of his tribe. Rumors of his presence persisted, but he escaped capture until he wandered alone and starving into Oroville, California, in 1911.

After being studied, poked, and prodded, he spent the years after employed by the Hearst Museum, essentially put on display and billed as "the Last Wild Indian" to demonstrate Yahi crafts and share traditional songs and stories for white audiences (as many as 24,000 visited him in his first six months). He gained considerable

Boiling Springs Lake is reminiscent of Yellowstone's geothermal features.

fame and renown but fought off illness after illness before succumbing to tuberculosis in 1916.

After his death, scientists extensively studied him before cremating all of Ishi except his brain, which was sent to the Smithsonian, where it remained for seventy-five years. But in 1997, the four federally recognized Maidu tribes formed a council to find and repatriate his remains. After three years of navigating a stonewalling bureaucracy, the tribes succeeded. He is now buried in a secret location near Deer Creek in Lassen National Forest, where his family resided.

Mammoth Cave is the largest cave system in the world—and much of it remains to be mapped.

Mammoth Cave National Park

Kentucky | nps.gov/maca | Visitation: 654,450

Mammoth Cave National Park stands divided between two worlds. With the world's longest known cave system beneath its grounds and a vibrant forested ecosystem above, the park's location in the Green River Valley offers a study in contrasts. Delving deep into its geology and ecology reveals a narrative that spans millions of years, chronicling the earth's transformative processes.

The heart of Mammoth Cave National Park is undoubtedly its sprawling underground network—a 400-mile maze of caverns, passages, and tunnels that speleologists haven't finished mapping. It's bigger than the second- and third-biggest cave systems on earth combined, and some scientists think there could be as much as 600 more miles of caverns.

Mammoth Cave began roughly 350 million years ago. As seas covered the region, sediments composed largely of shells and marine organisms accumulated, creating layers of limestone interspersed with layers of caprock. Subsequent uplifts and erosional processes exposed the limestone, and cave formation began. Rainwater absorbs carbon dioxide from the atmosphere and soil, becoming a weak carbonic acid solution. This acidic water seeped into the ground and began to dissolve the limestone along fractures and bedding planes, carving out vast underground chambers and passageways. Over time, these passages expanded and interconnected, resulting in the expansive labyrinth we see today.

These processes gradually sculpted awe-inspiring formations, including stalactites hanging from cave ceilings, stalagmites rising from the ground, flowstones resembling frozen cascades, and draperies—elegant, wavy sheets of mineral deposits that resemble folded fabric hanging from above.

Adaptation runs wild in the black of Mammoth Cave. The perpetual darkness birthed creatures like the eyeless cave fish and the translucent Kentucky cave shrimp. These troglobites (animals adapted to cave life) evolved over eons, forgoing sight and pigmentation to develop other heightened senses that make the most of their challenging environment.

Outside of the cave's cool confines, mesophytic (moisture-loving) forests cover Mammoth Cave topside. This ancient forest type has persisted since before the last ice age and includes a rich mix of oaks, hickories, tulip trees, and maples. Beneath the high canopy, the park's understory pops with seasonal wildflowers like trillium and lady's slipper orchids. Ferns, mosses, and fungi capitalize on

Hikers can spot wild turkeys on the Buffalo Creek Trail.

Aboveground, Mammoth is covered in hardwood forest.

the shade and humidity, forming a complex, multi-layered carpet. The canopies provide shade and house herbivores like white-tailed deer, while bobcats sneak through the underbrush. Above, warblers warble and woodpeckers drum on rotting tree trunks.

The calm waters of the Green and Nolin Rivers also meander through the park, supporting freshwater fish, amphibians, and the occasional otter. The rivers also play a crucial role in shaping the land today, eroding banks and depositing sediments that will become stone over millennia.

For over four millennia, Native Americans utilized the cave for rituals, mining gypsum and other materials, and burial. In the nineteenth century, the cave was mined for saltpeter, a crucial ingredient in gunpowder. Later, it became a tourist attraction with guides leading tours by candlelight. Until recently, no one understood how far these caves went.

An enslaved person named Stephen Bishop went farther than most. Beginning in 1838, he explored and mapped many of its passages. The movement to protect Mammoth didn't begin until the early twentieth century and experienced serious resistance—especially since the government used eminent domain to confiscate the 50,000 acres that would become a national park in 1941.

Today, the park provides a range of facilities, including the Mammoth Cave Campground, Mammoth Cave Hotel, a visitor center, and several picnic areas. Beyond the cave, the park boasts more than 70 miles of backcountry trails suitable for hiking, horseback riding, and biking, plus miles of navigable river for boating and fishing. The park provides a range of tours designed to cater to different physical abilities, ensuring everyone can experience the wonder of the caves.

You can visit Mammoth in any season, but spring brings wildflower colors and autumn sets the trees afire. The climate outside is most comfortable in the transitional seasons, but the cave always hovers near 54 degrees year-round.

ZONES OF INTEREST

Mammoth Cave
The centerpiece of Mammoth is its extraordinary cave system, and the best way to explore is by joining a ranger-led tour. These tours provide expert guidance and interpretation, and they ensure safety while navigating the complex cave system. Tours exist for a wide range of abilities—here are some of the best.

Historic Tour
This is perhaps the most popular tour, taking visitors through some of the most iconic parts of the cave. You'll see places like the Rotunda, one of the largest rooms in the cave, and the Ruins of Karnak, an array of enormous columns. This tour is moderately strenuous and covers 2 miles in 2 hours.

Domes and Dripstones Tour
This tour showcases both the massive, high-domed chambers of the cave and delicate dripstone formations, including the Frozen Niagara, one of the most photographed features of the cave that looks like a waterfall turned to stone. This tour is considered moderate, covering 0.75 mile in 2 hours, including several flights of stairs.

Grand Avenue Tour

This longer, more strenuous tour allows visitors to experience a variety of cave landscapes, from vast passages to intricate formations. Covering 4 miles in 4 hours, this tour is recommended for individuals in good physical condition.

HIKES

First Creek Lake Trail

The First Creek Lake Trail is a lovely 4.8-mile round-trip trail that meanders through the serene Kentucky woods, away from the bustling crowds visiting the cave.

Starting from the Brownsville entrance on the west side of the park, you'll follow the Nolin Lake shoreline. Begin by heading south along the tranquil lakeside shaded by large sycamore and cottonwood trees.

Continue along a gently undulating trail, catching occasional glimpses of the lake and birds and squirrels. After 2.4 miles, you will reach a secluded peninsula extending into the lake, perfect for a picnic or a quiet moment.

The flat trail gains little more than 200 feet, though some short, steep sections may challenge novice hikers. Return along the same path.

Buffalo Creek Trail

The Buffalo Creek Trail's 8-mile round-trip journey offers a more challenging and secluded hike through the heart of the park.

Begin at the trailhead near the Maple Springs Group Campground. The trail, marked by orange blazes, starts with a gradual ascent into a hardwood forest populated with oak, hickory, and tulip poplar. In 1.5 miles, you'll cross a wooden footbridge over gurgling Buffalo Creek.

Continuing onward, you will climb to an elevation of 900 feet 2.5 miles in. You'll be able to see the rolling hills of the Green River Valley unfolding before you. After another mile, you'll reach a ridge

Ranger-led tours of varying difficulty explore Mammoth's vast depths.

with panoramic views. In the distance, the Green River glints in the sunlight. Rest, hydrate, and enjoy the view.

Following the ridge, the trail winds down through mixed forest before reaching the turnaround point at the intersection with the Collie Ridge Trail. Take a breather, enjoy a snack, and return along the same path.

HIDDEN GEM

The **Wild Cave Tour** at Mammoth Cave National Park is an intense, physically demanding expedition designed for seasoned explorers and adventurous novices. Over 5 miles that might feel much longer because of the technical nature and roller-coaster elevation gain and loss, the tour lasts 6 hours and takes visitors off the beaten path into the less-explored sections of the cave. Participants on this challenging tour typically must be at least 16 years old and meet certain physical requirements.

The Wild Cave Tour is known for its challenging maneuvers. You will be climbing up and down steep, slippery surfaces, often using only cables or ropes for support. Crawling will also be a significant part of your experience, through passages like Bare Hole, and

Over centuries, water transforms limestone into curtain-like shapes.

you'll need to squeeze through tight areas like the claustrophobic "Backscratcher."

Throughout the tour, you'll be led through spectacular caverns, passageways, and pits that most visitors never get to see. You'll witness geological formations like flowstones, stalactites, and stalagmites, and you might also traverse sections like Bottomless Pit, Cleaveland Avenue, and the scary-sounding "Rumble Room." Each brings a unique set of challenges and wonders, though there's no guarantee you'll see them all, depending on conditions.

Given the physical demands of this tour, you'll want to wear durable, protective clothing that can get dirty, as well as sturdy, closed-toe shoes with good grip. The park service will provide helmets, headlamps, and kneepads. Gloves are also recommended.

These exhilarating, adventurous explorations of Mammoth Cave require physical stamina, agility, and comfort with tight spaces and dizzying heights that disappear into the black. If you're up for the challenge, the Wild Cave Tour offers a caving experience like no other.

(For an extra thrill, the **Violet City Tour** takes you through some of these passageways as original explorers did: by lantern light alone.)

Mesa Verde National Park

Colorado | nps.gov/meve | Visitation: 505,194

Near the Four Corners area of the Southwest where Colorado, New Mexico, Arizona, and Utah meet you'll find Mesa Verde—the rare park established primarily to protect urban civilization. The catch: This urban civilization started 800 years ago. But they lasted in this arid place much longer than American society has so far, thriving atop the mesas and in over 600 spectacular, miraculously preserved cliff dwellings for more than 700 years, from AD 600 to 1300. Yet so much about them remains shrouded in mystery.

The cliff dwellings of Mesa Verde National Park are a testament to the architectural genius of the Ancestral Puebloan people. Known for their impressive stonework and farming skills, they crafted each structure from sandstone blocks, which were shaped using harder stones. They set the stones in place with a mortar made from soil, water, and ash. They then placed small stones, or "chinking," within the mortar to add stability to the walls.

The plastered walls mean the interiors might've been covered in colorful murals long faded and lost to time. Each room or plaza possesses symmetry and purpose, and their strategic positioning within the alcoves in often hard-to-access locations seems to indicate the Ancestral Puebloans prized protection from elements and potential adversaries. Most rooms feature circular pits dug into the ground called kivas, which served as social gathering spaces and centers for ritual activities.

As skilled farmers, Ancestral Puebloans grew maize, beans, and squash on the mesa tops where they lived before migrating to the cliff dwellings. Scientists now believe they used them during the winter months, while the rest of the year was likely spent in farming communities on the mesas.

Remnants of petroglyphs are scratched into many walls in Mesa Verde. These carvings, created by removing the desert varnish to reveal the lighter sandstone beneath, often depict anthropomorphic figures, animals, and geometric designs. The exact meanings of these petroglyphs remain a mystery; beyond spiritual significance, they might have been used to record events, convey complex narratives, or mark territory.

Over time, the Ancestral Puebloans migrated from the area for reasons that remain the subject of ongoing study. Factors such as climate change, soil degradation, and social upheaval are often considered. Regardless of their departure, they left behind an enduring legacy in the form of Mesa Verde's cliff dwellings.

Mesa Verde's 800-year-old cliff dwellings preserve a little-understood culture.

Today, their descendants continue to thrive in the Hopi, Zuni, and Rio Grande Pueblo communities, who all preserve and pass down some rituals from their Ancestral Puebloan roots. Despite its age, this is a place of living history still represented in today's Indigenous societies. This astounding cultural resource became the first UNESCO World Heritage Site within the United States, and over 5,000 archaeological sites here continue to yield discoveries and important insights.

While the cliff dwellings draw the most attention, the park sprawls over 52,485 acres of high desert and montane ecosystems, characterized by a mosaic of pinyon-juniper woodlands, mixed conifer forests, and vast stretches of sagebrush scrubland. A visit in late spring reveals a landscape ignited with the hues of Indian paintbrush, evening primrose, and claret cup cactus. Pinyon jays' squealing echoes through the canyons, while rock squirrels scamper throughout long-abandoned residences. Bighorn sheep balance on precipitous cliffs with grace, and in the quiet corners of the park, you might catch a glimpse of more elusive creatures: bobcats, coyotes, or (rarest of all) a mountain lion.

Visiting Mesa Verde requires a delicate balance of timing and patience. The park is open year-round, but the best time to visit is in the late spring or early fall when temperatures are moderate and the summer crowds have thinned. Many of the premier sites require tickets for ranger-led hikes, though there are a few hidden gems for enterprising visitors.

HIKES

Petroglyph Point Trail

The Petroglyph Point Trail carves a path into the echoes of time. A 2.4-mile loop of mild to moderate difficulty, this trail offers more than a walk; it's a journey into the heartbeat of the park's ancient history.

The trailhead begins at the Chapin Mesa Archaeological Museum. From there, the path veers right at the fork, pointing toward Spruce Tree House, the third-largest cliff dwelling in the park. Although currently closed for preservation efforts, one can still appreciate the structure's astonishing complexity from a distance.

After your initial climb, you descend into the Spruce Tree Canyon on a trail originally worn in by the feet of Ancestral Puebloans themselves. As the quietude of the canyon wraps around you like an old blanket, the canyon's sandstone walls stand tall on either side, streaked with dark desert varnish across the red and beige layers of sandstone.

The ascent out of the canyon might leave you breathless, both from the effort and the sight that greets you. At the halfway mark, a

The Petroglyph Point Trail culminates in a 35-foot-wide panel of symbols carved into the desert varnish.

spectacle of ancient history presents itself in the form of the Petroglyph Panel. A dense collection of carved symbols, human and animal figures, the panel is a fascinating if indecipherable message of creativity and storytelling beamed in from the past. Handprints, lizards, mountain goats, whorls and spirals, and unidentifiable fantastical creatures crowd a 35-foot-wide panel.

Each carving is a voice from the past, a whisper from an era that has long faded into time. One can't help but wonder about the people who etched these symbols, the stories they hoped to tell, the legacy they yearned to leave.

After the petroglyphs, the trail ambles along the rim of the canyon. The landscape morphs around you, turning from dense woodland to a semiarid tableland studded with sagebrush and scrub oak. On a clear day, you might spot the distant peaks of the La Plata Mountains plastered against the sky.

The trail loops back to the Chapin Mesa Museum, but each step on the Petroglyph Point Trail brings you closer to an understanding, a shared moment with the Ancestral Puebloan people that transcends time.

Point Lookout Trail

The Point Lookout Trail travels a 2.2-mile round-trip path with an elevation gain of around 400 feet up a moderate but rewarding climb to one of the best views in the park.

Your journey begins near the Morefield Campground, at the trailhead marked Point Lookout. Follow the path as it curls southward and begins a steady ascent. The path is well marked, but keep an eye out for occasional trail signs to guide your way.

Point Lookout offers wide views over the Four Corners region.

As you venture farther, the landscape morphs gradually around you. Shrublands of mountain mahogany and serviceberry give way to scattered pinyon-juniper woodland, punctuated by brilliant bursts of wildflowers in some seasons. In spring, vermillion Indian paintbrush dots the landscape, while in summer, blue flax and cliffrose bloom to fill the air with gentle perfume.

The trail itself winds over sun-drenched sandstone and under soft, cool shade of blue-gray junipers. A consistent but manageable climb delivers new and increasingly captivating vistas. The expanse of Montezuma Valley unfurls to the west, while the Mancos Valley stretches out to the east. The best is reserved for the end of the trail, at the summit of Point Lookout.

Here, atop the weathered sandstone and beneath the endless Colorado sky, you can see across what feels like the entirety of the Four Corners region. To the south, the Sleeping Ute Mountain slumbers on the horizon, and to the east, the La Plata Mountains showcase snowcapped peaks gleaming in the sunlight.

Grab photos and descend the same path back to the trailhead. Spoiler: The photos won't do the hike justice.

Knife Edge Trail

On Mesa Verde's quieter side, you'll find the splendid, under-visited Knife Edge Trail. At 2 miles round-trip, the path sees mild elevation change, making it an easy but rewarding trail for those seeking a tranquil and scenic experience away from the cliff dwelling crowds.

Look for the signed Knife Edge trailhead near Morefield Campground and begin your journey along the trail that was once a dirt access road leading to the early twentieth-century Park Point Fire Lookout.

As you step onto the trail, Mesa Verde's characteristic semiarid ecology supports sagebrush and rabbitbrush swaying in the breeze on either side of the trail. Pinyon pines and Utah junipers rise along the trail at occasional intervals.

The Knife Edge's lack of petroglyphs or cliff dwellings keeps it quiet.

As you progress, remnants of an old telephone line that once connected the fire lookout come into view. Weathered poles stand guard along the trail, their wires long stripped away.

The trail meanders along the edge of the mesa, which gives the trail its name. To one side, the land drops sharply, giving way to sweeping views of Montezuma Valley and, on clear days, beyond to the distant horizon. The view glows during dawn or dusk, when a rising or setting sun casts light and shadow across the rolling landscape and paints the sky in shades of amber and gold, while the valley below lies cloaked in an ethereal mist.

While the trail avoids the grandeur and history of ancient cliff dwellings or the mystique of petroglyphs, it makes up for it with desert solitude and wide views. Retrace your steps to the trailhead, one step at a time.

By vertical relief, Mount Rainier is the tallest mountain in the Lower 48 by far.

Mount Rainier National Park

Washington | nps.gov/mora | Visitation: 1,674,294

Mount Rainier never gets old for a Seattleite. Watching the mountain fade from rosy pink to cool indigo as the sun sets, stealing a glimpse of her imposing shoulders through swirling fog on a winter day, admiring her carved facets from a plane window—she never seems anything less than the most impressive, ineffable mountain in the Lower 48.

In many ways, she is. At 14,411 feet above sea level, Rainier is only the fifth tallest in the Lower 48. But its extreme topographic prominence means 13,246 feet of it fill your naked eyes. That's over 3,000 feet more observable mountain than the actual tallest, California's Mount Whitney.

Early climber John Muir proclaimed the view from the bottom superior to the view from the top. Having seen both, I'm not sure I agree—but it's at least as good, which means you don't have to stand atop this overgrown ice cream cone to take in the full measure of the mountain.

Rainier's sheer mass and the turbulent riot of geology, climate, biology, and history residing on its sprawling flanks allows for a universe of world-class exploration. The park boundaries contain entire mountain subranges wrought from the peak's volcanic effluvia, groves of skyscraping trees that predate the Magna Carta, and 155 billion cubic feet of ice spread over 27 named glaciers (that's more than you can find in all the other Cascade volcanoes, Rocky Mountains, and every ice tray in America combined).

As you'd imagine, these wondrous attributes make Rainier extremely popular—and it's only 50 miles as the crow flies from the briny oysters and killer breweries of the Emerald City. That's both feature and bug.

Rainier is an active volcano—a slumbering giant with a fiery heart concealed beneath a calm exterior of rock and ice. It began its life over half a million years ago, shaped by thousands of eruptions, landslides, and the patient carving of glaciers. With over 35 square miles of permanent ice and snow cover, Rainier boasts the largest single-peak glacier system within the United States.

It was once over 16,000 feet tall, but an apocalyptic eruption sometime in the last 5,000 to 7,000 years projectile-vomited 2,000 feet of mountain across hundreds of square miles in the form of ash, lava, office-building-size boulders, and terrorizing high-speed mudflows known as lahars, which bulldozed the landscape before barreling into Puget Sound. Humans inhabited the area at this time, and Native tribes recorded it in oral tradition passed down today. The mountain's older name is Tahoma or Tacoma, and to some it means "don't forget the water," "mother of waters," or "place where the waters begin."

Glaciers are the stars of Mount Rainier, unfurling down its flanks like craggy-blue dog tongues. The Emmons Glacier, with its cavernous crevasses and seracs, has the largest surface area of any glacier in the Lower 48. The Nisqually Glacier, visible from the park's Paradise area, is a dynamic, ever-changing sculpture, and the most studied. The Carbon Glacier has the lowest terminus and is the thickest, with the largest volume.

The ice may govern the park's natural systems, but it yields to lower elevations blanketed by dense forests of Douglas fir, western red cedar, and western hemlock. These provide habitat for black-tailed deer, Roosevelt elk, black bears, cougars, and many more.

As you ascend, the forest gives way to subalpine meadows, where the endemic Rainier white marsh marigold and Maguire primrose bloom. Here, the whistle of marmots and pikas and the chittering of the Clark's nutcracker fill the air.

Above the tree line, the alpine zone, harsh and beautiful, cradles life in its nooks and crannies. Hardy cushion plants and lichens cling to rocks, and the sure-footed mountain goat skips between cliffs.

In summer, fields of wildflowers bloom in high meadows, vibrant against the stony cookies-and-cream hue of the mountain. Autumn drapes the park in the soft russet of turning maple and blueberry shrubs. Winter dunks the mountain in some of the heaviest snows on earth, offering a constant supply for snowshoers and skiers. Spring breathes life back into the landscape, with waterfalls gushing from melting snowpacks and wildlife rousing from winter hideaways. The snow usually won't disappear from mid- to high-elevation trails until late July, sometimes later.

In 1899, Mount Rainier became the fifth national park in the United States. It welcomes countless visitors and explorers with a blend of easy retreat and grueling adventure. The first American Everest summiteers cut their teeth on this peak—the only mountain outside of Alaska that approaches a Himalayan experience (albeit without the extreme altitude). It's still considered a crucial test piece for anyone who dreams of tackling Denali, Everest, or the Seven Summits. Each year, thousands attempt to conquer the 14,411-foot peak, a quest demanding physical stamina and technical prowess. Just under 50 percent make it. It's a serious climb on a serious mountain; some die.

But don't worry! There's a boatload of mellower, hidden adventures found in the park's 236,000 acres—plenty that won't risk succumbing to altitude sickness, hypothermia, falling in a crevasse, or being crushed under tons of ice.

ZONE OF INTEREST

Carbon River Entrance

Located on the park's remote northwest corner, this region is a realm of temperate rain forest nourished by abundant rainfall. It's one of the least-visited sections of the park, but that's a bit baffling:

The Carbon River entrance is the least-visited portal to Rainier.

The Carbon Glacier in the lowest-elevation glacier in the Lower 48.

Despite the rain, its low elevation of 1,900 feet means it's typically accessible year-round via the paved Carbon River Road.

The Carbon River Road was once open to vehicles, but since its construction in the 1920s, catastrophic floods from the swollen river running next to it have regularly washed it out. Realizing the futility of repairs, the park closed it at the entrance station and allowed it to return to nature as an especially wide trail. The trail meanders alongside the Carbon River for 5 miles to the Ipsut Creek Campground, a once drive-in campground now accessible only on foot or bike.

One can continue farther along the Wonderland Trail to the Carbon Glacier, the lowest-elevation glacier in the lower 48 states. The glacier's raw, gritty toe lies 17 miles round-trip from road's end—but you can greatly speed up your trip by riding a mountain bike to Ipsut Creek and tackling 10 of those miles on two wheels.

Either way, you'll pass through a world enrobed in green—western red cedars, Douglas firs, and western hemlocks, some over 500 years old. The understory is a messy riot of ferns, mosses, and lichens coming in a thousand shades of green.

The river itself tumbles on your left throughout as a tumultuous stream, carrying glacial silt and rocks from the heights of Rainier. You may spot a Roosevelt elk meandering through the forest or catch the flight of a northern spotted owl. Closer to the ground, fat banana slugs make their slow journeys across the rain-soaked landscape.

The Carbon River area receives copious amounts of rain—over 90 inches annually. Outside of the summer months, prepare to embrace the rain. This is easy: The forest glows during rainfall, mists weave through the trees, and the entire forest twinkles with droplets. The air grows richer, earthier, and the high canopy helps shelter you from all but the heaviest downpours.

I saw no one on an early-morning winter scouting jaunt on a bluebird January day. Signs of water-borne destruction were everywhere, and you could see how the processes of the mountain can destroy roads and toss bridges like King Kong across a river valley. Ranger Falls and serene Green Lake are well worth the side trip.

While this area doesn't have easy views of the mountain itself, 0.5 mile past the Green Lake trailhead the view opens to stone monoliths framing the valley like a miniature Yosemite Valley. Hard pavement gives way to softer gravel and dark, sandy glacial silt after 2 miles or so. There isn't much parking, but by the time I returned from the Carbon Glacier I had seen fewer than twenty people—remarkable for any sunny day in Rainier.

HIKES

Green Lake Trail

The Green Lake Trail is an 8.5-mile round-trip journey through old-growth forest to a still green pool surrounded on three sides by steep cliffs, with Tolmie Peak rising behind. Elevation gain clocks in at a modest 1,150 feet and is contained entirely on the final ascent to the lake.

Begin at the Carbon River entrance of the park. Follow the Carbon River Road Trail, a remnant of a road now overgrown and returned to nature. After 1.6 miles, the Green Lake Trail branches off to the right, marked by a sign.

The trail weaves through western red cedar and Douglas fir, crossing several streams on the way. The forest gradually thins out, opening to the lake cradled within a steeply cut cirque.

Mother Mountain Loop

The bold, challenging Mother Mountain Loop treks 19 miles to circumnavigate Mother Mountain in the remote northwest corner of the park. With an approximate elevation gain of 4,500 feet, it covers undulating terrain on the edge of the park but delivers bomber views and relative solitude in a moderate-to-strenuous backpack or a giant day hike.

Begin at Mowich Lake, the largest and deepest lake in the park. Start on the trail to Ipsut Pass, a moderate ascent through a forest of Douglas firs. The trail then descends to Ipsut Creek and the

Find sweeping panoramas all over the Mother Mountain Loop.

Carbon River (your first day's camping spot if you wish to make this a multiday hike).

From the Carbon River, the trail ascends again toward Seattle Park, a large series of meadows that explode with wildflowers in the summer. Pass by the mystical Spray Falls before beginning your climb to Spray Park. Then the trail cuts across the northwest slope of Mother Mountain toward the saddle known as Knapsack Pass. This section can be particularly challenging, but the sweeping panoramas make it worthwhile.

From Knapsack Pass, descend toward the Mowich River, crossing several streams on the way. The trail brings you back to Mowich Lake, marking the end of your journey.

Eastside Trail

The Eastside Trail spans 26.2 miles from Chinook Pass to the Ohanapecosh Campground, with an elevation gain of around 3,400 feet. It's a moderately difficult trek that keeps crowds at bay by trading Rainier views for a wealth of old-growth forests, roaring rivers, and hidden falls. It features several access points along its length; the

Ancient trees fill the Grove of the Patriarchs.

best thing to do is break out a map and plot a route that works for your allotted time. Individual sections can work as day hikes, or you can combine them with other trails to form a multiday loop (don't forget permits).

From Chinook Pass, the trail descends through subalpine meadows, offering splendid views of Rainier's eastern face (some of the best views are from here to Tips Lake). The trail then descends into the American River valley, providing a serene riverside hike beset by Douglas firs, western red cedars, and western hemlocks, some over 1,000 years old. The trail continues its descent until it reaches the Ohanapecosh River, where a large bridge offers a thrilling crossing over the rushing river. From there, the trail ascends to the Stevens Canyon Road before reaching your destination, the Ohanapecosh Campground.

For a day hike, consider the section from the Grove of the Patriarchs to Silver Falls. It's a 3-mile round-trip trek that offers a sampling of towering old-growth forests before concluding at Silver Falls, where the Ohanapecosh River roars over a rocky cliff, creating a white froth of water that shines like molten silver.

Shriner Peak Lookout

Shriner Peak Lookout's trail climbs a brutal 3,400 feet in under 4 miles; the path is steep and offers little shade and few water sources. But that keeps it empty, so you'll win champion views of Rainier for yourself. Bring lots of water and start early to mitigate the heat.

From the Shriner Peak Lookout trailhead, off WA 123, the trail immediately begins its ascent, switchbacking through a forest of fir and hemlock. As you climb, the trees give way to manzanita bushes and open slopes left from old burn areas.

Halfway up, you'll find St. Andrews Creek, the only reliable water source along the trail. After this, the climb resumes and doesn't let up until you reach the summit. As you climb, watch for pikas darting among the rocks and listen for the clarion call of gray jays. The Shriner Peak Lookout is perched on the peak, offering a

The view from Shriner Peak Lookout.

Spray Park is famous for its profusion of wildflowers.

splendid panoramic view of Mount Rainier, the Ohanapecosh val-ley, the Cascades, Goat Rocks, and Mount St. Helens.

The lookout itself was built in the 1930s by the Civilian Con-servation Corps, one of the many such fire lookouts scattered across the park. With a permit, you can stay overnight at a back-country campsite near the lookout. This trail also gets more pleas-ant in fall, when cooler temps ease the journey and brightly colored underbrush lights up the route.

HIDDEN GEM

Outside of climbing the peak itself, circumnavigating the entire mountain on the 93-mile Wonderland Trail remains a life-list expe-rience for many who visit Rainier. But snagging a coveted permit can be extremely difficult. The **Northern Loop**'s 43-mile trek offers a quieter alternative that encircles the northern region of Rainier, with a knee-busting total elevation gain of around 9,000 feet. This adventure is not for the faint of heart, but the rewards are sublime.

Start from the Sunrise Visitor Center. Head west on the Sourdough Ridge Trail toward Frozen Lake, where you'll join the Wonderland Trail for a spell. Descend into the White River valley

before beginning a climb toward the Granite Creek Campsite—your first day's goal.

The second day brings you into sprawling meadows and tow-ering peaks, and to the lovely Fire Creek Camp. As you navigate the Windy Gap and descend to the Carbon River, you'll pass the historic Dick Creek Camp, another potential spot to rest.

Day three is a test of endurance as you continue ascending on the arduous but rewarding Northern Loop Trail, but fantastic views of the mountain goad you along. As you traverse the Yellow-stone Cliffs (andesite columns formed from volcanic activity mil-lennia ago), look for the ideal campsite at either Yellowstone Cliffs or Windy Gap.

Your final day begins with a descent into the magical Spray Park, often flower-pocked in summer. Stop to admire Spray Falls, then begin your final ascent through another glorious meadow, Seattle Park, before rejoining the Wonderland Trail, leading back to Sunrise.

National Park of American Samoa

American Samoa | nps.gov/npsa | Visitation: 12,135

Trace your finger on a map 2,600 miles southwestward from Hawaii and you will find a handful of tiny emerald gems scattered across the cobalt Pacific. Welcome to American Samoa, a US territory that, while little known, is home to one of the most unique national parks in the United States—the National Park of American Samoa.

National Park of American Samoa spans sun-kissed beaches, lush rain forests, coral-rich waters, and extinct volcanoes. Straddling both land and sea, this 13,500-acre park provides a vibrant sanctuary for both a plethora of unique species and Polynesian culture.

The islands rose from ocean floor volcanoes, breaking the surface to form the land we see today. The last eruption in American Samoa occurred 100 to 200 years ago on the island of Aunu'u. Over time, coral reefs formed around these basaltic peaks, creating the foundations for the islands.

Five kinds of rain forest types—coast, lowland, ridge, montane, and cloud—dominate the peaks and valleys of the islands. The canopies of each teem with an array of tropical bird species, including the vibrant Samoan fantail, the elegant white-collared kingfisher, and the endangered Samoan starling. Spot them along Tutuila's Pola Island Trail, where at the end you can watch seabirds perform an aerial ballet around the craggy, uninhabited Pola Island.

If you spot especially large black wings blotting out the sky around twilight, it's probably not a bird. The islands' forests echo with the chatter of fruit bats, the only native mammals in the park. These "flying foxes" can often be seen roosting in the rain forest canopy or gliding in search of food.

Humans came to American Samoa 3,000 years ago, when Polynesian sailors navigated the open Pacific to find this remote paradise. This rich cultural heritage is a cornerstone of the park's identity. The Samoan culture, or *Fa'asamoa*, is an integral part of the park experience, so much so that park land is both leased from and co-managed by local *aiga*, or families. This ensures that traditional Samoan ways of life continue within the park and are shared with visitors.

Traditional Samoan houses, or *fale*, dot the coastline. Visitors can learn the local way of life by participating in homestays, which often encourage engagement with the community.

National Park of American Samoa is co-managed by Samoan families.

Getting here requires a 5.5-hour flight from Hawaii or a 15-hour pond hop from California. As the only national park site south of the equator, the park is warm and rainy all year, though June to September dries out a bit.

ZONE OF INTEREST

National Park of American Samoa hosts a small network of trails, but if you've made it this far, it pays to get wet. More than 4,000 acres of the park are underwater—and here biodiversity explodes exponentially. Sea turtles, dolphins, and over 950 species of fish dwell in the coral reefs and gin-clear water beneath the waves. World-class snorkeling lies a short splash from many of the park's empty beaches.

One of the best is Ofu Beach on teeny, remote Ofu Island. Charter a local boat or plane from the main island town of Pago Pago on Tutuila to reach the 35-acre reef. Be patient and flexible: Schedules can vary depending on weather, and flights and charters aren't guaranteed every day.

Once you arrive and dive into Ofu's typically calm waters, you can spot over 150 kinds of coral in waters where visibility exceeds 100 feet. Take a deep breath and enjoy your private paradise.

HIDDEN GEM

Rose Atoll

If you've made it this far, keep going: 180 miles and a rocky 10-hour boat ride east of Pago Pago is **Rose Atoll,** an uninhabited ring of coral reefs, sandbars, and two teensy islets enclosing a central lagoon in a perfect square. It is the southernmost point of land under US jurisdiction, and the Rose Atoll National Wildlife Refuge protects huge amounts of oceanic wildlife, including sharks, tuna, mahi mahi, barracudas, rare reef fish, dolphins, nesting birds, hawksbill and green turtles, and one of the biggest populations of giant clams.

You might want to hurry. Since the highest point in Rose Atoll rises barely above sea level, increasing sea levels mean the scant bits of sand and vine-laden vegetation could soon sink below the waves.

Unless you're a marine biologist, getting here will require some serious finagling. The US Fish and Wildlife Service maintains a rigid permitting and review process to allow entry to this protected and sensitive area. But if you succeed, congratulations: You've landed in arguably the most remote spot in the United States. Also . . . can I come?

The island of Olosega as seen from the top of Ofu.

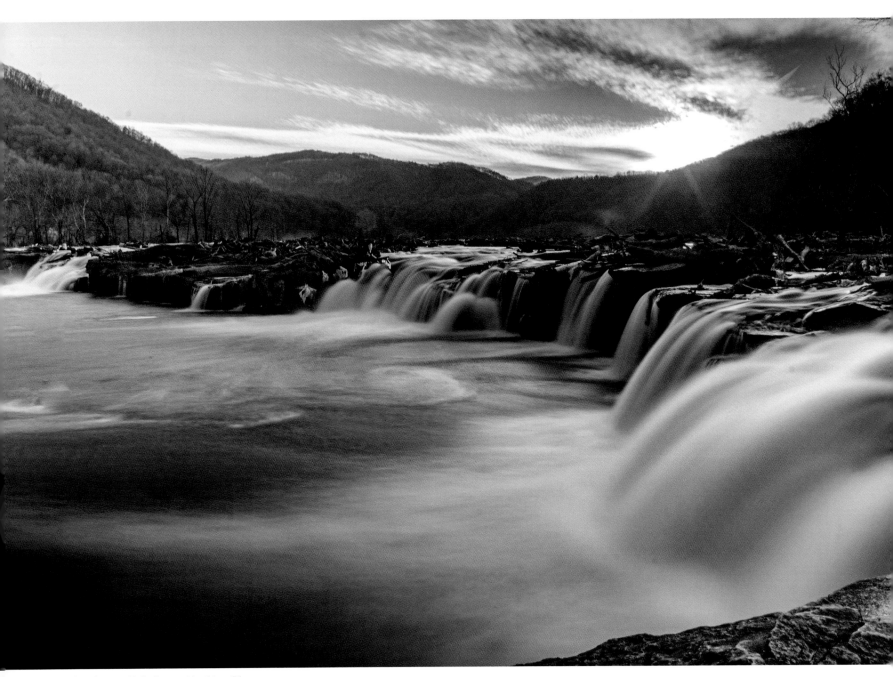

Sandstone Falls lies on the New River.

New River Gorge National Park and Preserve

West Virginia | nps.gov/neri | Visitation: 1,707,223

Rechristened in 2020, New River Gorge is brand-new national park, but it's been part of the system as a national river since 1978. (Along with Great Sand Dunes, it's the rare park outside of Alaska with the "preserve" designation, which means hunting and other traditional subsistence activities are still permitted in certain parts of the park.) Like many new parks, it retains a mixed-use flavor where extensive human settlements and artifacts commingle with pristine forests, a thriving wild watershed, and raucous, world-class rafting rapids.

Despite the name, the New River is one of the oldest waterways in North America. It also challenges conventional river behavior, flowing north rather than south or west, carving through the land rather than skirting around it like other rivers in the region. Some call it the "Grand Canyon of the East."

The river's deep gorge reveals rock layers over 300 million years old that chronicle the rise and fall of mountains, the birth and death of seas, and the inching of continental plates as they skate slowly on lava.

A diverse temperate forest thrives on its slopes; here, tall tulip trees, sweetgums, and over 60 species of oaks create a dense canopy and an understory haven for wildlife. White-tailed deer tread in the undergrowth, while wild turkeys strut under towering trees. Over 240 species of birds fill the air with song, from vibrant warblers to fierce peregrine falcons launching off cliffs. The river and its tributaries teem with many species of fish and amphibians.

Indigenous peoples thrived here for thousands of years. The remnants of their culture can be found in the stone tools, pottery, and mysterious petroglyphs etched on the rocks.

The Industrial Revolution transformed the region. Logging and rich seams of coal brought miners and the land-scarring infrastructure required to transport goods. The river became a highway, moving coal and timber to growing cities along the Eastern Seaboard. Ghost towns and abandoned mines stand everywhere as poignant reminders of the region's industrial past.

The New River Gorge National Park is a year-round destination. Spring welcomes wildflowers, while summer is ideal for rafting, climbing, and fishing on tumbling whitewater. Autumn colors the slopes in yellow and red, and quiet winters bring snow and Mid-Atlantic cold.

The New River offers challenging whitewater for many skill levels.

The hills light up with fall colors in New River Gorge.

ZONE OF INTEREST

One of the best ways to experience the New River Gorge is to get into the guts of the gorge on the water. With a variety of rapid classes and breathtaking scenery, the New River provides an adrenaline-pumping adventure for both beginners and seasoned rafters.

The Upper New River is perfect for beginners and families. It features mostly Class I–II rapids with a few Class III challenges thrown into the mix. The pace allows rafters to enjoy the beautiful surroundings, take a dip in the river, or try out inflatable kayaks.

The Lower New is renowned for its big waves and consistent rapids. It contains Class III–V rapids and is recommended for those with some rafting experience or those seeking a thrill. Famous rapids in this section include "Surprise," "Railroad," and "Double Z." This section ends at the New River Gorge Bridge, an iconic steel arch bridge that's one of the longest and highest of its kind in the world.

Several professional outfitters in the area provide guided trips, equipment, and safety briefings. They can also design day or multi-day trips to suit your group's desires and needs.

HIKES

Turkey Spur Trail

A modest mile-long trail, the Turkey Spur meanders to splendid views of the gorge and river below. The elevation gain is 250 feet, enough to set your heart racing but not so much to make you call it a day. From the Grandview Visitor Center, you'll traverse an easy path full of chirps from unseen birds, dashing squirrels, and the distant roar of the river.

Keeneys Creek Trail

In 3 miles, this trail brings you to the remnants of West Virginia's industrial past on a relatively flat hike that follows an old railroad grade along Keeneys Creek.

As you walk, the trail will narrate a tale of that bygone era: abandoned coal towns, derelict coal tipples, and old bridges and trestles.

Long Point Trail

The Long Point Trail is a 3.2-mile hike (round-trip) that presents you with a panoramic view of the New River Gorge Bridge, the river, and the gorge itself over a moderate elevation gain of around 400 feet.

You'll weave through a blend of woods and meadows, painted with wildflowers come spring. The trail ends at a spectacular viewpoint—a cliff that overlooks the gorge and the distant bridge.

Stone Cliff Trail

For those seeking a leisurely stroll by the river, the Stone Cliff Trail is a solid pick. This 3-mile trek runs along the river following an old road that once served the Stone Cliff coal mine. The mine is long gone, and in its place, the river and the forest have returned to recolonize the landscape.

North Cascades National Park

Washington | nps.gov/noca | Visitation: 40,351

Despite being located less than 3 hours from two sprawling metropolises (Seattle and Vancouver, BC) and featuring over 400 miles of trail in 500,000 acres of some of the most spectacular scenery in the system, North Cascades is the *second-least-visited national park in the Lower 48*. Let that sink in for a sec.

It owes its near-superlative position to a bit of a technicality. None of the park's actual borders touch a paved road, and it's buffered on all sides by national forest and two national recreation areas, Lake Chelan and Ross Lake. When those national recreation areas combine with the park to form the North Cascades National Park Service Complex, the visitation rockets up to a little over a million. Damnit.

But here's the big silver lining: A million of those folks never leave the electric-teal shores of Ross Lake or the pavement of the achingly scenic North Cascades Highway, both of which snake through the mountains and bisect the park. This means if you make it into the backcountry, you have it mostly to yourself. And thanks to a limited permitting system, for backpackers it's Valhalla.

I say "if" because the North Cascades extracts a steep penalty from hikers. I mean that literally: The Cascades are widely regarded as the steepest, most rugged mountain chain in the continental United States, and you can see only a sliver of their spellbinding beauty without ascending one or more knee-knocking passes on climbs often in excess of 4,000 feet. This thwarts day hikers on all but a few trails. But stout trampers and backpackers lucky enough to score a coveted permit will discover an under-the-radar landscape as awe-inspiring as any of its national park brethren: Seas of glacier-capped peaks stud the horizon. Cascading waterfalls hurtle off cliffs to mist the air and disappear into deep valleys stacked with ancient, mammoth trees and veined with ferocious aquamarine rivers. It trades a central defining feature like Rainier or Half Dome for a glut of the best alpine scenery around.

It could also credibly steal the title of "Glacier" from that other park. Around 300 glaciers cover the park's peaks, more than any other national park outside Alaska. These icy behemoths carve valleys, feed waterways, and nourish endangered species like the gray wolf, fisher, and spotted owl.

A moonless night in the North Cascades.

They melt into rivers that welcome all five species of Pacific salmon (can you name them?*). Black bears, lynx, bobcats, and mountain lions stalk through the understory along with elk and deer, while mountain goats and bighorns nimbly pick their way across sheer cliffs. Rarer charismatic carnivores live here, too—wolverines and grizzlies, the latter in numbers so small (perhaps less than ten) they might as well be ghosts.

North Cascades' ecosystems range from wet temperate rain forests of spruce and fir in the west to dry ponderosa pine forests in the east. More than a thousand species of plants thrive in these shifting, overlapping realms. Summer splatters meadows with wild-flowers in bright colors set against the grays and whites of stone and ice. In late summer, huckleberries and blueberries sprout in numbers too huge to fill the belly of any bear or backpacker.

For over 8,000 years, native peoples like the Nlaka'pamux, Chelan, Skagit, and Methow traversed these mountains, moving with the seasons, fishing the rivers, and gathering plants for medicine and food. In recent times, Euro-American settlers pushed

*Chinook (king), sockeye, chum, coho, and pink

Shuksan is one of the most photogenic peaks in the North Cascades.

into the area questing for gold, timber, or furs. But the severity of the terrain thwarted these efforts as well as attempts to build railways or other paths through. The only successful human endeavor besides recreation involved the construction of large dams to power expanding Seattle. But those are specks on a southern toe of wilderness that extends practically unbroken from here to Alaska.

The park can feel untamed, untouched, unyielding. It demands respect and perhaps a bit of sacrifice from those who would know it. Much of the park is accessible only by foot—or hand, foot, and spike: The stellar alpine climbing challenges here have earned this area the nickname "The American Alps" and became the proving ground for climbing legends like Fred Beckey.

The source of this alpine wondery is a bit more obscure. Geologically, the North Cascades are a conglomerate mess of volcanic rocks and metamorphic schists, gneisses, and granites. Each teeny pebble and towering peak has been variously bubbled, cooked, sintered, melted, uplifted, folded, glaciated, iced, thawed, scraped, and eroded over 400 million years. The melt and uplift behind their current profile likely started 40 million years ago, but we can't be sure—the geology here constitutes some of the most complex and least understood in the world.

You don't need bomber climbing skills to experience the best the park has to offer. Fitness, grit, and the willingness to shoulder a pack will take you far enough to shed modern life, slow down, and feel the built world shrink away. All paths here lead to big helpings of solitude, tranquility, and personal achievement. And when you emerge from this capital-W Wilderness, the big-city beers and burgers are close by.

HIKES

Hidden Lake Lookout

The Hidden Lake Lookout trail delivers in spades everything North Cascades National Park is famous for: deep woods, gurgling creeks, stout climbs, electric wildflowers, loads of berries, high meadows and ridges, bare granite, and colossal views of glaciers and spiky peaks. "Very strenuous but very rewarding" pretty much sums it up.

The trail to the Hidden Lake Lookout tops out at nearly 7,000 feet.

The 4.4-mile one-way trail starts at the Hidden Lake trailhead, located off Cascade River Road. It's roughly a 10-mile drive east of Marblemount on a road that quickly devolves into a potholed, rutty mess. Sedans sometimes make it depending on the year and conditions, but 4WD and high clearance are recommended.

The path begins by winding through a lush, green forest, climbing steadily but keeping you cool with lots of shade. At 2 miles in, you'll emerge from the forest into a large meadow often filled with blooming wildflowers in the summer.

After the meadow, you'll ascend switchbacks up the mountain's face for another mile and a half, entering the subalpine and alpine zones. This section gets steep and doesn't let up; take it slow and steady. The vegetation gradually transitions from forest to low shrubs and alpine flowers; look out for berries along this section in late summer/early fall.

The last mile of the hike levels out along the ridge to the lookout to give a bit of a nice respite after the arduous climb. As you approach the lookout, keep your eyes open for marmots, pikas, and the occasional mountain goat.

The trail ends at the Hidden Lake Lookout, a fire lookout perched at 6,890 feet above sea level. The lookout, which is still occasionally used for its original purpose, offers eye-popping views of prized North Cascades climbs, including Eldorado Peak, Forbidden Peak, Boston Peak, and Sahale Peak. Clear days see Mount Baker and Mount Rainier punching at the clouds in the distance. The lookout cabin is open to the public on a first-come, first-served basis for overnight stays, but space is extremely limited. (You need a permit to camp at the lake, which lies beyond the park boundary.)

If you wish, you can descend to the lake through a trailless cross-country zone. More impacted campsites exist uphill from shore in two grassy patches, but you'll need to secure a permit for those, too.

This trail's 3,300 feet of elevation gain can be tough for those unaccustomed to steep, high-altitude hiking. Snow can linger on the trail well into the summer, and during early and late seasons, an ice axe and crampons may be necessary.

Cutthroat Pass + Snowy Lakes via PCT

Across from the more popular Heather–Maple Pass loop, the hike to Cutthroat Pass reveals an alpine world of broad meadows, jagged peaks, and pristine lakes. It's the North Cascades at its most raw and dramatic. In the autumn, the pass blazes gold with prized larches, a rare conifer that turns color.

To begin your journey to Cutthroat Pass, drive up the North Cascades Highway (WA 20). Across from Rainy Pass and the Heather–Maple Loop trailhead, turn left to find the trailhead for Cutthroat Pass, located down a short gravel road at the Pacific Crest Trail (PCT) parking area.

The trip is 10 miles round-trip to Cutthroat Pass (farther if you head to Snowy Lakes), with an elevation gain of a bit more than 2,000 feet. You can also get there via Cutthroat Lake, but this segment of the famous PCT offers a broad, well-maintained path.

Starting amid dense forests, the trail quickly ascends through switchbacks, revealing views of the surrounding peaks. As you climb, the forest gives way to sprawling meadows dotted with wildflowers in summer months. Ever-expanding views of the North Cascades goad you on as you continue.

Reaching Cutthroat Pass, you're greeted with insane vistas: Peaks rise in every direction, with valleys plunging deep below. To the southeast, the view extends down to the Methow Valley and, on clear days, farther still. Cutthroat Lake gleams far below, and campsites dot the ridge—no permit required (this is before the park boundary).

If you're feeling adventurous and want to hike farther, get a permit and push on to camp at Snowy Lakes, a spectacular side trip from Cutthroat Pass in exchange for another 5ish miles one-way. Continuing the PCT from Cutthroat Pass, the trail dips down and crosses a basin before traversing several steep ridges. After 4 to 5 miles, you'll encounter a trail junction with the Snowy Lakes path

Larches turn golden in September and October at Cutthroat Pass.

veering up and to the right on a stiff climb. The Snowy Lakes are a set of turquoise pools set against the backdrop of towering peaks like the Golden Horn.

HIDDEN GEM

Easy Ridge in North Cascades National Park is anything but: This royal grinder of a backpacking trip requires multiple days, significant elevation gain, and solid route-finding skills. The trail is typically completed as a part of the Easy Ridge–Chilliwack River loop. It's not recommended for beginners, and preparation is key. This is part of what makes it exciting and empty. (Also, don't confuse it with Easy Pass off WA 20 in the park—also a stunner, also hard).

The journey begins at the Hannegan Pass trailhead, ascending steadily through lush forest over 4 miles and 2,100 feet until you reach Hannegan Pass. Enjoy the first of many sweeping views here, taking in the Chilliwack River Valley and the glaciated peaks surrounding it. Ending here or with a quick detour climb up Hannegan Peak is a great option for a day hike. (There's a non-permitted campsite before the pass.)

From Hannegan Pass, you'll lose 1,600 feet as you descend into the valley along the Chilliwack River Trail, crossing the official park boundary. This part of the journey offers cooler temperatures and a respite from the climb. Several established backcountry campsites can be found along the river, a good option for the first night.

Mile 10–15 (elevation gain approximately 2,800 feet): The next 5 miles are where the real challenge starts. Depart from the Chilliwack River Trail to ford the river (there's no bridge) and begin a steep 2,800-foot ascent toward Easy Ridge. Occasionally a stuck log can form a makeshift crossing, but use extreme caution and cross in wide, shallow sections (look for riffles). In periods of high flow, you're skunked. From here, a reliable map, compass, and knowledge of how to use them are crucial. Once across, you'll need to find a sometimes-obscured user trail; it's faint and often overgrown. It cuts straight up the mountainside in a grueling climb.

Once on the ridge, the trail follows it for another 3 to 5 miles, offering a spectacular panorama of mountains, glaciers, and steep-sided valleys on all sides. Vegetation thins and you'll ascend granite ramps as you get higher and higher. After 5 miles of ridge-walking, you'll find a few dirt patches or flat rocks that offer life-list views across the Cascades and into Canada. You can follow the ridge all the way to a steep, messy, crumbly scramble to where a fire lookout once was. Now there's a single rusting chair, but it's a mighty throne

The toilet at North Cascades' Sahale Glacier Camp is perhaps the finest in the National Park Service.

for the view: The terrifying Picket Range—considered among the most remote and rugged in the United States—spikes the horizon, and the wild Baker River drainage splays out below (a place scientists point to as a possible refuge for the North Cascades' tiny grizzly population).

Basecamp here for a night or two. After you've soaked it in, begin your descent from Easy Ridge down to the Chilliwack River again. You'll cross the river and rejoin the Chilliwack River Trail, which will lead you back to the junction with Hannegan Pass Trail.

Total elevation gain: 6,900 feet over 30ish miles.

This route requires you to ford the Chilliwack River twice, which can be dangerous or impossible during high water. It's also more of a route than a well-marked trail, especially in the Easy Ridge area. You should be experienced in wilderness navigation and comfortable with hiking on rough terrain. Always check the weather forecast and trail conditions before embarking on the journey. With that in mind, the Easy Ridge route offers an unparalleled, unforgettable opportunity to experience the full wild beauty of the North Cascades.

Olympic National Park

Washington | nps.gov/olym | Visitation: 2,947,503

Jutting into the open northern Pacific Ocean, the Olympic Peninsula is surrounded by water on three sides. Its 8,000-foot peaks cull 150 or more inches of precipitation a year, which feeds crevassed glaciers, rain forests filled with exceptionally tall conifers, and massive blue-gray rivers that snake through the forest back to the sea.

In the center, Olympic National Park sits atop it like a vast patchwork quilt, stitching together several ecosystems into a singular marvel. It's as if Mother Nature chose this corner of the world to flaunt everything that makes the western slope of the Pacific Northwest—sea to mountaintop—a world-class wilderness. Visiting Olympic is like indulging in a sampler platter of the finest wild lands from this part of the planet.

Here, you'll find lush temperate rain forests, where dripping mosses, ferns, and other epiphytes cling to every available surface and reframe your idea of how many shades of green there can be. Ancient Sitka spruces, western red cedars, and coastal Doug firs reach over 300 feet into the sky, some starting as seedlings 200 years before King John signed the Magna Carta. A short drive away you can trace wind-sculpted coastal stretches. Sandy shores get pounded relentlessly by king tides and angry Pacific waves. Venture back inland far enough, and the alpine meadows give way to jagged snowy peaks clad in glaciers and sharp black stone.

It started 34 million years ago, when tectonic forces pushed the basaltic seabed upward—bending, folding, and exposing the raw material that glaciers would later sculpt into striking peaks and deep, U-shaped valleys. Big rivers churn in the valley basins, each trafficking tons of rich sediments milled from above. The glaciers persist now, grinding down spires and coloring the rivers milky blue or Ovaltine, depending on the height of flow and season.

Rain rules everything in Olympic. This place receives more than any place in the Lower 48—an average of 14 feet a year, though sometimes as much as 21 feet. North Pacific storms slam into the high Olympics, where the immovable wall wrings out the clouds like a sponge. The omnipresent moisture brings forth an explosion of life, from miniature fungi to epic conifers. It comes in surprising variety: Drizzles, mists, downpours, deluges, fogs, sprinkles, cats and dogs, mizzles. They all maintain and nurture a year-round growing season, especially in the lower-elevation rain forests like the Hoh, Quinault, Bogachiel, and Queets.

The sun sets on Rialto Beach.

The Olympic coast's 70-mile-long wild stretch of beach holds precipitous cliffs, sandy beaches, secluded coves, and sea stacks looming offshore. Its intertidal zones, offshore waters, and estuaries harbor a multitude of life forms. Anemones, starfish, mussels, and crabs fill the tide pools. Seabirds such as puffins, murres, and gulls nest on the sea stacks. The waters are frequented by marine mammals including sea otters, harbor seals, orcas, and gray whales. Bald eagles and peregrine falcons rule the skies, while endemic Olympic marmots, black bears, bobcats, beavers, black-tailed deer, cougars, recently reintroduced fishers, and too many birds to count roam the coastal forests and occasionally dip into the beaches. The rivers host all five species of Pacific salmon in champion sizes and runs.

For thousands of years, Indigenous tribes like the Quinault, Hoh, Quileute, Elwha Klallam, Port Gamble S'Klallam, Skokomish, Jamestown S'klallam, and Makah have called this place home, dressing in water-repellent cedar and traversing the waterways in canoes carved from the biggest trees. These tribes nurtured a profound connection to the land that persists today. These cultures and

A bridge spans Olympic's Sol Duc River.

Olympic's high meadows open to glacier views.

their rituals—fishing, hunting, clamming, the dueling feast known as the potlatch—are built on the obscene bounty of resources shed by the Olympics.

Many tribes explored the interior long ago, but Euro-American explorers came relatively late. The late 1800s saw several thwarted by the immensity and density of Olympic's wild interior, but in 1889 the six men of the infamous Press Expedition (so called because it was rallied by Seattle's then-largest paper) embarked on a harrowing six-month journey full of busted boats and dead donkeys. The expedition started up the Elwha River and exited the Quinault, and the tales of this great expedition would later play a pivotal role in solidifying Olympic's reputation as a fierce roadless wilderness in need of preservation—especially once logging concerns began eating away at old-growth forests.

In the early twentieth century, awareness grew that forests are worth more than their chopped and whittled products, and Theodore Roosevelt declared Olympic a national monument in 1907; it gained additional protections and became a park in 1938. Its ascension to UNESCO World Heritage Site expanded its esteem, although the shuttered mills remain a sore spot for many in the timber towns on the edges of the park.

Olympic remains the rare park with no road crossing its interior, preserving a raw wilderness character despite its relative proximity to Seattle. The best way to absorb it is to chart a route on foot across 600 miles of painstakingly maintained trails. It's the rare place where it's possible to go from sea to summit and back all on foot, if you have the time and energy. But you need only a few short steps on a day hike to feel transformed.

ZONE OF INTEREST

Staircase Entrance and Area

Though Olympic National Park welcomes millions of visitors annually, only a modest 5 percent venture into the Staircase region. The reason? It's not the park's grandest spectacle or its most accessible corridor. But its remote location and lesser infrastructure mean that Staircase is less frequented than big draws like Hurricane Ridge or the Hoh Rainforest.

The region derives its unique name from an early and ambitious 1890 expedition led by US Army Lieutenant Joseph P. O'Neil. Upon encountering a particularly steep canyon and an impassably

The Skokomish River tumbles toward the Staircase entrance.

steep rock bluff while following the Skokomish River, they built a cedar staircase to get over it. This "devil's staircase" is long gone, replaced by the Shady Lane Trail.

All Olympic's biodiversity is on display here: It's not uncommon to find Roosevelt elk grazing in the meadows or to spot a black bear foraging in the distance. And a network of trails offers options for all abilities.

The relatively easy 2-mile Staircase Rapids Loop Trail follows the northern bank of the Skokomish River, guiding visitors through lush forests and past the foaming rapids that give the trail its name.

Shady Lane Trail is another gentle, beginner-friendly option that travels 1.9 miles round-trip with great views of long Lake Cushman. During springtime, it comes alive with a profusion of wildflowers.

For those seeking a more strenuous journey, North Fork Skokomish River Trail stretches over 13 miles, leading hikers deep into the heart of the Olympic wilderness. It heads up to First Divide, a high pass with views of craggy peaks, and can connect to the Duckabush River Trail for longer treks.

The challenging 14.2-mile round-trip Flapjack Lakes Trail delivers unparalleled beauty for those willing to undertake it. The

journey ends at the Flapjack Lakes, twin alpine lakes surrounded by grassy meadows and spiny, snowcapped peaks.

HIKES

Grand Ridge Trail

Hurricane Ridge draws the hordes, but Grand Ridge is the highest continuous trail in the park, characterized by 360-degree panoramic views, subalpine meadows, and rugged mountain terrain for its entire length. It runs 7.5 miles point to point from Obstruction Pass to Deer Park, but given the logistics it is best accomplished as a 15-mile out and back. It sees a tiny fraction of Hurricane's crowds, especially if you begin at Deer Park.

Grand Ridge commences at Deer Park, one of Olympic's more secluded entrances. From the town of Port Angeles, head south on US 101. Soon after, make a right onto Deer Park Road, a steep and winding route. The 18-mile drive up is an adventure in itself, with narrow lanes and switchbacks, but your reward awaits immediately at the top: the trailhead and a serene campground are already perched at tree line near 5,400 feet.

When fog clears, views of Vancouver Island can be seen from Grand Ridge.

From Deer Park, you ascend to Grand Ridge, walking the spine of the Olympic Peninsula. The landscape alternates between alpine and subalpine ecosystems, meandering through vast meadows sprinkled with wildflowers in a riot of colors during late spring and summer. Early on, watch for the delicate fronds of the maidenhair fern in any season. As you progress, the terrain gets rockier, and vegetation takes on a stunted form.

Steep ridges fall off on both sides of the route. On one side, the trail offers panoramic views of the Olympic Mountains, while the other side boasts vistas stretching to the Strait of Juan de Fuca and, on clear days, to Canada's Vancouver Island.

At 5.5 miles in, Mount Olympus roars into view, goading you on the final mile. Near the 6.5-mile mark, detour up empty Elk Mountain for commanding views of the entire peninsula; there's no need to descend to Obstruction Point unless you've parked a shuttle car.

Cape Alava Loop

The mountains give way to the vast Pacific throughout Olympic, and the Cape Alava Loop offers a two-for-one stunner that takes you through primeval forest to reach the crashing Pacific and back, sprinkling in a bit of ancient Native history.

The adventure begins at the Ozette Ranger Station. From Port Angeles, head west on US 101. Around 20 miles past Forks, turn left onto Hoko-Ozette Road. This winding lane will take you directly to the trailhead after roughly 21 miles. An ample parking lot and the ranger station await, making it easy to kick-start your coastal escapade.

Cape Alava Loop's initial stretch introduces you to a dense, verdant rain forest, with boardwalks navigating through cedar, spruce, and fern-laden undergrowth. The scent of damp earth and the distant roar of the ocean guide you onward.

Soon, the dense canopy gives way to the rugged Olympic coastline, where rocky outcrops stand sentinel against crashing waves. Tide pools dot the landscape, and vast stretches of sandy beaches, punctuated by driftwood, beckon for mid-hike breaks.

Cape Alava is near the northwesternmost tip of the United States.

At Wedding Rocks, between Cape Alava and Sand Point, Makah ancestors etched petroglyphs of whales, hunters, and boats into rock using bone and stone. Centuries old, these accounts relay the daily lives of the Makah, and they remain sacred and demand respect—observe but don't touch.

Wend southward along the beach toward Sand Point. These are some of the most scenic beaches on the Washington coast, offering abundant tide pools along the way. These little microcosms fill with starfish, anemones, and the occasional crab playing hide and seek. Additionally, keep an eye out for otters frolicking in the surf, orange-billed oyster catchers picking at shellfish clinging to rocks, or, if luck is on your side, a distant whale spout on the horizon.

As you loop back, the beach nearing Sand Point Trail offers breathtaking views, especially during sunset when sea-stack monoliths create hulking silhouettes against a sky streaked in reds, pinks, and oranges in the last golden light.

The combined loop, taking you from the Ozette Ranger Station to Cape Alava and then returning via Sand Point, spans roughly 9 miles. While navigating the coastal section, especially around areas like Wedding Rocks, being aware of tide timings is crucial. High tide can make certain stretches impassable. Always consult a tide chart before heading out.

There are designated wilderness camping sites along the coast as well as dispersed camping. However, a permit, obtainable from the Ozette Ranger Station or the park's visitor center, is mandatory.

The boardwalks can get slick, especially after rain. The coastal sections, meanwhile, involve a mix of sandy beaches and rocky terrain. Good, grippy hiking boots are indispensable.

HIDDEN GEM

On a sodden February day in Olympic, a cheeky ranger once told me that if all the Sasquatches in the Pacific Northwest gathered for a town hall, it would be in the **Queets Rainforest.** Of all the hallowed mossy rain forests in Olympic, the one lining the wily Queets River is the wildest, most secret, and most inaccessible. The few who go here are guaranteed to experience all the skyscraping trees, chest-tall fields of sword ferns, and misty rapids of all the other more popular rain forests without company.

This is because the glacier-fed Queets River itself puts up a mighty barrier to entry. After bumping down a rough and potholed road (check with the NPS for conditions—it regularly closes from landslides), you'll arrive at the trailhead and immediately must cross the giant Queets River to reach the actual beginning of the trail on the north side of the river, opposite the mouth of the Sams River. This is no small feat: In most months and during periods of rain or high flow, the river is too fast and dangerous. The park advises you not to cross unless the river is flowing at less than 800 cubic feet per second (check online), which usually occurs only in late summer and early fall before the rains come. Even then, a river ford could bring bone-chilling water waist high (it might lower to knee high in the driest years). Bring trekking poles, unbuckle your pack, and prepare for a difficult and dangerous crossing. (Some years there's a marker on the other side to help point you to the trail; other years there isn't.)

Getting to the Queets Rainforest requires a risky river ford.

Once you are on the other side, however, a hushed silence will swallow you into the Queets as you follow 11 miles of mostly flat, unmaintained trail into the forgotten rain forest. Maintenance is nonexistent here, so blowdowns and obstacles are common, and route finding is necessary to work around the forest's reclamation of the trail. Along the way you'll find abandoned homesteads being gulped back by the forest, and at 2.4 miles before Coal Creek, a spur trail leads to reportedly the world's largest Douglas fir. Recent reports suggest the trail is impassable, but knowing you're near it makes the air hum with supernatural energy. You don't have to imagine what it looks like: Other superlative Sitka spruces, western hemlocks, and western red cedars lord over the trail in near-redwood-size proportions.

Lonely campsites exist along the route, especially at mile 4 and at Spruce Bottom at mile 5 (permits required). Bear sign and Roosevelt elk droppings litter the trail; don't be surprised if you see them, but keep your distance. Beyond Spruce Bottom you'll encounter a virgin rain forest that could be the most untouched in the park, but beyond that the trail dies in the mess left by 2014's Paradise fire. Return the way you came, steel yourself to make the crossing again, and give Bigfoot a high-five if you see her.

Petrified Forest National Park

Arizona | nps.gov/pefo | Visitation: 520,491

In the desert badlands of northeastern Arizona near the border of New Mexico, one national park features literal gems strewn everywhere, sparkling in the sun. They lie in a 150,000-acre jumbled desert under the open sky, tiny as thimbles and big as felled tree trunks. Many of them were tree trunks.

Petrified Forest likely holds the world's largest stores of mineralized wood, but it's the story of two ecosystems overlaid on top of each other, separated by millennia and the transmogrifying power of the earth. Around 225 million years ago, during the Late Triassic period, the arid desert we see now was located near the equator and enjoyed a subtropical climate closer to present-day Costa Rica. A massive river system bigger than any known today dominated the region, its braided channels choked with giant insects, amphibians, and crocodilians. Ferns and horsetails lined the banks, and a canopy of hulking trees spread from there—conifers, cycads, and gingkoes reaching 200 feet into the sky.

When trees along the riverbanks died, they fell into rivers swollen with sediment, which would carry these logs downstream. The dense, mineral-laden waters prevented the wood from decomposing as it normally would. Instead, the logs became buried in sediment.

Over time, groundwater seeped into the logs. This water was rich in silica, derived from volcanic ash. The silica molecules began to bond with the molecules in wood cells, and over the course of millions of years, the silica crystallized into quartz, replacing the wood's organic material. This process, known as permineralization, preserved the original structure of the wood, including the cells and growth rings, in sharp detail.

Different minerals in the groundwater—iron, manganese, carbon—gave the quartz crystals different colors. Iron oxides resulted in red, yellow, and orange colors; manganese produced blues, purples, and blacks; and carbon contributed to blacks and grays.

Over millions of years, the earth's crust shifted and uplifted. Erosion washed away the softer rock layers, revealing the petrified wood below. The petrified logs in the Petrified Forest National Park are the remains of those ancient trees, turned to stone by time, water, and geology.

Entire logs have been turned to stone in the Petrified Forest.

Humans predated the desertification of the area: Paleoindians of the Folsom, Clovis, and other cultures followed bison and mammoths into the rich, cool, rain-fed grasslands that dominated this area 13,000 to 6,000 years ago. Though the land dried out, later residents learned to farm maize. By 500 BC, the petrified forest became a desert environment, but Ancestral Puebloans adapted to cultivate squash, corn, and beans. They built great stone pueblos aboveground and spun intricate pottery before a long drought in the 1400s forced them to join nearby Zuni and Hopi settlements. The Spaniard Francisco Vasquez de Coronado was the first European to

set foot here, shortly before being stymied by the Grand Canyon hundreds of miles to the west.

It didn't take long for ol' Teddy Roosevelt to take notice of this spectacular place and declare it a national monument in 1906; it got upgraded in 1962. Historic Route 66 once ran through, bringing road trippers and stranding at least one of them (a rusting 1932 Studebaker sits snug in the dirt on park grounds). We've since assigned colorful, evocative names to many of the park's main attractions: Painted Desert, Crystal Forest, Black Forest, Rainbow Forest. Each is festooned with stained crystals in smoky quartz,

Some perceive Blue Forest's logs as having a bluish tint.

purple amethyst, yellow citrine, jasper, and opal. Treasure literally coats the ground.

But if you're thinking of taking some for yourself—don't. I'm not being a humorless scold: Beyond wrecking the natural beauty of the place, taking even a grain of petrified wood is rumored to bring a curse of bad luck. Over decades the park has received hundreds of pieces of returned petrified wood and crystals in the mail, many with handwritten notes of apology and declarations of misfortune.

Letters have come from as far away as the Bronx, Italy, and Germany. But because rangers and scientists have no real way of knowing the provenance of any of these rocks (and coverage of the curse typically causes an upswing in returned rocks and letters), they cannot reliably return them to their original place. Instead, all returned rocks end up on a "conscience pile" within the park, a separate island for orphaned stones.

HIKES

Blue Forest

The Blue Forest Trail's unofficial status keeps its 3-mile round-trip, moderate-elevation tread off most hikers' radars. This trail has no marked route, so you'll need to rely on landmarks, a compass, or GPS to navigate.

Find the trailhead off a dirt road 0.5 mile north of Blue Mesa Road. There's a small dirt pullout to park, then head east down into the badlands. As you descend, you'll start to see the namesake stark blue-gray badlands, a result of the high concentration of bentonite clay, a volcanic ash derivative, in the soil. Over the millennia, weathering and erosion have carved these badlands into intricate ravines and sharp ridges.

The petrified logs here have a blueish tint, blending in with the surroundings. As you tread carefully on the uneven terrain, you may also spot fragments of petrified wood scattered around, some gleaming flakes of polished quartz. The palette goes beyond the blue: You can spot layers of purples, grays, reds, and oranges, especially under the shifting sun.

It's worth reinforcing that you should refrain from collecting petrified wood or any other natural and cultural artifacts, and tread lightly to minimize impact on this delicate environment.

Blue Forest's off-the-map status affords you the luxury of enjoying the beauty of the park in relative solitude, but with that comes the responsibility of taking extra precautions. Make sure you have enough water, sun protection, and possibly a downloaded map or a GPS device, as cell reception can be spotty to nonexistent.

Red Basin Clam Beds

Witness an ancient seabed that once flourished with life on a jaunt through the Red Basin Clam Beds. This trail also isn't officially marked, offering solitude and a sense of exploration away from the usual tourist routes provided you're prepared and comfortable with some route finding across its moderate 3 miles.

The trailhead is located off a dirt road north of Pintado Point. There's no established trail, so you'll need a good map or GPS and a solid understanding of how to navigate with them. The route quickly drops into the Red Basin, a colorful depression that lives up to its name with washes of vibrant red and orange sediment.

As you explore the basin, you'll come across a high concentration of fossilized clam beds. These are remnants from the Late Triassic period, 210 to 220 million years ago, when this area was a vast river system that emptied into a shallow sea. Over time, sediment buried the clams, meticulously preserving them as detailed fossils.

Throughout the hike, you'll also see scattered chunks of petrified wood in varying sizes, remnants of the trees that once lined the riverbanks. The contrast between the red clay and the multicolored petrified wood pops brightly, making for striking photography.

Martha's Butte

This lesser-known trek to an isolated butte in Petrified Forest National Park offers an excellent opportunity to step off the beaten path and explore the park's quieter side. It's 2 to 3 miles round-trip, depending on how much you choose to explore, and the elevation gain is relatively minimal, making this a suitable adventure for hikers of different levels.

The trailhead for Martha's Butte can be found off Petrified Forest Road, north of Newspaper Rock. It's an off-trail, cross-country route, but the butte itself is a clear landmark that's visible from the start, so it's hard to get lost.

The route takes you across rolling grasslands dotted with scattered hunks of petrified wood. Look closely, and you may spot multicolored fragments shining with quartz crystals of

Red Basin is filled with fossilized clam beds.

In addition to petrified wood, you can observe petroglyphs and ancient village ruins near Martha's Butte.

rainbow-like diversity. Wildflowers add dashes of color to the landscape in the spring, and park wildlife often frequents this less-traveled area.

Martha's Butte itself is a dramatic sight rising from the grasslands. As you approach, you'll see petroglyphs made by Ancestral Puebloans. The presence of these petroglyphs suggests that this place held significance for those who lived here long ago, though the precise meaning and usage has been lost to time.

Another defining feature of Martha's Butte is the remnants of a prehistoric village site at its base. This archaeological site offers a fascinating glimpse into the past, and the park is working on further archaeological investigations to learn more about the people who once inhabited this region. Observe from a distance and take care not to disturb anything.

Onyx Bridge

The Onyx Bridge hike delves into a remote section of Petrified Forest National Park over 4.5 miles on an off-trail, minimally marked route. Good orienteering skills, a map, and a reliable GPS device are necessary.

To access the trailhead, travel along the park road to the Painted Desert Inn. To the north is the signed trailhead for Onyx Bridge. From here, you follow the trail, which descends steeply into Lithodendron Wash.

Proceed past petrified logs scattered in the foreground—remnants of a Late Triassic forest. In the background, badlands resist centuries of wind and water erosion to rise in banded colors.

The centerpiece of the hike is the Onyx Bridge itself—a large, intact petrified log spanning a small gully. This "bridge" is an impressive 30-foot-long specimen of a petrified Araucarioxylon tree, lying in the path of a dried-up riverbed. Despite the name, the Onyx Bridge is not composed of onyx. Early explorers mistook the colorful petrified wood for onyx, and the name stuck. Resist the

The 30-foot log at Onyx Bridge is approximately 210 million years old.

temptation to climb on the Onyx Bridge itself in order to preserve the structure.

HIDDEN GEM

It seems a bit hat-on-a-hat to mention a hidden gem in a park literally made of hidden gems, but when in doubt, ask a ranger. The park maintains a detailed **guide to off-the-beaten-path hikes** in a physical binder at the visitor center. Ask, and a ranger can guide you through a veritable bible of off-trail, unofficial hikes that wind through empty corners of Petrified Forest. Photos help describe the routes, and because Petrified Forest National Park consists of mostly open terrain punctuated with easily identifiable landmarks, it's an exceptional place to dip a toe into off-trail exploration.

Craggy Pinnacles is California's newest national park.

Pinnacles National Park

California | nps.gov/pinn | Visitation: 341,220

Small, unassuming Pinnacles National Park lies a hundred miles south of San Francisco in the Salinas Valley. Yosemite takes twice as long to get to but sees sixteen times the visitors. Pinnacles' landscape isn't as iconic, but solitude and quiet come easy on the 32 miles of trail clustered in its 26,000 acres of pointy volcanic spires, talus caves, and cliffs. Founded in 2013, it's the newest of California's parks.

The park's craggy landscape owes its existence to the ancient Neenach Volcano that erupted and formed some 23 million years ago near present-day Lancaster, California. The park is not located near Lancaster anymore: Over millennia, the San Andreas Fault shunted this colossal volcanic remnant to where it now sits, 195 miles away in the Salinas Valley. Erosion whittled the soft, brittle tuff and rhyolite of the Gabilan Range into the profusion of boulders, rock walls, and columns that now dominate the terrain.

In this geological maze, hikers can thread their way through narrow gorges, beneath monoliths and spires, and through bat-filled caves that plunge them into profound darkness. In the heat of the day, these caves offer a retreat from the sun.

Pinnacles is home to an array of species perfectly adapted to its chaparral, woodland, and riparian environments. California condors, a gigantic vulture-like bird of prey with a 10-foot wingspan, represent a notable success story. Once near extinction, these birds found sanctuary among the park's crags and pinnacles, and while they exist in limited numbers (twenty-six or so), their large size and penchant for riding thermals high above in search of carrion means you have a decent chance of seeing them anywhere in the park. On the ground, the Townsend's big-eared bat and 12 other species flit in the talus caves, and tarantulas and kangaroo rats bounce around the scrubby terrain. Look closely at the flowers: More bees exist here than anywhere else—about 450 species in total.

The Chalon and Mutsun peoples were the park's first known human inhabitants, leaving behind a rich record of their existence through petroglyphs and bedrock mortars going back thousands of years. Spanish missionaries showed up in the 1700s, bringing diseases and displacing the Natives.

When to visit: The turn of the season from winter to spring sees a bloom of wildflowers across the park. Fields of larkspur, poppy, and buckwheat paint the park with strokes of color. The summer, however, can be unforgiving, with temperatures soaring above 100 degrees. Autumn and winter are quieter seasons, a time to appreciate the park in its more subtle moods, though it can be wet and chilly.

North Chalone's summit is the highest point in the park.

Pinnacles National Park offers a range of trails that cover varied terrain, from creekside walks to challenging climbs. While popular routes can get busy, especially on weekends, several less-frequented hikes can take you into the park's quieter corners.

Remember that many trails in Pinnacles are exposed, with little to no shade, so bring plenty of water, sun protection, and a map or GPS device for off-trail routes. Some routes might involve scrambling over rocks or through tight spaces. The park service installed metal railings and chopped steps into stone in certain places to help steady hikers.

HIKES

South Wilderness Trail

The South Wilderness Trail at Pinnacles National Park is a gem tucked away in the park's more secluded southern reaches. Begin your journey at the Chaparral trailhead on the west side of the park.

There's a parking area here, but it can fill up quickly on busy days. Aim to arrive early in the morning for a better chance at securing a spot and to beat the heat, particularly during summer.

The route is 7.7 miles round-trip and brings 600 feet of elevation gain, making it a good option for a day hike. You can, however, extend your hike by adding other trails if you're feeling up to the challenge.

The South Wilderness Trail takes you through open grasslands and chaparral, showcasing a different side of Pinnacles National Park. Keep an eye out for wildflowers in the spring. This trail also presents an excellent opportunity for bird-watching: You may spot species like the California quail or, if you're lucky, the California condor soaring above.

Bring plenty of water as there's no source along the trail and the area can get hot, especially during the summer months. Wear a hat and sunblock, as the trail has minimal shade.

North Chalone Peak Trail

The North Chalone Peak Trail climbs to the park's highest point, adorned with an abandoned fire lookout. You will begin in the park's volcanic heart before departing for the golden hills of the chapparal.

Start at the Bear Gulch Day Use Area and begin hiking on the Moses Spring to Rim Trail Loop, which takes you to Bear Gulch Reservoir, a good spot to tank up before your climb.

From the reservoir, take the Chalone Peak Trail, which leads you on a steep climb toward the peak. Cross a wire pig fence installed to keep out the invasive pests. The last section of the trail, right before the peak, is a particularly steep section of service road, but stick with it and you'll gain 360-degree views of the Salinas Valley, Bear Valley, and the Farallon Islands on a clear day.

The trail is 8.4 miles round-trip. Although it's a challenging hike, it's feasible to complete it in one day if you're in good physical condition and start early. The elevation gain for this trail is around 2,040 feet. The most significant elevation gain happens as you're ascending toward the peak.

Balconies Cave to High Peaks Loop

Bring a headlamp for this one. On an exciting and moderately strenuous trail, you'll scramble through the dark, narrow passages of the talus cave and emerge on the other side of the park to broad vistas of the pinnacles in the High Peaks region.

The hike begins at the Old Pinnacles trailhead, where you'll find a parking area and basic facilities. It's advisable to get there early in the morning to secure a parking spot.

From the Old Pinnacles trailhead, take the Balconies Trail, which will lead you to the Balconies Cave. To traverse the cave, you will need a light source and comfort with mild, fun scrambling. *Note:* The cave can sometimes be closed due to flooding or to protect the bat populations that live inside, so it's a good idea to check with the park beforehand.

Watch for bats deep inside Balconies Cave.

After passing through the Balconies Cave, follow the trail up a steep incline and several switchbacks toward the High Peaks.

This loop's 9 miles and 1,500 feet of elevation gain make it a full day's adventure—you'll want to budget as much as you can to account for time spent exploring the cave.

The tallest trees on earth occupy less than 5 percent of their former range.

Redwood National Park

California | nps.gov/redw | Visitation: 409,105

When you are among the redwoods, it's hard not to feel like you've stepped out of time into a lost world inhabited by ginormous, ancient creatures beyond understanding. And while you won't see any dinosaurs, the sheer mass of the living things around you in this mysterious world feels positively Jurassic.

It is: *Sequoia sempervirens* (Latin for "ever-living") come from the Jurassic era, and dinosaurs once roamed through the redwood forests that once dominated the continent. Hollywood took this literally, filming *The Lost World: Jurassic Park* here decades after George Lucas used it to embody Endor, the forested Ewok planet of *Return of the Jedi*. And while the park does draw its fair share of starstruck location seekers, they concentrate in specific areas. Large tracts of the forest are still full of hushed, empty beauty.

The park is a patchwork of state and national parks managed together: Redwood National Park and Del Norte Coast, Jedediah Smith, and Prairie Creek Redwoods State Parks combine to cover 139,000 acres. It's an area marked by deep silence, where misty fog clings to the surface of the deeply grooved bark and feeds the redwoods through their leaves. The earthy scent of fern and moss mingles with the brine of the nearby Pacific.

Redwoods are holdovers from an era when towering trees dominated. Their historical spread contracted after the dinos died, but 20 million years ago they still covered 2 million acres of California and Oregon, their range hugging the coast to access the fog that keeps them damp and growing slowly to extreme sizes over 2,000 years. Encroaching settlers and a thirst for raw material to support burgeoning California cities shrank the forest to its present size (about 3 percent of its range at the time of westward expansion).

Redwoods have long been a battleground for the warring factions of extractive and conservation interests, and the trees' survival is a testament to the result of impassioned advocacy informing policy. The trees won decisive protection with their ascension to national park status in 1968 and integration with state redwood parks in 1994.

The sense of mystery that pervades any time spent under a redwood has concrete origins. We still don't know why they grow as tall or live as long as they do, though we have a few intriguing clues. Foot-thick bark and high tannin content in the wood wards insects away, eliminates disease, and renders insect damage minor. That armor also protects them from fire, and their foliage is out of reach for all but the hottest blazes (which unfortunately are more common in our age of climate

Banana slugs can reach 10 inches long.

change). They can grow from a seed dropped from a cone or sprout as a clone from fallen specimens. Unfortunately, the bigger they are, the harder they fall: The lack of a taproot and shallow root systems (often no deeper than 10 feet) make these 300-foot giants vulnerable to toppling from high winds. This is how most redwoods die.

The biodiversity of the park flows out from the big trees and connects to countless other large conifers like Doug firs and western hemlocks as well as the sorrels, ferns, and mushrooms that regenerate and recycle the soil layer. In sprawling meadows you'll find Roosevelt elk, a particularly large subspecies named for the president who did much to preserve America's wild spaces. Black bears, bobcats, and river otters hide out here. Coho salmon trace their cyclical journey through wild rivers like the Smith—the only intact, undisturbed waterway in California. They're chased by seals, sea lions, and orcas. Farther out gray whales, humpbacks, and porpoises breach the choppy waters.

The native peoples of the region—the Yurok, Tolowa, Karuk, Chilula, and others—recognized the spiritual significance of these trees long before European settlers arrived. To them, the redwoods remain entities of profound respect, serving both practical and sacred purposes.

The best time to visit the park is from late spring to early fall, though it is open year-round. In summer, that crucial fog drifts in from the Pacific Ocean and provides the trees with much-needed moisture, lending the park a mystical, otherworldly aura. In other seasons, as much as 100 inches of rain falls on the park.

Redwoods is the rare park that allows access to all its magic from season to season, offering incentive to avoid summer and the crowds it brings. Marquee locations like Fern Canyon and Tall Trees Grove now require limited reservations from May to September. As always, obtaining a backpacking permit any time of year is the surest way to spend some alone time with the giants.

HIKES

Hope Creek/Ten Taypo Loop

Sometimes profound hiking experiences come in small packages. The compact yet captivating Hope Creek/Ten Taypo Loop clocks in at 3.5 miles, but it packs a dizzying array of natural wonders on its relatively modest footprint.

To access the Hope Creek/Ten Taypo Loop, head toward the Prairie Creek Redwoods State Park sector. From the town of Orick, take US 101 north for 6 miles until you reach the well-marked exit for Newton B. Drury Scenic Parkway. Turn right and continue for a couple of miles, looking for a sign indicating the trailhead. Parking is available alongside the road.

From the moment you step onto the trail, towering redwoods greet you, and an intricate maze of ferns, mushrooms, and fallen needles makes for a cushiony carpet that complements the skyward aspirations of the redwoods.

As you traverse the Hope Creek segment, you'll wind through many groves of redwoods filtering down shafts of sunlight through the canopy. Small, burbling Hope Creek accompanies you for parts of the hike. Transition to the Ten Taypo section, and the landscape starts to undulate, introducing you to an array of creeks and modest elevation changes. Some of the trees along the route are over a thousand years old. Keep an eye out for bright rhododendrons and other blooming species adorning the forest floor in spring. This area is home to diverse wildlife, including banana slugs, black-tailed deer, and perhaps Roosevelt elk (the largest subspecies of this ungulate).

Redwood Creek Trail

The Redwood Creek Trail is an immersive journey into pristine Redwood National Park, offering an up-close experience with countless champion redwoods and the opportunity to spend the night surrounded by these silent giants.

The trail follows Redwood Creek, meandering through a mosaic of old-growth redwood forests, riparian ecosystems, and alluvial flats. Expect to see towering redwoods, fern-draped undergrowth, and wildlife such as Roosevelt elk, black bears, and various bird species. The clear waters of Redwood Creek are also home to salmon and steelhead during specific times of the year. The world's tallest tree, 380-foot Hyperion, stands somewhere off this trail, its location a secret to protect it from crowds or others who might harm it.

It's 16 miles round-trip, but there are opportunities for shorter hikes, and with minimal elevation gain, most hikers can make short work of it.

Hyperion, the world's tallest tree, lies somewhere in Redwood Creek.

The trail begins near the town of Orick, at the end of Bald Hills Road. From the trailhead, follow the well-marked trail as it descends gradually toward Redwood Creek. You will start to see the colossal trunks of redwoods after a mile—you can't miss 'em. After 4 miles, you will cross the first of several footbridges. Continue to follow the trail along Redwood Creek.

At around 8 miles, you'll reach the Tall Trees Grove, a remote stand containing some of the tallest trees on earth. Here, you can explore the grove or find a spot to rest and enjoy your surroundings before making the return journey. But if you score a camping permit from the park's visitor center, prepare for a humbling evening searching for brilliant stars peeking out from the highest canopy.

A few backcountry sites are available all along Redwood Creek Trail, with the most coveted in the area around Tall Trees Grove. You might not see Hyperion itself here, but you'll swear you can feel its presence nearby.

Coastal Trail

Hugging the wild edges of northern California's coastline lies a trail where two iconic landscapes of Redwoods collide: the soaring trees and the craggy, untamed Pacific coast. The 35-mile Coastal Trail threads the needle between sky-reaching forests and empty shores.

This pathway offers multiple segments varying in length and difficulty. A popular starting point is the Kuchel Visitor Center near Orick. From US 101, take the exit for Orick and head toward the coast, following signs to the visitor center. There, you'll find ample parking and trail information.

The Coastal Trail ping-pongs through the two ecosystems throughout: One moment you're walking through cathedral-like groves of ancient redwoods; the next, the sun-dappled canopy opens up to reveal the expansive Pacific Ocean. Cliffside vistas give sweeping views of craggy rocks and swirling tide pools below, while stretches of sandy beaches provide opportunities to stop, stretch out, and contemplate at the water's edge (or swim, if you're exceptionally brave).

Redwood state and national parks also preserve miles of unspoiled Pacific coast.

Highlights include Enderts Beach, a pristine, secluded area perfect for picnicking and tide pool exploration; lush, prehistoric Fern Canyon (featured in movies like *Jurassic Park*); and Gold Bluffs Beach, a marquee spot for watching Roosevelt elk graze as the sun sets the sky afire. Several campsites exist along the route, with Nickel Creek and Gold Bluffs Beach as two of the best for beach-bum backpackers. These sites require permits, so plan in advance.

Many segments of the Coastal Trail can be tackled as day hikes, like the Trillium Falls Trail loop or the hike to Enderts Beach and back. The coastal climate can be unpredictable, so be prepared for sudden changes including rain and wind. For portions of the trail near water, it's essential to consult tide charts to ensure you're not cut off or cliffed out by rising waters.

HIDDEN GEM

In the deepest, most unseen stretches of Redwood National Park, the world's tallest tree hides from the eyes of both the curious and those who would harm it. Named **Hyperion** for one of the twelve Titans of Greek mythology, this entity is no god, but its proportions could certainly fool you. Standing at an astonishing 380.3 feet high, Hyperion is the tallest tree known to humankind, and it has existed since before you or any relative you can name.

Even among coast redwoods, a species famed for its extraordinary height, Hyperion stands superlative. The tree is as tall as a thirty-eight-story building, surpassing the Statue of Liberty from heel to torch. Hyperion's crown contains as many as 550 million leaves, and it's the seventh-largest tree in the park.

The discovery of Hyperion is as fascinating as the tree itself. In 2006, naturalists Chris Atkins and Michael Taylor found it during one of their many forays into the park. Armed with laser rangefinders, they measured it from the base to the top. A climber who scaled the tree later that year confirmed the results.

The location of Hyperion was a closely guarded secret, with only a select few officially knowing its exact whereabouts. This secrecy is for a purpose: Hyperion's status as a natural marvel attracts the powerful motivation and destructive force of human curiosity. Foot traffic can compact the soil, hindering root growth. Carved initials can damage the bark. In an ideal world, Hyperion would stand alone, unmarred by the masses. But in recent years, as word of its exact location spread, many people have found their way to the tree, carving illegal trails, threatening the delicate surrounding ecosystem, and leaving behind piles of garbage and human waste.

To curb the risk, the park service now patrols regularly and prevents anyone from coming within a mile of Hyperion. Doing so could earn trespassers a $5,000 fine and up to six months in jail.

If risking harm to an organism that has persisted through countless summers and winters, storms and fires, and earthquakes and droughts isn't enough to deter you, consider this: Most experts regard Hyperion as a rather unimpressive specimen at ground level, and the human eye can't see more than 150 feet of the tree. Look for more impressive ground-level specimens in Tall Trees Grove, and remind yourself that Hyperion is somewhere out there safe, taller than everything else in the world.

Rocky Mountain National Park

Colorado | nps.gov/romo | Visitation: 4,115,837

The 3,000-mile spine of the continent we call the Rocky Mountains stretches from Alaska into Mexico and cradles several national parks. So why does this park in northern Colorado get to hog the name?

Being the "Most High" seems reason enough. With more than sixty peaks over 12,000 feet, the highest paved through road in North America, and alpine tundra above 11,400 feet occupying more than a quarter of the park, Rocky (yes, locals call it that, like the boxer or the squirrel) has more rarified thin air in its 415 square miles than any other park in the system. It's an iconic symbol of the American West renowned for mountain vistas, diverse ecosystems, and abundant wildlife—and since it's all a stone's throw from Denver, it's maybe the easiest way to kiss the sky.

The park's elevation ranges from 7,860 feet to 14,259 feet, encompassing a vast range of environments. The lower montane ecosystem consists of ponderosa pine forests and grassy knolls, and is home to elk and mule deer. Moving up in altitude, the subalpine ecosystem is filled with spruce-fir forests and supports creatures like black bears and bighorn sheep (and nonnative mountain goats). Above tree line, the alpine tundra hosts mosses, forbs, and flowers adapted to its poor soils and harsh, windy, cold conditions. Here, unique mammals like the pika and marmot whistle the day away and hoard food for winter under boulders, while birds of prey hunt for them overhead. The grouse-like ptarmigan never leaves this zone, turning white with the snow and shuffling through the drifts in feathered booties. In marshes and wet meadows, especially on the west side, you can see moose.

(Wolves are on the way, too: In a controversial decision that will likely get tied up in years of litigation and bureaucracy, Colorado voters recently approved wolf reintroduction on the western slope of the state.)

Geology here boils out of a long, dynamic history. In brief: Over 1.8 billion years ago, the area was composed of gneiss and schist. Then, 1.4 billion years ago, an upwelling of magma intruded into the older rock, forming granite. Around 70 million years ago, uplift raised the Rocky Mountains, and during the last ice age, glaciers molded the mountainous terrain, creating U-shaped valleys and sharp arêtes.

A bull elk in rut bugles in Moraine Park at Rocky Mountain National Park.

For at least 10,000 years, the region served as a cultural crossroads for Native American tribes, including the Ute and Arapaho. Though they probably didn't spend the year in the brutal, resource-starved interior, they hunted and gathered on its fringes and established the trail route over the peaks that would become Trail Ridge Road. Later, in the mid-nineteenth century, Euro-Americans began to explore the area, primarily prospectors and homesteaders. Brief gold rushes quickly flamed out, leaving tools, implements, and makeshift towns to recede into the landscape. After decades of local advocacy, the park was officially established on January 26, 1915.

It's now the fourth-most visited national park and often feels it. From late May to late October, visitors must reserve their spot on a timed-entry permit system. It's important to check the park service website prior to visiting, as there are different tiers of access for different parts of the park, and the policy could undergo changes or revisions from year to year.

For hikers, the hassle is worth it. There are over 350 miles of hiking trails, ranging from flat lakeside strolls to challenging peak climbs. Bird-watching (over 270 species), picnicking, fishing, horseback riding, stargazing, and a wide range of technical climbing thrills casuals and experts alike. In winter, loads of people defy bone-chilling cold with activities like snowshoeing and cross-country and backcountry skiing. At 14,259 feet, Longs Peak is the tallest in the park and a famed 14er, but its status as a popular crucible for a wide range of visitors (many unprepared) makes the crowded Keyhole route hard to recommend (unless you possess the climbing skill or time to avoid it and go for a more obscure route).

Rocky seduces the REI hordes every weekend of the year, whether they come from Boulder or Boston or Bangalore. Spending a permitted night in the backcountry is the best way to give 'em the slip. But it's a credit to this high-country kingdom that sharing the experience with crowds barely diminishes its impact. Everyone is smiling, everyone is gasping for air. Enjoy the Rocky Mountain high.

HIKES

Lake Verna via East Inlet Trail

The Lake Verna via East Inlet Trail is a fantastic, lesser-traveled hike in the park that offers an abundance of natural beauty and wildlife.

The trail begins at the East Inlet trailhead near the west-side town of Grand Lake, which is quieter than the bustling Estes Park on the east side of the park. The trailhead has a large parking area with restrooms and picnic tables, but arrive early to ensure a spot.

The trail itself is 14 miles round-trip with an elevation gain of 1,500 feet, making it a moderately challenging hike. Snow can linger into early summer, and fall can bring early snowstorms, so always check current conditions before heading out.

Starting off, you'll cross a bridge over the East Inlet Creek and gradually climb through a beautiful forest of aspens and conifers. Half a mile in, you'll reach Adams Falls, a popular turnaround spot for beginner day hikers and photographers. The trail continues past the falls and climbs along the creek, where you may spot moose and other wildlife in the thickets.

Reserve backcountry sites to spend a night at Lake Verna.

As you hike farther, the trail levels out, and you'll emerge into a broad meadow where elk are often seen grazing. Here, you get the first views of the towering peaks surrounding the valley. The trail continues to meander along the creek, gradually gaining elevation.

At around 5.5 miles, you'll arrive at Lone Pine Lake. The serene, glass-like waters of the lake offer a perfect place for lunch, with the added bonus of potentially fewer people. A backcountry campsite is available here for those who wish to spend the night, but keep in mind that you will need a permit.

From Lone Pine Lake, the trail becomes steeper and more challenging, winding through rugged terrain for another 1.5 miles until you reach Lake Verna, the final destination. Lake Verna's serene waters are nestled at the foot of a dramatic glacial cirque. You can reserve a backcountry campsite at Lake Verna, making it an excellent choice for an overnight trip. Return the way you came.

Lake Nanita via North Inlet Trail

This rewarding, if challenging, route offers hikers the opportunity to experience some of the best that Rocky Mountain National Park has to offer in a big but rewarding trek.

Starting from the North Inlet trailhead, located near the town of Grand Lake on the park's west side, the trail stretches for 24

Lake Nanita ends in a steep valley surrounded by soaring peaks.

miles round-trip. Because of its length and 3,000 feet of elevation gain, this route is generally undertaken as an overnight backpacking trip. It's a bit of a haul to the semi-obscure trailhead, but this means you'll likely see fewer hikers on this trail.

The first few miles of the trail offer a gentle incline, meandering through verdant meadows and stands of aspen and lodgepole pine. You'll pass Summerland Park, a beautiful meadow where elk are frequently spotted. (In fall, this is a great place to watch rutting males battling it out for female favor.) At 3.5 miles in, you'll reach Cascade Falls, a delightful waterfall that cascades down a series of rock steps. If you're looking for a shorter day hike, this is a great spot to return to the trailhead.

As you continue, you'll start a series of switchbacks weaving higher into the mountains. The path will take you through a mixture of forested areas and open meadows, with several creek crossings along the way. There's a good chance of spotting wildlife throughout this portion of the trail, including moose, deer, and a variety of birds.

After 10 miles, you'll reach Lake Nokoni, a beautiful alpine lake nestled in a steep cirque. This makes a great spot for a rest and a snack before you tackle the final stretch to Lake Nanita.

The trail from Lake Nokoni to Lake Nanita climbs steeply over a rocky ridge. Be prepared for a challenging climb, but your efforts will be rewarded when you reach Lake Nanita, the largest and deepest lake in the park. Nestled in a dramatic granite cirque, Lake Nanita's still, sapphire waters offer a spectacular spot to relax and soak in the views.

The North Inlet and Pine Marten campsites along the trail can be used for overnight stays, but they require a permit, so be sure to reserve one in advance. You can return the way you came or, if you're up for an epic backpacking loop, combine this with the Tonahutu Creek Trail for a loop trip that doubles your helping of some of the park's choicest scenery.

Bluebird Lake

Bluebird Lake in the Wild Basin area of Rocky Mountain National Park spans 12.6 moderate miles round-trip, gaining around 2,500 feet in elevation. The trail is best used from June until October. Snow can linger well into the summer and fall, so check current conditions before setting off.

The trail begins at the Wild Basin trailhead, which is located off CO 7. Trundling on a gravel road to reach the trailhead holds back some visitors, but the trailhead has a limited number of parking spaces.

From the trailhead, you'll initially follow a relatively flat trail through a mixed conifer and aspen forest. One mile in, you'll encounter Copeland Falls, a beautiful cascading waterfall that's easily accessible off a spur from the main trail.

Continuing past Copeland Falls, the trail gently ascends through a series of meadows and forests. You'll cross several footbridges over North St. Vrain Creek and continue to Calypso Cascades, a dazzling tiered waterfall 2.5 miles into the hike.

Beyond Calypso Cascades, you'll reach Ouzel Falls, a powerful 40-foot waterfall named after the ouzel birds that are often seen in the area. The trail offers several vantage points to view the falls.

From Ouzel Falls, the trail begins to steepen, climbing through more forest and a series of switchbacks. You'll pass through a

The 13,430-foot Mummy Mountain is the eighth tallest in the park.

high-country riparian ecosystem, home to a variety of bird species, making this a great trail for bird-watching.

Six miles in, you'll reach your destination: Bluebird Lake. Cradled in a bowl beneath Ouzel Peak and Mahana Peak, it's a stunner and a welcome spot to take a break and enjoy a lunch with an incredible view.

Backcountry camping is available by permit at a designated campsite near Bluebird Lake if you wish to extend your hike into an overnight trip.

Mummy Mountain

In the northern part of Rocky Mountain National Park, prominent Mummy Mountain lords over the horizon as the eighth-highest peak in the park. On a 14.7-mile round-trip hike that includes a thigh-busting elevation gain of over 4,500 feet, it's a fierce but quiet 13er that will greatly satisfy experienced, hardy hikers in search of thin air and relative solitude.

Begin at Lawn Lake trailhead, which is located off Old Fall River Road. It's worth noting that snow closes this dirt road from October through late May or early June, so check the park's website for current conditions. Arriving early is advisable as the small lot can fill up quickly.

The trail initially follows the path of the Roaring River, which was created by the Lawn Lake Dam failure in 1982. The first 4.3 miles lead to Lawn Lake, a serene alpine lake surrounded by rugged peaks. The ascent is gradual, passing through mixed pine forests and offering occasional glimpses of the surrounding mountains.

Past Lawn Lake, you'll arrive at a junction with the Black Canyon Trail. Stay to the left to continue toward Mummy Mountain. Here, you'll reach "the Saddle," a flat, tundra-like area nestled between Mummy Mountain and Fairchild Mountain.

At this point, the trail becomes less defined and the true climb begins. You will need to negotiate steep, rocky terrain and some loose scree as you make your way up to the ridge. This part of the hike is off-trail and requires a good level of fitness, as well as some route-finding skills.

Once you reach the ridge, the grade lessens, and you'll continue northwest toward the summit. The top of Mummy Mountain provides jaw-dropping views of the Mummy Range, the greater park, and the eastern plains extending to what feels like Kansas. On a clear day, you might spot hulking Longs Peak in the distance.

The severe altitude ushers in quick weather changes, and afternoon thunderstorms are common in the summer after noon. Start

The mighty Colorado River begins as little more than a mountain stream.

early and be prepared to turn back if the weather worsens—summit fever isn't worth a life-ending zap.

A few backcountry campsites are available along the trail if you wish to turn this into an overnight hike. Make sure to secure a permit in advance.

HIDDEN GEM

The Colorado River, one of the most significant rivers in the western United States, originates in Rocky Mountain National Park in northern Colorado. The **river's headwaters** can be traced to the park's high mountain peaks, where snowmelt collects in small streams that coalesce into the mighty, oft-fought-over river that sustains several metropolises thousands of miles downriver. Imagine: The waterway that keeps carving the Grand Canyon starts as raindrops here.

The Colorado River officially begins at La Poudre Pass, near the park's northern boundary. Here, the river is a piddling, gentle stream meandering through a wetland meadow at an elevation of over 10,000 feet. The pass is part of the Continental Divide, with water to the west flowing into the Colorado River and water to the east making its way to the Mississippi River.

From La Poudre Pass, the nascent Colorado River flows west through the Kawuneeche Valley, a tranquil valley on the park's western side. The Kawuneeche Valley is notable for its wet, marshy meadow habitat flanked by dense coniferous forests—ground zero for hydrophilic moose.

One of the most striking aspects of the river's journey through Rocky Mountain National Park is the dramatic transition in ecosystems. Starting in the alpine tundra, the river descends through subalpine and montane ecosystems, gaining volume with each foot it descends.

The Colorado River Trail in the park provides hikers with a chance to explore the river's headwaters. From the picnic tables at the trailhead, you'll first encounter the river 0.5 mile in on the trail. Meander 3.7 miles to Lulu City, an abandoned mining encampment that once housed as many as 500 miners and hangers-on. At 4.5 miles in, you'll cross a bridge over the Colorado that many count as the headwaters, though the trickle that serves as the official source lies high above.

It's hard to imagine that a 1,450-mile river flowing through seven US states plus two Mexican states and providing water for millions of people and thousands of acres of farmland actually begins as a patch of dirty snow (though it gains much of its volume at its confluence with the Green River in Utah, near Canyonlands National Park). The journey from the high peaks of the Rocky Mountains to its terminus in the Gulf of California is one of the most epic hydrological journeys on the planet. It all starts here.

Saguaro National Park

Arizona | nps.gov/sagu | Visitation: 1,010,906

From Looney Tunes cartoons to classic Westerns, few things conjure the American desert Southwest like the saguaro. Silhouetted against a blazing sun or standing witness as the Roadrunner deadfalls Coyote under yet another boulder, they punctuate the background with their blunted human shapes, looking ready to gossip once all these silly, warring creatures depart the sandy Sonoran mountains.

In a sun-blasted, parched corner of southern Arizona, these massive, columnar cacti take center stage at their eponymous park. They're known to reach ages of 150 to 200 years and heights approaching 50 feet. In the spring, they sprout crowns of radiant white flowers, a brief bloom brilliant enough to serve as the state's flower. By summer, succulent red fruits dangle from the saguaro's limbs, tempting wildlife and humans alike. Extremely sensitive to frost and cold, they only grow in the Sonoran Desert from central Arizona to Sonora, Mexico, at altitudes up to 4,500 feet.

The cactus grows just a few inches in its first decade of life, usually under the protective shade of an ironwood or mesquite. Saguaros don't produce flowers until thirty-five years of age, and arms don't sprout for sixty or seventy-five years. Roots splay out like veins a few inches under the sandy substrate, ready to absorb all the water they can after a rain. When this happens, the slimy flesh below its waxy, needled surface expands like an accordion to hold the liquid. It contracts in times of drought. With so much water constituting its body mass, each vertical foot of a saguaro can weigh up to 80 pounds; a circular, woody internal skeleton helps support this weight. Very old specimens sprout several arms, and a few rare individuals showcase fan-like crests erupting from their tops. Right now, the population is very healthy: As many as 2 million saguaros live in the park, providing food, shelter, and other benefits to many other species.

The park is split into two districts: the Tucson Mountain District to the west, and the Rincon Mountain District to the east. Each showcases a distinct side of the region's geologic story. To the west, the Tucson Mountains arose from violent volcanic activity, their craggy slopes composed of an agglomeration of rock fragments from an ancient eruption. The Rincons, on the east, are an archetype of fault-block mountain building, their steep eastern front and gentle western slope pitched like a table upended on one side.

The park's wide elevation range—2,000 to 9,000 feet—allows for broad biodiversity. Lower desert zones house creosote bushes and mesquite trees, whose roots plumb the depths for precious

Saguaros can live up to 200 years and grow to 50 feet tall.

water. There are twenty-four other species of cactus besides the giant saguaro, most concentrated at lower elevations on the western side of the park. Ascend the Rincons, and the vegetation shifts to include yucca, juniper, and oak. At the highest elevations, coniferous forests drape the landscape, washing most of the taste of the desert away. The sky islands that crown the tallest peaks are particularly unique, topped with lush vegetation thriving in cooler temps and increased moisture.

Since its inception as a national monument in 1933 (it expanded and gained national park status sixty-one years later), Saguaro National Park has safeguarded a unique slice of the Sonoran Desert where Gila monsters (one of two poisonous lizards known to science) and javelinas seek shade beneath ironwood and palo verde trees, and coyotes stalk actual roadrunners (not kidding). Surprisingly, the desert landscape hosts hundreds of species of bees, highlighting the saguaro's role in bolstering desert pollinator diversity.

Bobcats and mountain lions blend into the taupe hills, while the Sonoran Desert tortoise plods slowly through the sands. High in the skies, Harris's hawks fly, while lower to the ground hummingbirds sip nectar from blooming cacti and desert flowers. Over 200 other birds can be found here, as well as rattlesnakes, many species of lizards, black bears, ringtails, eagles, countless insects, and a rare coati.

Humans have always found ways to thrive in this barren place, leaving petroglyphs, pottery shards, and ancient irrigation canals as evidence of their artistry and ingenuity. The Hohokam people, a culture that mysteriously vanished around AD 1450, nurtured corn, beans, and squash with those ancient waterways. Their descendants, the Tohono O'odham, Pima, and Hopi, still hold the saguaro sacred as a symbol of endurance and sustenance. They still make wine, syrups, and jams from the fruit. The Spanish, following Native American trails, introduced livestock to these lands, altering the landscape. Later, American prospectors and pioneers, drawn by the promise of silver, gold, and a new life, left their own imprints.

Today, each half of the park sandwiches urban Tucson, a city of more than a million less than 10 miles away. With such proximity to a major urban area, the park can fill quickly, but hardy hikers who depart the main drives (and bring plenty of water) can still find solitude on over 165 miles of trail within the park. Plenty wind past countless giant saguaros—each of which seems to pose according to its own whimsical personality.

HIKES

Tanque Verde Ridge Trail

The Tanque Verde Ridge Trail is a tough but rewarding route that traverses the eastern Rincon Mountain District of Saguaro National Park. It gives a great overview of the biomes you'll encounter in this section of the Sonoran Desert while peppering in panoramic views.

The trailhead is located at the Lower Javelina Picnic Area, off the Cactus Forest Loop Drive. Initially, the path winds through a

The Tanque Verde Ridge Trail features forests of whimsical saguaros.

classic desert landscape thick with saguaro cacti, cholla, and palo verde trees. A mellow ascent graduates into a sustained climb where ocotillo, agave, and juniper trees start to appear.

Three miles in, you'll reach a saddle that offers sweeping views of Tucson and the Santa Catalina Mountains to the north. This is an excellent spot to catch your breath and refill the tank. If you're looking for a moderate hike, you can turn back from here.

For those looking for a more strenuous journey, continue along the ridge. The trail becomes rockier and steeper. The views get better and better with the effort, offering a panorama of Tucson and the surrounding desert below.

At the 6.9-mile mark, you'll find the Juniper Basin, where a designated backcountry campsite can be used with a permit. This is a great place for overnight backpacking, offering a chance to enjoy the desert's tranquility under a star-studded sky.

Farther on at the 9-mile mark is Tanque Verde Peak, another backcountry campsite. If you've made it this far, congrats: You've crushed a climb of over 3,000 feet. The peak itself is still a little farther, and the view from there is a fitting reward for your efforts.

Over twenty-four other species of cacti live in Saguaro.

The trail continues to the summit of Rincon Peak at 17.8 miles, but most hikers opt to turn back at either Juniper Basin or Tanque Verde Peak.

Sweetwater Trail

This splendid trek is in the Tucson Mountain District of Saguaro National Park. Located a bit outside of the main park, the trail provides hikers with a quieter experience while still offering an impressive exposure to the beauty of the Sonoran Desert.

Find the trailhead at the end of Tortolita Road, a few miles west of the Tucson city limits. The route begins relatively flat as it meanders through a rich forest of saguaro cacti. Barrel cacti, cholla, and other desert-adapted plants speckle the landscape in their shadow. In the spring, the desert bursts into bloom with varied cactus flowers.

The trail marches upward, traversing a few washes with views of Wasson Peak to the west, the highest summit in the Tucson Mountains, an ever-present goal on your constant zigzag. You'll get bonus views over Tucson and the surrounding desert on the return part of this out-and-back hike.

Halfway along the trail, around the 4.5-mile mark, you'll encounter a junction. The trail to the right takes you to the Hugh Norris Trail and to 4,687-foot Wasson Peak. The left trail continues the Sweetwater Trail, which also leads to the peak, albeit on a more challenging route. If you wish to extend your hike, both routes provide opportunities for further exploration and more magnificent views.

Most of the year, the Sweetwater Trail offers little shade or water sources. It's essential to start early, particularly in the summer, and bring plenty of water and sun protection. Hikers should also watch out for snakes, scorpions, and other desert biters.

Douglas Spring Trail to Bridal Wreath Falls

This 5.2-mile round-trip hike in the eastern Rincon Mountain District follows a dry riverbed before it starts climbing into the Rincon Mountains to end at an oasis and the cascading seasonal Bridal Wreath waterfall. The terrain transitions from desert floor to rocky hillside, providing views of saguaro forests, riparian habitats, and rocky cliffs.

From the trailhead, the path gently meanders through the characteristic landscape of saguaro cacti, cholla, and other desert vegetation. Gradually, the terrain becomes rockier, and you'll start a moderate ascent into the foothills of the Rincon Mountains. Along the way, the trail offers panoramic views of the Tucson Valley.

At 2.7 miles into the hike, a side trail will divert you to Bridal Wreath Falls. Depending on recent rainfall, you'll be greeted by a glistening cascade flowing down a rugged cliff face at the end of this spur. Return to the Douglas Springs Trail and head back to the trailhead, or continue on Douglas Spring Trail to reach a namesake campground 6 miles from the trailhead (permit required). Camp here in the chaparral overlooking the desert valley.

Sequoia National Park

California | nps.gov/seki | Visitation: 980,567

You can't look at a giant sequoia for the first time and emerge unchanged. Elephants, blue whales, dinosaurs, megalodons—they all bow down to a single tree. Known as General Sherman, this most massive living organism on earth stands 275 feet tall and measures a staggering 36 feet in diameter at its base. At 2,200 years old, few living things are older. Twigs extend off its trunk bigger than the biggest tree in your city. Its orange bulk glows with power, inevitability, wisdom.

As you enter the heart of Sequoia National Park, the air seems to shimmer when multiple sequoias surround you. Named for Sequoyah, the Native American polymath who invented the Cherokee syllabary, these majestic trees endure, marking time in their wood over millennia. When you look at these living columns reaching into the sky, far more ancient than any human monument, you will be surprised at how insignificant you feel. You will be more surprised that it feels so good.

The origin and evolution of *Sequoiadendron giganteum* goes back to dinosaur times. They debuted on earth over 200 million years ago, and climate shifts altered their distribution significantly over time; today, wild sequoias are found only on the western slopes of the Sierra Nevada in California in a few scattered groves.

Sequoias belong to the cypress family (Cupressaceae), but there are only two other members of the Sequoia genus: taller cousin the coastal redwood (*Sequoia sempervirens*), and the dawn redwood (*Metasequoia glyptostroboides*). All once grew across much of the Northern Hemisphere.

Sequoias are adapted for long survival. Their bark can be up to 2 feet thick and contains a high tannin content, which helps protect the tree from fire, insects, and diseases and helps them live for over 3,000 years. Their cones, while relatively small, can hold up to 200 seeds. Sequoias have some of the smallest seeds among trees: A single ounce can contain up to 91,000 seeds.

Sequoias depend on fire for reproduction. Sequoia cones are sealed with a resin that requires fire to melt it, allowing the cones to open and release their cargo. Heat from fire can cause the cones high up in a tree to open and drop their seeds to the forest floor below. Fires also clear undergrowth and expose bare mineral soil, which is ideal for sequoia seed germination and growth.

While sequoias can reach incredible heights, their root system is relatively shallow, typically extending only 6 to 8 feet deep. However, they spread out sideways up to 250 feet, intertwining with the roots of other sequoias to create an interlocking root system that provides stability and support.

The heart of Muir Grove is the trailless understory where one can walk under these giants.

Sequoias are the largest single organisms on earth.

When it comes to the trees' namesake park, the geography that houses these giants is among the finest in the world. Sequoia is managed along with Kings Canyon, its sister park to the north, although nature doesn't distinguish between the glut of towering Sierra Nevada peaks, deep forests, steep gorges, and raging rivers that spill over the imaginary boundaries between the two. Ancient tectonic forces and icy glaciers sculpted them both, and it's a roll of the dice that Mount Whitney—at 14,505 feet above sea level the highest summit in the park and the contiguous United States—lies on the Sequoia side.

Despite the arid climate of the region just beyond the Sierras, Sequoia National Park hosts a surprisingly rich array of life. Black bears, mule deer, and more than 200 bird species call the park home, finding sustenance and shelter beneath the towering canopy and along rippling mountain streams. The mixed conifer forest that fills the rest of the park may not draw the same attention as the giants, but its complex ecology plays its part in supporting all that biodiversity.

The park has seen its share of human drama. The native Monache tribe called this region home, subsisting on acorns, deer, and the rich hunting and gathering found primarily in the foothills and valley bottoms. The Mono and Yokuts lived among these trees for thousands of years and used the sequoia's bark and seeds for various purposes. They held a deep respect for these trees and the forests they anchored. European settlers arrived in the mid-nineteenth century, drawn by the allure of gold. Their legacy is a bittersweet one, as their greed led to rapid deforestation and disruption of the Monache way of life. They killed most through smallpox infection; the rest were relocated. Though it lives on in the flag and is memorialized in the "Bear Republic" nickname for the state, the last California grizzly was killed here in 1932.

When those settlers from Europe arrived, the size of these trees amazed many who encountered them. Some sequoias were cut down for exhibitions, such as the Discovery Tree in Calaveras Big Trees State Park, felled in 1853. Hucksters tunneled through others, like the famous Wawona Tree, to attract tourists. However, the wood of sequoias, while voluminous, is brittle and not ideal for building. This saved many from logging.

Not all human interaction with the park was marked by exploitation. Sequoia became the second national park in the United States after Yellowstone in 1890. Early champions included John Muir and other proto-conservationists—many former loggers who understood that some forests deserved a reprieve from economic expedience. Park borders expanded in 1978 to include the remote, wild Mineral King area.

Like Kings Canyon, 96 percent of Sequoia is designated wilderness; while Sequoia attracts twice as many visitors, there's plenty of quiet Sierra to find for yourself. Even with company, a walk among these ancient giants both humbles and uplifts with an offering of permanence in a universe of constant change.

Mineral King lies at the end of a scenic but hair-raising road.

ZONE OF INTEREST

Mineral King

Mineral King is a secluded and less-visited area in the southern part of Sequoia National Park—largely because of challenging access. The 25-mile road to Mineral King, while scenic, is winding, narrow, and steep, with eye-popping cliffs on one side for much of its length (and few guardrails!). It takes 1.5 hours from the town of Three Rivers at the park's Ash Mountain entrance. This challenging journey, however, rewards those willing to venture with access to some of the park's most stunning and tranquil landscapes.

Day Hikes

Monarch Lakes Trail

This trail is a popular day hike in the Mineral King area—which means you might see a handful of people. The trail is 9 miles round-trip with an elevation gain of 2,500 feet. The journey begins at the Sawtooth trailhead, located at the end of the Mineral King Road. You'll hike through a forest of lodgepole pines, ascending steadily until you reach the Timber Gap, which offers beautiful panoramic views. After a series of switchbacks, you'll reach Monarch Lakes, set in a dramatic alpine landscape. The upper lake, located in a cirque at the base of Sawtooth Peak, allows for a leisurely lunch amid striking glacially carved terrain.

Eagle Lake Trail

This strenuous 7.2-mile round-trip hike leaves the Mineral King trailhead to gain 2,200 feet and quickly ascend through a dense forest on the way to Eagle Lake, a shallow tarn nestled in a glacial cirque with aquamarine waters reflecting the surrounding cliffs. Take a dip in the chilly waters before returning via the same route.

Backpacking Trips

Franklin Lakes and Franklin Pass

With the hair-raising Mineral King Road behind you, the 5.7-mile one-way climb up 2,500 feet of mountain to reach Franklin Lakes might strike some as a breeze. From Mineral King trailhead, follow the East Fork Kaweah Valley before veering off at a junction halfway to climb to the lakes. After a series of grueling switchbacks, you'll reach Franklin Lakes. For those with backcountry permits, this is a beautiful place to set up camp. Beyond Franklin Lakes is Franklin Pass, another 2.5 miles up a series of tougher switchbacks. From the pass, you'll gain righteous views of the Great Western Divide and the completely wild Kern River Valley beyond.

Paradise Ridge and Paradise Peak

For a longer backpacking trip, consider the Paradise Ridge route, which is 25 miles round-trip. The route follows the Sawtooth Pass Trail to Monarch Lakes, then veers off toward Crystal Lake before climbing steeply up the ridge. From Paradise Ridge, you can make the challenging scramble up to Paradise Peak for incredible 360-degree views.

HIKES

Redwood Canyon Trail

The Redwood Canyon Trail is a lesser-known but beautiful route located in the heart of Sequoia National Park. At 10 miles in length,

Several of the park's largest and oldest trees are found on the Redwood Canyon loop.

this loop trail offers moderate difficulty with some uphill sections but is manageable for most hikers.

The trail starts at the Redwood Canyon trailhead, accessible from a dirt road that branches off from Generals Highway. The trailhead has a small parking area.

From the trailhead, you have the choice of two paths. The right-hand trail, known as the Sugar Bowl loop, descends into a stunning grove of mature sequoias. The left path, or Hart Tree loop, takes you to the magnificent Hart Tree, one of the park's largest sequoias, featuring a cavernous fire scar large enough to walk through.

If you choose to start on the right-hand trail, you'll meander down into Redwood Canyon, experiencing an enchanting dense grove of sequoias. You'll be walking among some of the world's oldest and largest trees, which provide a unique sense of scale and a tangible connection to natural history.

At 1.5 miles into the hike, you'll come across a junction that connects the Sugar Bowl and Hart Tree loops. Depending on your chosen route, you can either loop back to the start or continue farther.

If you decide to continue onto the Hart Tree loop, you'll find a relatively flat trail that winds through a mixture of lush forest and open chaparral. Along the way, you'll pass the Fallen Goliath, another notable attraction. This immense tree fell naturally and offers a unique opportunity to get an up-close view of a sequoia's root system.

Farther along the Hart Tree loop, you'll come across a small but beautiful waterfall, a gurgling creek, and several serene meadows—all perfect for rests or snack breaks.

Once you've completed the Hart Tree loop, you can follow the trail back to the junction and then follow the Sugar Bowl loop back up to the trailhead.

The Redwood Canyon Trail doesn't offer established campsites, but backcountry camping is allowed with a permit—it's a fantastic place to spend the night out among the big trees.

Alta Peak

The Alta Peak Trail offers some of the most spectacular views in the park in exchange for a 14-mile round-trip crusher with elevation gain of over 3,900 feet.

Alta Peak serves up some of the best views in all of Sequoia.

The trail begins at the Wolverton parking area, located near the Lodgepole Visitor Center. From the parking lot, you'll find the well-marked trailhead and a path that guides you through a mixed forest of white fir and lodgepole pine. The first part of the hike is a steady uphill climb. As you gain elevation, the forest gradually gives way to manzanita bushes and other high-altitude vegetation.

At 1.9 miles into the hike, the Panther Gap junction briefly detours to a fantastic overlook of the Middle Fork of the Kaweah River and the surrounding mountains.

Stay straight at the Panther Gap junction to continue your ascent. As you go higher, trees thin out and the path gets rocky and rough. At around 6.5 miles, you will arrive at Alta Meadow, a lovely subalpine meadow nestled between seated high peaks. You guessed it—take a break, grab a snack, and enjoy this view.

From Alta Meadow, the trail gets steeper as it makes a final push toward Alta Peak. The landscape changes again, with the meadows giving way to exposed, rocky terrain, with scattered whitebark and foxtail pines. This part of the trail can be a slog but press on for your ultimate reward.

Once you reach the top of Alta Peak, at over 11,000 feet, you'll be smacked by epic views of the Great Western Divide and the High Sierra. On a clear day, you can see as far as the Central Valley.

After taking some time to rest and enjoy the views at the summit, you'll retrace your steps down the mountain to the trailhead. Remember, this steep hike is as demanding on the return, so save some energy, calories, and water for the journey back.

Little Baldy Dome

The Little Baldy Dome gives you the chance to tackle Half Dome in miniature. Over a mellow 3.3 miles round-trip, this trail climbs roughly 600 feet, making it a manageable trek for younger hikers.

The trailhead is located off Generals Highway, north of Dorst Creek Campground. There's a small parking area on the side of the road where you can leave your vehicle. From there, look for the signed trailhead and head off into the forest.

Little Baldy is like a bite-size Half Dome.

You're quickly surrounded by a mixed conifer forest interspersed with towering sequoias and vibrant green ferns, all popping out on a gradual incline. The path meanders through the woods, steadily gaining elevation. You're under shade most of the time—a welcome relief during the warmer summer months. Switchbacks mitigate the ascent's steepness until the pitch increases and the trail begins to ascend more rapidly as the terrain changes from forest to granite halfway in.

After 1.6 miles of hiking, you will arrive at the top of Little Baldy, a modest granite dome with windows on the Great Western Divide, the Silliman Crest, and the valley below. The hike back down to the trailhead follows the same path you came up on. Though it's downhill, be cautious of the loose granite terrain, which can be slippery.

Muir Grove

The Muir Grove Trail is a quieter route in Sequoia National Park, perfect for those seeking solitude and a more intimate experience with the giant sequoias. Named for the legendary naturalist John Muir, this 4-mile round-trip trail offers a moderate difficulty level, with 800 feet of total elevation change.

To reach the trailhead, you'll start from Dorst Creek Campground, which is located roughly midway between the park's northern and southern entrances along Generals Highway. There's a parking area near the campground's registration booth where you can leave your vehicle.

From the campground, a well-marked trail cuts west into the forest. The trail starts with a descent and winds through a mixed conifer forest of white fir, sugar pine, and incense cedar. The hike is generally peaceful and serene; be quiet and look for black bears, deer, or various bird species.

After a mile, you'll reach a junction. Keep to the right to continue toward Muir Grove. From here, the trail begins a gentle incline, with a series of switchbacks that climb up to a ridge. Along this section, you'll have some nice views of the surrounding mountains and valleys.

After another mile, you will descend into Muir Grove. This grove is a quiet sanctuary that houses some of the park's most majestic sequoia trees. The grove's centerpiece is the Dalton Tree, one of the largest sequoias in the park. Marvel at these colossal trees, walk among them, and soak in the sheer size and scale.

Muir Grove doesn't contain any formal trails, so you're free to explore at your own pace. Bask under the giants, then retrace your steps to Dorst Creek Campground.

There are no established campsites along the Muir Grove Trail itself, but Dorst Creek Campground is close by for those looking to extend their stay.

HIDDEN GEM

Not all hidden gems require grueling sacrifice or backbreaking effort. Nineteen miles up Mineral King Road, the **Atwell Mill Campground** is the only drive-up campground where you can pitch a tent and sleep under a grove of looming sequoias. Additionally, the Atwell Grove itself features a lovely collection of ramrod-straight sequoias in subalpine terrain—the highest collection of sequoias in the park. It's a lovely way to spend an evening before pressing on to the rugged trails at the end of Mineral King, or recharge and relax after completing one of the many High Sierra thigh burners out of that trailhead.

Shenandoah National Park

Virginia | nps.gov/shen | Visitation: 1,576,008

Though the theory has evolved many times, national parks were initially established to protect a place we perceive to exist in a natural state of grace that predates or resists our encroachment. We make efforts to safeguard their pristine delights for future generations to enjoy, yada yada yada. (This original conception is of course deeply problematic, as Indigenous peoples inhabited and shaped most parklands for thousands of years before the arrival of settlers and Eurocentric ideas about extraction or conservation.)

Shenandoah is the complete opposite. At the time Shenandoah was authorized for park status by Congress in 1926, it wore the scars of 200 years of continuous human occupation. All its old-growth hardwood forest had been logged at least once over, and farming, ranching, and settlements had already woven themselves into the landscape. But soon after, the state of Virginia began a bold nine-year campaign of extrication, using eminent domain and other powers to purchase land or otherwise remove residents who had lived here for generations. (The sting of that controversy persists to this day—ironic, given that many of these residents' ancestors forced out the region's original Indigenous inhabitants.) Upon park establishment in 1935, officials allowed a few old-timers to live within the park's borders for the rest of their natural lives. The last one died in 1979.

The results speak volumes. Five years into being a park, the land was 85 percent forested; by 1987 that grew to 95 percent forested. That number has stayed more or less constant, but this unique regrowing of a forest primeval affords scientists the opportunity to observe and study how fluid and competing populations of oak, oak hickory, poplar, maple, birch, pine, and tulip tree ebb and flow throughout generations. These trees will one day become a future generation's old-growth forest.

Those forests are draped over a narrow strip of 200,000 acres of ancient Appalachian Mountains rising to heights of over 3,000 feet. Shenandoah is fewer than 100 miles from the nation's capital, so millions can access the hushed forests, splashing waterfalls, and boulder-topped peaks found here. Far more flock to western stunners like the Grand Teton, Grand Canyon, Mount Rainier, and Arches. The ones who do come to Shenandoah stick mostly to the 105-mile Skyline Drive and its seventy-five picture-perfect, drive-up overlooks. As a result, you can find long pockets of quiet on over 500 miles of stellar trail.

Shenandoah was occupied for hundreds of years before it became a park.

And lovely trails they are: Old Rag Mountain is an eastern-park crucible with a hairy scramble at the summit; 75-foot Dark Hollow Falls leads a pack of shimmering cascades; and 100 miles of the OG long trail, the Appalachian, cut a green tunnel through wild trilliums, ferns, mountain laurels, and 800 flowering plants filling the understory. Bird-watchers' binoculars stay busy scanning for 190 bird species, from the flashy red cardinal to the swift peregrine falcon. A score of amphibians and 32 kinds of fish join mammalian standbys like bobcats, coyotes, white-tailed deer, and black bears. All this biodiversity is overlaid on the weathered billion-year-old rock of a worn-down mountain range that predates the ancient Appalachians.

Though the natural world has returned to determine the flavor of the park, human history lies barely concealed below the surface. The land was the ancestral home of Native American tribes such as the Manahoac and Monacan, communities who lived in symbiosis with the land by hunting, fishing, and foraging in the mosaic of forests and rivers. Their legacy remains in the toponymy of the park: "Shenandoah" is widely but perhaps dubiously believed to derive from a Native American word meaning "Daughter of the Stars." Given the fantastic night-sky views here, it remains apt even if it's apocryphal.

In recent times, the Civilian Conservation Corps (CCC) heavily influenced the shape and experience of the park. Established in 1933 as part of President Franklin D. Roosevelt's New Deal policies to provide employment during the Great Depression, it put young, unemployed men to work on improvement projects in public lands. They built Skyline Drive through feats of heavy labor, including dynamite blasting through mountains and the careful laying of roadbeds to minimize environmental impact. The CCC was also instrumental in constructing the network of hiking trails, including ones that lead to Old Rag Mountain and Dark Hollow Falls. They also built campgrounds and picnic areas, making the park more accessible and user-friendly.

The young men of the CCC also planted hundreds of thousands of trees and shrubs, helping restore habitats for the park's flora and fauna and stopping rampant soil erosion and habitat loss. Visitor centers, campgrounds, picnic areas, trails, and more: The CCC laid the foundation for what Shenandoah National Park has become today—a well-preserved, accessible oasis for all.

HIKES

Sugarloaf Loop

A quiet loop trail located in the northern district of Shenandoah, this loop trail offers hikers a peaceful stroll through wooded areas, with opportunities to spot wildlife and enjoy views of the surrounding mountains on a gentle 3.6-mile hike suitable for most hikers. The trailhead is located at the Skyland Resort stables, at mile 42.5 of Skyline Drive.

The trail begins at the stable and meanders through a pleasant mix of oak, hickory, and pine forest. The path is well marked with yellow blazes to guide you. An initial flat section starts to climb gradually as you approach the summit of Sugarloaf Mountain.

The trail winds around Sugarloaf Mountain, offering glimpses of the valley below through the tree cover. Reaching the peak might require a bit of a scramble, but the topography is generally gentle.

Halfway through the hike, you'll reach the highest point, where a wooden bench offers a chance to rest and take in the views of the Blue Ridge Mountains. Although the summit is forested, there are still spots where you can find solid windows for photos.

The trail then descends gently on the opposite side of the mountain, leading you through a shady canopy of trees. As you continue down the trail, keep an eye out for wildflowers and wildlife. Deer, foxes, and a variety of bird species are commonly seen in this area.

As you complete the loop, you'll connect with the horse trail that leads back to the stables where you started.

South River Falls Trail

The South River Falls Trail is a moderately difficult trail in the central district of Shenandoah National Park that leads to the third-highest waterfall in the park on a 4.7-mile loop.

You can access the trailhead from the South River Picnic Area at milepost 62.8 on Skyline Drive. The trail initially descends steadily through a mixed forest filled with both hardwoods and pines. In spring, the understory may be dotted with bright wildflowers, including mountain laurel.

The first section of the trail takes you to an overlook, 0.9 mile in. Here, you can admire the South River Falls from afar, watching as the water tumbles impressively down 83 feet into the rocky canyon below. Snap a shot and have a snack before continuing.

The trail drops steeply as you approach the base of the falls. You can follow the trail down to the pool at the bottom of the falls, which allows you to appreciate its full height and power.

After visiting the base of the falls, the trail begins to ascend and loops back to the picnic area. It continues through more thick forest—watch for wildlife such as deer, birds, and (rarely) black bears.

Shenandoah's hills blaze with autumn colors.

Sections of the loop trail are quite steep in places, and the rocks can be slick after rain, so hikers should wear sturdy footwear and take care while navigating these sections.

Little Devils Stairs

Little Devils Stairs is a challenging 5.5-mile loop located in the northern district of Shenandoah National Park featuring a steep, rugged climb along a beautiful canyon.

You can find the trailhead outside the park in the Keyser Run Fire Road parking lot, off the Weakley Hollow Road. The trail begins by crossing Keyser Run and then quickly starts to ascend along the stream.

A stout ascent comes quickly and may require intermittent scrambling. The trail soon snakes up a narrow, gorge-like canyon where you'll encounter multiple larger cascades and small water-falls tumbling down the moss-covered boulders and leaping off

South River Falls pours 83 feet from cliffs above.

high cliffs. Midway through the ascent, a small trail branches off to the left to provide a closer look at one of the waterfalls. It's pleasant detour away from the main trail.

The steepest part of the climb ends as you reach the top of the canyon. From here, the trail intersects with the Keyser Run Fire Road. This is a wide, gentle trail that descends back to your starting point.

Halfway down the fire road, you'll pass the Bolen Cemetery, a poignant reminder of the families who once lived here before the establishment of the park. The cemetery is a small, fenced area containing a few headstones.

The fire road leads back to the trailhead, completing your loop.

Some of Teddy Roosevelt's formative years were spent hunting bison in the park that now bears his name.

Theodore Roosevelt National Park

North Dakota | nps.gov/thro | Visitation: 746,862

Theodore Roosevelt National Park, located in the rough badlands of western North Dakota near the border with Montana, remains one of America's least-known but most intriguing national parks. Quiet and windswept, it tells of two Roosevelts: the brash-but-scrawny New York youngster who arrived in the Dakota Territory in 1883 at age twenty-four to hunt bison, and the man who left transformed into a steadfast and vocal advocate for protecting our wild places. One could make a credible argument that the inspiration for a broader parks system began here.

Natural history begins well before the twenty-sixth president. The layers of striated rock, carved and eroded by the elements over eons, came from an ancient inland sea. Sedimentary rocks, deposited over millions of years, were worn by wind, water, and ice into deep ravines, steep cliffs, and towering spires. The South Unit's scenic loop drive and North Unit's scenic drive offer views of the painted badlands, where bands of color signify different geological eras. As the sun dips below the horizon, the rocks ignite in a fiery display of oranges, reds, and purples. Venturing deeper into the rock yields discoveries of the fossilized remnants of prehistoric creatures who roamed this landscape over 60 million years ago. Dinosaurs, crocodiles, palm trees—essentially, a mother lode of fossils that could supply *Jurassic Park* with new attractions each season.

The dinosaurs disappeared, but bison descended from the ones Roosevelt hunted still graze on the mixed-grass prairies alongside wild horses and pronghorn antelope. Mule deer move like shadows through the juniper forests, while coyotes, foxes, and bobcats stalk the small creatures of the night. Meadowlarks, ferruginous hawks, golden eagles, and wild turkeys stalk the skies and grasses.

While Roosevelt's name is attached to the park, he came late to the magic of the badlands (a word he hated). For thousands of years, the land sustained the Mandan, Hidatsa, and Arikara tribes—known collectively as the Three Affiliated Tribes.

The tribes navigated the intricate channels of the sinewy Little Missouri River—gathering food, utilizing trade routes, and letting it guide their intricate agricultural cycles through floods and droughts. Women typically cultivated corn, squash, sunflowers, and beans, while men hunted from the herds of bison, elk, and deer that stretched ever onward pre-settlement. Evidence of their earth lodges still marks the land, and their villages consisted of complex, fortified settlements with central plazas for ceremonies and social activities.

Their towns served as hubs of cultural exchange long before and after Europeans arrived. Plagues introduced by European settlers, intertribal warfare, territorial pressures, and forced relocations marred their collective history. Today, the sacred sites within the park give us a chance to remember the tribes' resilience and the stories of their ancestors. The River Bend Overlook, although a product of the Civilian Conservation Corps in the 1930s, serves as a vantage point to appreciate the timeless bond these tribes continue to have with the land. The Mandan called it "Maah Daah Hey," which translates to "long-lasting place" or "grandfather" land.

Long after the tribes' decline, Roosevelt returned to establish the Elkhorn Ranch. He wanted to grapple with the hardship of frontier life and mourn the loss of his wife and mother, who died on the same day. He admitted that he never would have become president without his earlier experiences in North Dakota, and his subsequent returns to heal through frontier living informed his conservation philosophy. You can still visit the site of the Elkhorn Ranch today, where the foundation stones remain.

HIKES

Caprock Coulee

This quiet, serene 4.3-mile loop trail starts from the Caprock Coulee parking area and takes you on an exploration of diverse landscapes in Theodore Roosevelt National Park.

As you start your journey from the trailhead, the route leads through mixed-grass prairie, displaying wildflowers in the spring and early summer. Listen for meadowlarks, watch for prairie dogs scampering about their towns, and keep an eye out for bison grazing in the distance.

The trail soon winds into a small coulee, offering an intimate experience of the unique badlands topography. Coulees are deep ravines or gullies, often dry, with steep sides.

Colorful badlands erupt from the prairie on the Caprock Coulee Trail.

At the midpoint of the hike, you'll encounter the Buckhorn Trail intersection. Here, you can choose to extend your adventure onto the Buckhorn Trail or continue along the Caprock Coulee loop. The latter option will lead you up a steep incline to a ridge from where you can survey the stark beauty of the badlands from on high.

The trail takes you through caprock formations—hard, erosion-resistant layers of rock that often look like ledges or caps on the softer underlying sedimentary layers.

Toward the end of the trail, you'll descend back toward the trailhead through prairie lands and scattered juniper patches. Take a pause, breathe in the fresh air, and revel in the quiet solitude on this less-traveled trail.

Lower Paddock Creek Trail

The Lower Paddock Creek Trail stretches 4.6 miles one-way and is generally flat, making it a moderate hike suitable for most people to experience the profound solitude of the prairie. The trail starts at Peaceful Valley Ranch, heading southward, and ends at the intersection with the Talkington Trail.

From Peaceful Valley Ranch, the trail leads you into mixed badlands and prairie along the contours of the winding Paddock Creek. It's a dried-up waterway for most of the year, but it can morph into a rushing creek after heavy rainfalls.

The entire trail features now-rare native grass species like bluestem, grama, and buffalo grass. Wildflowers bloom in spring and early summer, dotting the landscape with splashes of color.

The 144-mile Maah Daah Hey Trail features parallel mountain biking trails just outside park boundaries.

Stay alert: It's common to spot mule deer, pronghorns, and wild horses grazing nearby. One of the park's bigger prairie dog towns lies just off the trail. These gregarious animals provide entertainment with their social antics, and they attract predators like coyotes, badgers, and birds of prey.

Halfway through, you'll pass a junction with the Ridgeline Nature Trail. As you continue on Lower Paddock Creek Trail, the landscape starts to open up, and you'll begin to see big views of the surrounding badlands.

Lower Paddock Trail, on the larger 144-mile Maah Daah Hey Trail, features parallel mountain biking trails just outside park boundaries.

As you near the end of the trail, you'll intersect with the Talkington Trail. From here, you can choose to extend your hike on the Talkington Trail or turn around and head back the way you came.

Lower Paddock Creek Trail is generally less crowded because of its length and the need to grab a pickup at the other end for a one-way hike. Backcountry camping is permitted, but there are no specific campsites along this trail. A permit is required for overnight stays.

Trunk Bay features the only underwater trail in the national park system.

Virgin Islands National Park

US Virgin Islands | nps.gov/viis | Visitation: 343,685

Tucked away in a Caribbean archipelago, Virgin Islands National Park encompasses 60 percent of St. John, the smallest of the US Virgin Islands. Extending beyond into the turquoise waters, this jewel also holds rocky hills, mangroves, and subtropical forests in addition to scenic beaches. But man, those beaches—they're the stuff of shipwrecked fantasy. Underwater, the park's reefs and sea-grass beds harbor a rainbow of aquatic life, from pokey giant sea turtles to nimble angelfish and the industrious parrotfish (which help create the island's beautiful beaches by chewing up coral and excreting lily-white sand).

On land, the tropical ecosystem plays host to towering mahogany trees and delicate orchids, where nimble mongoose hunt animals like the critically endangered St. Croix ground lizard.

The Indigenous Taino people left their presence in petroglyphs that can still be seen on the Reef Bay Trail. Then came a brutal era of slavery when the island's economy was driven by sugar plantations. The remnants now stand as haunting ruins scattered throughout the park. Emancipation came in the mid-nineteenth century, bringing an end to the plantation system but setting off a period of economic hardship that lasted until the mid-twentieth century.

In the 1950s, wealthy conservationist Laurance Rockefeller, moved by the island's unspoiled beauty, bought much of the land and donated it to the federal government, leading to the establishment of Virgin Islands National Park in 1956. This marked a new chapter in which the island came to rely on conservation and ecotourism.

ZONE OF INTEREST

Trunk Bay Snorkeling Trail

Nestled within the heart of Virgin Islands National Park, Trunk Bay's 225-yard-long, self-guided underwater snorkeling trail, situated in one of the most picturesque beaches in the world, offers snorkelers an unfiltered view into the park's underwater realm.

Swimmers on the trail will find themselves gliding through crystal-clear waters full of rainbow-hued parrotfish, curious sea turtles, and thousands of exotic fish species flitting among the coral.

Easy-to-follow underwater markers guide snorkelers in Trunk Bay.

Each stop along the trail is marked by an underwater plaque affixed to a concrete block on the seafloor, presenting valuable information about the coral reef ecosystem and the diverse marine life that calls it home.

While you explore, expect to encounter plenty of vibrant coral species, including staghorn, elkhorn, and brain corals. Keep an eye out for sea fans gently swaying in the currents and sponge colonies dotting the seafloor. Never touch or stand on the coral to help preserve this delicate ecosystem.

Visibility is generally excellent, thanks to the protected nature of Trunk Bay and the care taken to preserve its waters. The snorkeling trail is an all-levels experience; its calm waters are perfect for beginners while also offering enough diversity and beauty to delight experienced snorkelers.

Post-snorkel, take time to bask in the beauty of Trunk Bay's white-sand beach, surrounded by green, palm-laden hillsides and the vibrant blue Caribbean Sea.

Voyageurs National Park

Minnesota | nps.gov/voya | Visitation: 220,825

Pressed against the Minnesota-Canada border, Voyageurs is named for the French-Canadian fur traders who first traversed the sprawling web of waterways that define this park. But the land is the result of a much older tug-of-war between ice and rock.

The park lies within the Canadian Shield, a vast geological formation composed of some of the planet's oldest rock. These rocks formed over two billion years ago only to later get scoured, crushed, and reshaped by gargantuan ice sheets during multiple ice ages. As the glaciers retreated, they left a labyrinth of interconnected lakes and islands.

You can still glimpse the ancient bedrock in the rocky outcrops punctuating the waterways that wind through dense boreal forest. A sea of spruce, fir, and pine shelters creatures as diverse as moose, beavers, and gray wolves. Bald eagles fly overhead, while beneath the waters, northern pike, walleye, and the prehistoric-looking lake sturgeon patrol the depths.

The hardy French-Canadian fur traders who paddled these waterways in the eighteenth and nineteenth centuries portaged their canoes and cargoes across the wilderness in search of beaver pelts to meet the demands of European fashion. The voyageurs' stories and songs have become part of the fabric of this park, but theirs are predated by Native tribes like the Ojibwe, who have called this area home for centuries. Signs of the region's rich Indigenous heritage, from petroglyphs to burial mounds, remain scattered throughout the park, remnants of a history that connects to the tribes who still live nearby.

ZONES OF INTEREST

Paddling Voyageurs is by far the best way to experience its large network of lakes and waterways. Stable, silent kayaks in particular offer an intimate way to connect with the park's environment, though canoes are more popular and are available to reserve through the national park. (To prevent the spread of invasive species, you can't bring your own to interior lakes.) Remember to check weather forecasts before setting out, as conditions on these large bodies of water can change rapidly.

Here are some premier ways to experience Voyageurs by water.

Paddle the Park's Four Main Lakes

The park is home to four large, interconnected lakes: Rainy Lake, Kabetogama Lake, Namakan Lake, and Sand Point Lake. Paddling through these waterways, you'll have the chance to observe wildlife, explore islands, and visit historic sites.

Voyageurs features a network of interconnected lakes.

Northern lights erupt over Voyageurs' night sky.

Explore the Smaller Lakes

In addition to its major lakes, Voyageurs is dotted with numerous smaller lakes, perfect for more serene, intimate paddling experiences. Locator Lake and Cruiser Lake, for instance, are excellent for spotting wildlife and offer a tranquil setting away from the larger lakes.

Overnight Kayak Camping

For a more immersive experience, consider overnight canoe and kayak camping. The park has over 200 designated campsites accessible only by water. These sites, spread across the park's islands and lakeshores, offer a unique wilderness experience. Most require a reservation, so be sure to plan ahead.

HIKES

Cruiser Lake Trail

This 8-mile trail (one way) is the park's longest and most challenging trail. But it offers an unparalleled chance to appreciate the park's diversity in relative solitude.

Find the trailhead at Eks Bay, due north of the Ash River Visitor Center (accessible by water). You'll trek through mixed forest,

Camp overnight on the multiday Kab-Ash Canoe Route.

past still bogs, and along rocky ridges. Keep an eye out for moose and (rarely) wolves. The trail culminates at Anderson Bay on Rainy Lake, providing a tranquil place to rest and admire the beauty before hoofing back the way you came.

Blind Ash Bay Trail

The Blind Ash Bay Trail is one of the best short trails in the remote eastern end of the park. Starting near the Ash River Visitor Center, the 2.8-mile round-trip trail winds through a forest of pine and birch before reaching a series of boardwalks that take you through a wetland area. The trail ends with wide views of Blind Ash Bay.

Locator Lake Trail

The Locator Lake Trail keeps crowds at bay largely because access to the trailhead requires a boat. The trail is 2 miles long (one way) and takes you from the shores of Kab-Ash Trail to the secluded Locator Lake.

Along the trail, you'll march past towering pines and beautiful wildflowers. The end point's tranquil lake is perfect for a mid-hike picnic or a swim on a hot day. If you're lucky, you might spot a bald eagle or a loon. Best of all, you can stay the night: Locator Lake has

campsites and canoes for rent, accessible by permit and reservation at the visitor centers.

HIDDEN GEM

While water defines Voyageurs and has dictated preferred modes of travel since before its namesake fur trappers arrived, it also commands the most attention. But hikers can immerse themselves in deep northern-woods solitude hard to find elsewhere on the **Kab-Ash trail network**, a 28-mile one-way path that connects the communities and main park portals of Kabetogama and Ash River. Over the course of a few days or even a week, experienced wilderness travelers can plot a customized trek that wends through the silent old-growth forests, still marshes, and rocky ridges harboring abundant boreal wildlife. Perhaps best of all, you can reach the Kab-Ash route by road via four main access points (check for closures).

Why aren't there more visitors? Besides the lack of paddling opportunities, you'll spend much of the time in thick woods with sparse views. High-season summer months bring heavy heat, abundant bugs, mud, and encroaching greenery that can overwhelm the rarely maintained trail. But in fall, biting insects abate and the undergrowth peels back to reveal maples, blueberries, and aspens lighting your path in splashes of orange, crimson, and gold.

Without another soul around, you can attune yourself to beavers slapping the surface of bog ponds or moose, fox, and marten leaving tracks. If you're extremely lucky, you might catch a wolf darting into the underbrush: At least two packs are known to circulate in the area, but sightings remain rare. Finding scat or hearing a howl piercing the night remains much more likely.

Intermittent boardwalks aid you in crossing the biggest bogs, but you should be prepared for plenty of soggy sections. In winter, the path transforms into a ski trail and becomes even more silent as snow swallows up the soundscape. In any season, stepping away from the water on the Kab-Ash promises a soul-stirring adventure.

White Sands National Park

New Mexico | nps.gov/whsa | Visitation: 729,096

In the middle of New Mexico's Tularosa Basin, there's a place where the land itself defies belief. At the center of a ring of dark mountains and below a blue sky, where one might expect washes of sepia and sage, there lies a stark alabaster expanse. It looks like snow, but it's piled too high—and it doesn't melt, even in June.

Welcome to White Sands National Park, where bleached dunes ripple and crest like an ocean frozen in place, so white they seem like negative space. The sand here isn't the coarse, multicolored, conglomerate crystal variety you find in most deserts. Instead, it's pure gypsum—a mineral typically soluble in water, denied its destined dissolution by the Tularosa Basin's peculiar lack of outflow to the sea.

Gypsum, cast off from the surrounding San Andres and Sacramento Mountains, gets stuck in the basin. The torrents of summer monsoons wash it down mountainsides, onto the playa of Lake Lucero and Alkali Flat, where water evaporates to leave behind selenite crystals. Over time, the wind breaks down these crystals, lifting them skyward, setting them on a journey across the basin, where they come to rest as dunes as high as 50 feet, an ocean of white grains billowing in the arid breeze.

In this desert sea, life finds ways to thrive. Insects, small mammals, and reptiles, many camouflaged by a bleached pallor that mimics their surroundings, traverse and forage in the gypsum fields. Stubborn vegetation breaks the surface of the dunes: Yucca, cottonwood, sumac, and a host of fast-growing grasses all manage to find footholds in the shifting landscape.

Humans have visited for some ten thousand years. Folsom hunters, the farming Mogollon, the nomadic Apache, and later, European settlers all sought to comprehend this place and attempted to survive in the white sands. Few remained for long, but the residue of their passage—arrowheads, pottery shards, cabin walls—endured, discovered by later generations similarly mesmerized by this place.

In modern history, White Sands took a detour into ominous territory. These grounds host the site of Oppenheimer's Trinity—the world's first nuclear detonation. The echoes of that event linger, a chilling reminder of humanity's capacity to harness destructive forces we hardly comprehend. Sixty miles north of the park, a nuclear test bomb named "Gadget" sent off a nighttime flash whiter

White Sands' unique hue comes from gypsum washing down from surrounding mountains.

than the sands below it, spewing a mushroom cloud 38,000 feet into the sky and excavating a crater 0.5 mile across and 8 feet deep. Inside, the heat and intensity melted and fused grains of white sand into an eerie green glass known as trinitite.

While fewer than 10 miles of trail exist here, you can walk onto the sand (not the easiest going) and spend an evening in the dunes. On clear nights (even moonless ones), the white sand glows so brightly you won't need a headlamp.

HIKES

Playa Trail

The term "playa" refers to the dry lakebed found in the park, not a sandy beach. This self-guided, interpretive trail introduces the geology and ecology of White Sands National Park and is a welcome primer on how to understand and navigate this otherworldly landscape. It's located on a flat area near the dune fields, on an easy, accessible 0.5 mile trail suitable for all ages and fitness levels.

As you leave the visitor center, follow the road that leads to the Dune Drive. A mile down Dune Drive, you'll see the Playa Trail on your right. The trail is a flat, circular loop that navigates around the small playa. You'll find educational signs along the path that explain the geological history of the gypsum dunes and how the playas contribute to their formation. The trail is clearly marked and easy to follow.

On the trail, you might spot the darkling beetle, bleached earless lizard, and other creatures that have adapted to this environment. The Playa Trail also brings chances to see striking selenite crystals, which form when groundwater carrying dissolved gypsum evaporates, leaving behind large, transparent crystals that erode into sand.

Early morning or late afternoon are the best times to embark on this trail to avoid the scorching midday sun, and these times offer the best lighting for photography, casting long shadows that accentuate the texture of the dunes.

Alkali Flat Trail

Marked by red-tipped poles, the trail winds through an unending sea of white gypsum dunes, providing an expansive view of the stark landscape. Despite the name "Alkali Flat," the trail is far from flat; it involves a series of ascents and descents over the ever-shifting sand dunes.

The 5-mile trail begins at the Alkali Flat Trail parking area, 6 miles from the park's entrance along the Dunes Drive. You'll begin by traversing a series of smaller dunes before reaching the edge of Alkali Flat itself, the dry lakebed of an ancient Pleistocene-era lake. The area now showcases some of the tallest dunes in the park. The dunes seem to roll on endlessly in all directions, providing hypnotic vistas and a fierce sense of isolation.

Alkali Flat at sunset.

Markers guide hikers on the backpacking trail.

Look out for wildlife tracks in the sand and the resilient plants and animals that have adapted to survive in this harsh environment. Take a cue and adapt yourself: Carry plenty of water, use sun protection, and wear sturdy shoes. Navigational aids like a compass or GPS can be helpful, as it can be easy to lose the trail in the expanse of dunes. Remember that the red-tipped poles marking the trail can sometimes be obscured by shifting sands.

White Sands Backpacking Trail

You can spend an unforgettable night camping among the vast white gypsum dunes after a short 1-mile hike into the dune field. While you can explore further, there's little reason to since the monochromatic landscape that dominates remains largely static; it can be fun to look for wildlife sign, but take care not to get lost in the blinding dunes.

The trailhead starts from the backcountry camping parking area, which is located at the end of the Dunes Drive. From the parking area, you'll set off into the heart of the dunes along the trail, which is marked by a series of orange trail markers. The route winds through a dune-filled landscape, gradually leading you away from the park's main areas and deeper into the wilderness.

The ten numbered campsites are located off the main trail at intervals, so you will have to follow short spur trails to reach them. Each campsite has a flat area for setting up your tent, but other than that, the campsites are primitive, with no water or other facilities.

The fireworks begin at dawn and dusk when sunrise and sunset each paint the gypsum sand in shades of pink and purple. At night, the stargazing opportunities are some of the best in the world.

Campsite 8 is farthest from the trail and offers a more secluded experience, but some backpackers opt for Campsite 2 because of its unique dune formations and wide-open views.

The best times to hike are during the cooler parts of the day, particularly early morning and late afternoon. The park can get extremely hot during the summer months, so spring and fall are generally the best times for overnight backpacking trips, unless you want to bake alive in your tent.

Camping in the park requires a permit, which you can get from the park visitor center on the day of your trip. There's a limit on the number of people per campsite, and fires are not allowed. Make sure you're prepared for the possibility of strong winds, which can lead to sandstorms.

The eerie natural entrance to Wind Cave.

Wind Cave National Park

South Dakota | nps.gov/wica | Visitation: 592,459

The Black Hills of South Dakota are forested, big-sky, meadow-and-mountain country known for bison, prairie dogs, and intact native prairie. But below lies Wind Cave: 150 miles (and counting) of dense, maze-like caverns—the ninth largest in the world.

Its creation began around 320 million years ago when a warm, shallow sea left behind layers of sediment, including marine fossils, to accumulate on the seabed. As the sea receded, the sediments solidified and transformed into limestone.

The limestone bedrock in Wind Cave is characterized by its porous nature. Rainwater, mixed with carbon dioxide from the air, becomes acidic and forms a weak carbonic acid. As this acidic water seeps through the soil, it encounters the limestone rock and dissolves it over time, creating a network of cracks and fractures within the rock. Over thousands of years, these fractures widen, allowing water to flow through and enlarge the passages. As the passages expand, a cave system begins to form beneath the surface.

What sets Wind Cave apart from many other caves is a unique geological feature known as boxwork. Boxwork cave formations are characterized by delicate, honeycomb-like patterns of intersecting calcite fins. Calcite, a mineral deposited by water as it flows through the cave, fills the narrow cracks in the limestone. As the limestone erodes the more resistant calcite fins are left behind, forming these intricate patterns.

But Wind Cave gets its name from the "breathing" or wind-like sensation many visitors experience from air movement within the cave passages. This ventilation is driven by atmospheric pressure differences and temperature fluctuations.

The cave has numerous openings and narrow passages that connect to the surface. As atmospheric conditions like temperature or barometric pressure change outside the cave, air is forced through these openings and passages. This results in airflow within the cave, which blows on visitors exploring the cave.

The wind phenomenon in Wind Cave can vary in intensity and direction, depending on the prevailing atmospheric conditions and the interconnectedness or shape of the cave passages. It can manifest as gentle breezes or strong gusts.

Over time, the erosive forces of wind and rain that shaped the underground also sculpted the surface, transforming it into a mixed-grass prairie ecosystem. Bison, elk, pronghorns, coyotes, and

Bison graze on grasslands above Wind Cave.

prairie dogs all occupy spots on the interconnected food web. Wind Cave National Park has reintroduced the endangered black-footed ferret, which now thrives in its original habitat.

Native Americans have considered the Black Hills sacred for thousands of years (the area has featured prominently in the Landback movement, which seeks to return stolen land to Indigenous stewards). The Lakota Sioux believed that Wind Cave was the place where humanity first emerged from the underworld. The cave was "discovered" in 1881 by two European-American brothers, Jesse and Tom Bingham, after noticing the peculiar wind phenomenon.

Coming into prominence at a time of rapid expansion and irresponsible recreation, the cave was exploited for its commercial potential at first. The most audacious of these entrepreneurs was a dude named J. D. McDonald, who proclaimed himself the cave's owner and set up shop with his son Alvin, exploring and promoting it as a tourist attraction.

In an ironic twist of fate, it was the McDonalds' commercial venture that paved the way for Wind Cave's entry as the seventh US national park in 1903. From a place of exploitation, it transformed into a symbol of conservation, preserved so future generations could enjoy its bizarre geology and ecology.

While the small park has 30 miles of pleasant hiking through the Black Hills, the impressive cave below is the undeniable star. Joining a ranger-led tour is the best way to immerse yourself in the windy black. After, you'll be ready for the fresh air and sunshine of the trail.

ZONES OF INTEREST

Exploring the depths of Wind Cave requires joining a guided cave tour. The National Park Service offers versions that cater to different interests and skill levels.

Garden of Eden Tour

This introduction to cave exploration lasts 1 hour and covers 0.5 mile. Led by a knowledgeable guide, you'll traverse well-lit passages and encounter wild cave formations, including the lattice-like boxwork, a distinctive feature of Wind Cave.

Fairgrounds Tour

This immersive experience lasts around 1.5 hours and covers 0.6 mile. It goes deeper into the cave and explores a variety of cave formations while explaining the cave's history of exploration. Be prepared for narrow passageways and the opportunity to witness unique geological features up close.

Candlelight Tour

For a memorable (and frightening) adventure, consider the Candlelight Tour. Lasting around 1.5 hours and covering 0.6 mile, this

Wind cave is famous for its unique boxwork formations.

tour offers a glimpse into the past, re-creating the experience of early cave explorers. With only handheld candles for light, you'll navigate through narrow passages and gain a sense of the challenges faced by early cave enthusiasts.

Wild Cave Tour

This more adventurous and physically demanding experience can last 4 hours and cover 4 miles, all in the dark. Led by experienced guides, you'll crawl, squeeze through tight spaces, and explore hidden areas of the cave (scientists think only 5 percent of the cave has been discovered). Participants should be in good physical condition, comfortable in confined spaces, and unafraid to get wet, dirty, or muddy.

Cave tours have limited availability, and it's advisable to make reservations in advance. The National Park Service provides information on tour schedules, availability, and booking procedures on its official website.

Wrangell–St. Elias is the largest national park and part of one of the biggest undisturbed wildernesses in the world.

Wrangell–St. Elias National Park and Preserve

Alaska | nps.gov/wrst | Visitation: 78,305

Have you heard the one about the drunk Texan complaining to the Alaskan about being the second-biggest state? "Keep talking and we'll cut our state in two and make you third," said the Alaskan.

The same principle applies to Wrangell–St. Elias, the undisputed size king of national parks. "Immense," "colossal," "f***in' huge": None of those words seems sufficient to describe a wilderness that can swallow Death Valley, Yellowstone, Denali, Yosemite, and Glacier whole. The Malaspina Glacier alone is bigger than Rhode Island.

Everything you can think of when you picture Alaska exists here in profane amounts: nine of North America's sixteen tallest peaks; the largest non-polar glaciers, dead-ending in huge moraines and calving into tidewater bays; at least ten volcanoes; enormous, braided rivers filled with every salmonid in healthier runs than anywhere else; brown bears and other charismatic megafauna beyond counting. All that superlative majesty comes with its fair share of best-in-class terror: Potentially nightmarish weather anytime; exceedingly dangerous river crossings; hellacious mosquitoes; brown bears beyond counting.

But for advanced backcountry adventurers game to map out extensive expeditions and blow cash on bush planes, Wrangell–St. Elias is nothing less than Shangri-la. Treacherous rock and ice and deep forest and alder thickets hostile to travel comprise much of the interior. But there's also a profusion of high-altitude, ice-free tundra that makes for easy tramping and camping, if you know where to look. On that score, it helps to find a trusty local.

Locals have been here for a long time, but never in large numbers. Much of the interior was too harsh to support permanent human settlements, but humans began using the area 8,000 years ago, once glaciers began receding. Ahtna and Upper Tenana Athabascans lived on the edges of the interior, while Eyak and Tlingit people utilized the coast. European exploration didn't begin until Russians showed up from the Aleutians in the 1780s; quickly thereafter they found and explored the Copper River, establishing a fort sixteen years later. Prospectors discovered gold in 1899, launching

Wrangell contains some of the biggest non-polar ice sheets in the world.

a series of gold rushes that produced hundreds of millions of dollars' worth of ore before petering out in 1938.

Economic attention quickly turned to recreational possibilities, and Alaska governor and senator Ernest Gruening became an early champion for park status well before Alaska was a state. A dedicated global traveler, Gruening adventured extensively throughout Alaska, Mexico, Switzerland, and the Andes. But after flying over the Wrangells in 1938, he wrote to the US Secretary of the Interior to deem this area "the finest scenery that I have ever been privileged to see."

It was so remote, however, that it would take another forty years for anyone else to take notice. Wrangell–St. Elias became a national park in 1980 when Jimmy Carter signed the Alaska National Interests Lands Conservation Act (ANILCA) to permanently protect 104.5 million acres of public land. This sweeping federal declaration makes some Alaskans bristle to this day. But given that it's joined with Glacier Bay National Park and both Canada's Kluane National Park and Reserve and Alsek-Tatshenshini Provincial Park to form a single UNESCO World Heritage Site recognized as the biggest tract of internationally protected land in the world, it's probably safe to say there's no going back.

Approaching the Root Glacier, just beyond the town of McCarthy.

While one can debate Gruening's assessment of Wrangell–St. Elias National Park's status as the prettiest place, its status as wildest is fairly unassailable. This is wilderness at its biggest and most deafening, capable of overwhelming the steeliest nervous system with joy, fear, and awe—often all at the same time. Pretty words and pictures don't come close. You must get swallowed by Wrangell–St. Elias to understand.

HIKES

Hidden Creek Lake

Accessible from the quaint-but-remote former mining town of McCarthy, this 20-mile round-trip trek lets stout-hearted hikers navigate glaciers and tundra to arrive at a unique, glacially dammed lake that drains dramatically once a year over a single day of flooding.

Begin at the end of McCarthy, where beyond the wreck of the abandoned Kennicott mine you'll find the Root Glacier trailhead. A trail leads through berry bushes (make noise for bears) for 2 miles before ending at the toe of the Root Glacier. A few flat campsites give you the chance to stay the night and admire the icy, lolling tongues of the Kennicott and Root Glaciers and jaw-dropping 16,000-foot Mount Blackburn rising behind.

Now it's time to get on the ice. To continue, shuffle down the crumbly moraine, strap on crampons and step out onto the Root Glacier. The Root is unique because it's relatively flat and free of the dangerous jumble of an icefall; most crevasses are either shut tight or wide open and easy enough to walk around. You don't need ropes or an ice axe, but it doesn't hurt if these items bring you extra comfort. Still, some familiarity with glacier travel is recommended: Some of the crevasses are deep, and numerous moulins—vertical holes where rushing meltwater pours into the icy guts of the glacier—pock the route. They're both easy to avoid, but falling into one is curtains.

A spectacular 10ish-mile walk over ridges, hills, and ramps made of ice awaits. Day hikers can explore the Root Glacier and turn around (a GPS helps with marking your glacier exit for the return), or wind through this frozen maze to cross the Root and then Kennicott Glaciers before finding the entrance to Hidden Lake in the Glacier Gulch basin. You'll want to enter the lake at the north shore, where there are flat spots for camping. If you've got more than a day, you can explore the tundra above Glacier Gulch. You can further break up the trip by camping out on the ice.

McCarthy is accessible by a 30-minute bush plane flight or a 7-hour drive from Anchorage, but beware: Most car rental companies explicitly forbid you from driving the notoriously tire-puncturing McCarthy Road.

You don't need a permit, but filing an itinerary with rangers at the Wrangell–St. Elias National Park Visitor Center in Copper Center or from the local office in McCarthy is advisable.

Late June to early September offers the most amicable weather conditions, but always be prepared for Alaska's volatile climate.

Goat Trail

In a landscape bursting with colossal mountains, ancient glaciers, and a multitude of rivers, the Goat Trail serves up a heaping helping of all those and more on a life-list backpacking odyssey that demands a high degree of fitness, preparation, and experience. In exchange, you'll cruise through some of the finest and most pristine high country Alaska has to offer, skirting past 400-foot waterfalls and watching brown bears and Dall sheep trundle through meadows with 16,000-foot peaks in the background.

While there are many variations, at its core the Goat Trail is a 4- to 7-day, mostly off-trail route that meanders through the expansive Skolai Pass to Chitistone Canyon. With 21 miles of undulating wilderness (or much more, depending on side trips), this trail serves as an unforgettable journey into the heart of America's last frontier.

The Goat Trail follows animal tracks etched into steep mountain slopes.

The Goat Trail is not accessible by road. Your journey will usually begin with a chartered bush plane flight from either McCarthy or Chitina, which will drop you off at Skolai Pass. Another variation lands you high atop the Wolverine airstrip, which skips some bushwhacky terrain and big river crossings. You'll start above tree line at 5,500 feet and stay there for a bulk of the trip.

Upon landing at Skolai Pass, you'll be greeted by high-alpine meadows streaked in green and earth tones, complete with wildflowers and small streams running throughout. The mighty Russell Glacier dominates the distance, veined with giant crevasses. From the Wolverine airstrip, invisible game trails lead you across the open tundra, while skyscraping, glacier-clad peaks own the horizon. Grasslands slowly give way to a barren landscape dotted with boulders and shale.

Cross the numerous creeks and tundra sections of Hasen Creek Basin until you find the Goat Trail itself—a thin track scratched into a wall of steep scree. While it's not technical, it isn't for the faint of heart: Long stretches of exposure on a 2-foot-wide, crumbling sheep path will make you feel as if you're floating thousands of feet above the braided river valley below. A slip or fall here would Not Be Good.

You'll ascend the Goat Trail toward the narrow Chitistone Pass, a break between towering rock walls. Chitistone Canyon unfolds with awe-inspiring rock formations, while the usually ferocious Chitistone River roils through the canyon below. Most routes require a deep, swift crossing of the river, which you might need to wait out if flow is too dangerous. Look for riffled sections and do it early in the day, before glacial meltwater adds to the flow.

The trail then descends into Glacier Creek, where the terrain becomes a mix of tundra and forest—some of it onerous to push through. You'll make your way to takeout points at Lower Skolai Lake or the Glacier Creek airstrip.

You don't need a permit, but filing an itinerary with the park is smart; it's typically handled by either your air carrier or guide service. For most hikers, a guide company is ideal: They can handle the sometimes-complicated transport logistics, and for not too much more than the price of airfare, you'll often get cooked meals and a companion with built-in familiarity of the route. Don't underestimate this benefit in Alaska, where the best route often changes depending on weather, yearly conditions, time, and chance.

The ideal period to undertake this trek is from late June to early September when the weather is more stable, but again: This is Alaska. You can expect baking sun, torrential rain, or heavy snow any time of year. Bears are abundant, so bear spray, bear-proof containers, and knowledge of how to behave during potential bear encounters are essential.

Yellowstone National Park

Wyoming, Idaho, Montana | nps.gov/yell | Visitation: 4,501,382

It all started here—the world's first national park, "America's Best Idea," established in 1872. Encompassing over 2.2 million acres, Yellowstone is larger than the states of Rhode Island and Delaware combined. The park is home to the largest concentration of geysers on earth, with over 10,000 geothermal features. The Grand Prismatic Spring, with its vibrant rainbow colors, is the largest hot spring in the United States. And beneath the park's rugged beauty lies the Yellowstone Caldera, one of the largest active volcanic systems in the world (and a popular source of apocalyptic anxiety).

It earns its reputation as the Serengeti of the Lower 48: Dense forests of lodgepole pine, Douglas fir, and spruce cover the mountainsides. They shelter thriving gray wolf and grizzly bear populations. The biggest remaining herds of bison roam the grasslands as they always have. Pronghorns, the fastest land mammal in North America, bound across the sagebrush steppe, and the trumpeting bugles of herds of elk echo through endless mountain valleys. The second you cross its borders, you instantly understand why people all over the country and the world get hopelessly infatuated with Yellowstone, why generations return year after year and go home inspired to protect their own special places.

But I have a confession to make: The first time I visited Yellowstone, I was a bit underwhelmed.

Before you push me into Old Faithful or gore me to death with a plush gift-store buffalo, let me explain. I was a dumb twenty-one-year-old on his first cross-country road trip, fresh off a life-changing experience with the drop-dead-gorgeous park prom queen (Glacier, see page 99). Yellowstone's softer curves couldn't compare, and I quickly tired of waiting in traffic every time a bison pooped by the roadway. I never got to see the idiots straying off a boardwalk get their scalding comeuppance, and the wolves and grizzlies I'd mostly come for took PTO for the duration of my visit.

On subsequent trips, I learned it was my fault. The National Park Service estimates 98 percent of the people who visit Yellowstone never stray more than a half mile from their car; 90 percent never leave the 142-mile Grand Loop that accesses less than 1 percent of the park. I was part of the problem, clogging the asphalt, choking the limited entrances, and sighing in line while I waited behind screaming toddlers for an overpriced milkshake.

Grand Prismatic Spring at dawn.

But when I first stepped onto a trail a few years later, that all fell away. Hiking any distance in Yellowstone puts you directly in touch with what makes this place so special, and delving into the backcountry enhances that exponentially. There are over 1,000 miles of trail, most at high elevation (average height of the Yellowstone plateau: 8,000 feet). While out on those paths or wandering cross-country, you will experience the country much as the Shoshone, Blackfeet, Crow, Nez Perce, and Bannock tribes first did; and as mountain men and explorers like Jim Bridger and John Colter did after.

Don't be surprised if you encounter secret fumaroles, hot springs, or mud pots: The largest volcano in North America is long overdue for another blowup (the last one was 640,000 years ago). The rivers are cold, beautiful, and full of fish like trout; I've seen unusual birds like sandhill cranes and white pelicans poking in the reeds at river edges and along the bank of Yellowstone Lake, the largest high-elevation lake in North America.

After many more years spent visiting Yellowstone, for a while I came to think of it as a "sacrifice" park: a place where we allow vast infrastructure (10 visitor centers, 9 lodges, 2,000 campsites, 20 restaurants, 251 miles of road, 90 bathrooms) to intrude on the park's wild character. This would allow as many people as possible the opportunity to catch a biophilia bug that might power whole lifetimes of recreation, conservation, advocacy, fellowship, purpose, and meaning. Yellowstone could endure a measure of suffering so that wild places all over the world might gain a voice and persist unmarred "for the benefit and enjoyment of all the people." If that meant cuddling up to the screaming multitudes on the way to joining my fellow 2 percenters on the trail, so be it.

But if I let my mind drift back to Yellowstone now, most times I don't dwell on those crowds. Instead, I remember how I once stood still to let a hundred-strong herd of bison have the right of way as they forded the Lamar River. Or how I watched an elk cow narrowly escape a pack of young wolves after falling through the ice of a pond in a frosted meadow. Or when I tucked behind a sagebrush to see a

Bison jams are common on Yellowstone's roads.

Though controversial, wolf reintroduction has been a major wildlife success story.

young male bear emerge from his den, climb a snowy hill, point his nose skyward and take his first big sniffs of post-hibernation air. I remember how I did these things alone, or in the presence of one or two people of my choosing.

Then I remember that Yellowstone is no sacrifice at all. It's a gift.

ZONE OF INTEREST

Lamar Valley

The Hayden Valley gets a lot of the attention of wildlife seekers—but the Lamar Valley is arguably better and far less crowded. Situated in the northeastern part of the park, this expansive valley offers visitors a unique opportunity to witness an abundance of wildlife and find solitude amid the natural splendor.

Some scientists think the Lamar Valley hosts the densest population of predators in the Lower 48. It's prime habitat for wolves, which were reintroduced to the park in the 1990s, but also coyotes, grizzly bears, black bears, and elusive mountain lions. This is largely because the valley's lush grasslands and abundance of water sources attract en masse the herbivores they eat: Bison, elk, mule deer, pronghorns, and bighorn sheep all migrate through the Lamar in large groups.

It's a haven for bird-watchers, too. The riverbanks, meadows, and forests support bald eagles, golden eagles, ospreys, sandhill cranes, various owl species, and a plethora of migratory birds.

Another bonus: The Lamar Valley's expansive vistas stretch as far as the eye can see. With binoculars, it's easy to scan wide-open grasslands and panoramic spaces to catch wildlife milling from a safe distance. Its remote location and the absence of major tourist attractions keep crowds away and wildlife undisturbed. There are many hiking trails (the Lamar Valley and River Trails are good starting points), but exploring the Lamar Valley is often as simple as pulling over on the Lamar Valley Road and striking out into open meadows and forests.

With plentiful prey, the Lamar Valley has one of the highest concentrations of predators in the Lower 48.

Be patient and respectful, maintaining a safe distance from the animals for both their well-being and yours. Wildlife is typically more active during dawn and dusk, so consider visiting during these times for optimal sightings.

HIKES

Pelican Valley Trail

Pelican Valley lets you stroll through premier bear country—so premier that it's often closed for bear activity. Make sure to check for updates before heading out, and make plenty of noise and bring bear spray when you go. But plenty of other wildlife is abundant here, too: wolves, bison, and of course pelicans.

Access the Pelican Valley Trail from the trailhead located near the Pelican Creek Campground. From Fishing Bridge Junction, drive east on the East Entrance Road for 7 miles. Turn left onto the signed road leading to the Pelican Creek Campground.

Begin your hike from the trailhead near the campground. The trail follows the valley floor, winding through grassy meadows and alongside the creek. The toothy Absaroka Mountains pop out in the distance. Hike as far as you desire, then retrace your steps to return to the trailhead.

Pelican Creek Campground is conveniently located near the trailhead. The campground offers sites on a first-come, first-served basis. Water is available at the campground.

Sky Rim Loop Trail

The 21-mile lollipop loop Sky Rim Trail's 4,000-plus feet of elevation gain makes for a difficult backpack or a monstrous day hike—but you'll thrill to Yellowstone's finest high country and awe-inspiring views while hugging the edge of the Gallatin Range where Yellowstone bleeds into Montana. Starting from the Daly Creek trailhead outside the park, this loop delivers expansive meadows, rocky ridge walks, deep solitude, and an experience that challenges the most seasoned hikers. Plentiful camping gives hikers many options to compress or extend their trip along this trail.

The Daly Creek trailhead (sometimes spelled "Daily" on maps or permits) is accessible via US 191. It's 15 miles north of West Yellowstone and a stone's throw from the park boundary. (An alternate, longer version begins at Specimen Creek, which adds more miles of airy ridge walking but requires a shuttle.)

You'll need a backcountry permit if you plan on camping along the trail. These can be obtained from the Yellowstone Backcountry Office. It's advisable to book your permit well in advance during peak season (June to September). Snow can linger on high ground into July, and by October, early snowstorms are a possibility.

Day one from the trailhead to Daly Pass covers around 7 miles, starting by walking through a mix of forest and meadows along Daly Creek. As you ascend, the vegetation thins, and vast alpine meadows dotted with wildflowers take over, giving you the first glimpses of the stony Gallatin Range. Daly Pass has limited camping options, so make sure to arrive early to secure the best spots.

The next day's 5 miles of trail get rockier and steeper as you traverse the rim, but you'll get mind-blowing panoramas covering Yellowstone's vast interior. Clear-day views can extend into adjacent states. Highlights include Sky Point, a rocky outcrop offering 360-degree views, and your destination of Shelf Lake—a gleaming sapphire tarn with a couple of backcountry campsites.

On day three, leave Shelf Lake to make your way to Big Horn Peak and back (2 to 3 miles). The terrain remains rocky and alpine, demanding caution and solid footwear, but summiting Big Horn Peak delivers perhaps the best panorama of the trip. Look for mountain goats and bighorn sheep. Summiting Big Horn Peak is a must for the extra kick of adventure. Return to camp at Shelf Lake.

On your final day, depart Shelf Lake for the trailhead, retracing your steps along the rim and down through the meadows and forests to Daly Creek trailhead.

This is a water-scarce route for much of high season; prepare to bring in more than usual for an alpine trip, especially as seasonal creeks dry up beyond July.

Osprey Falls

Tucked into Sheepeater Canyon, Osprey Falls is one of the quieter cascades in the park. The trailhead is accessible off the Grand Loop Road, near Bunsen Peak. It's a moderately strenuous 8-mile round-trip hike that descends 700 feet to a view of the falls plunging over 150 feet into the Gardiner River. The descent into the canyon offers a rare chance to experience Yellowstone's volcanic rock formations up close. It delivers on the name, too: Occasional sightings of ospreys diving for fish occur along the river.

Osprey Falls is a quieter alternative to Yellowstone Falls.

Lone Star Geyser

If Old Faithful is a venerable star of Yellowstone National Park, attracting millions of spectators each year, Lone Star Geyser is the character actor who is always nominated but never wins. Often referred to as Old Faithful's quieter cousin, Lone Star Geyser provides an experience that is at once intimate and grand, far removed from the boardwalks and crowds of its more famous counterpart.

Situated a 2.5-mile hike from the Lone Star Geyser trailhead off Grand Loop Road, this beautiful cone geyser erupts every 3 hours, making its eruptions less frequent but equally magnificent. Lone Star's water jets up to 45 feet into the air, accompanied by a spouting steam plume. One of the most captivating features of Lone Star is the intricate mineral sinter that has built up around the geyser over time, resembling a porous, sculptural mound encapsulating the fountain. The eruptions last much longer than those of Old Faithful, sometimes continuing for half an hour, giving you ample time to sit back, relax, and soak in the spectacle.

A serene hike through lodgepole pine forests and along the Firehole River precedes the geyser itself. The hike itself is relatively flat, making it suitable for hikers of various abilities. It's also bike-friendly, offering an alternative mode of travel.

While Old Faithful has visitor centers, food services, and a range of other amenities, Lone Star Geyser offers none of these conveniences. The backcountry bonus means you'll need to bring in all water, food, and first-aid supplies. While Old Faithful's eruptions may be grander and famously more predictable, the experience can often feel more like a tourist event than an encounter with the raw power of nature. At Lone Star, you can appreciate the geyser's force as a part of a larger ecosystem.

Specimen Ridge

Specimen Ridge packs in wildlife viewing possibilities, scenic diversity, and a surprising foray into the park's paleontology in one sprawling trail. Beginning near Tower Junction and accessible

A short hike leads to spewing Lone Star Geyser.

via the Northeast Entrance Road or from the Lamar Valley, you'll find the trailhead near the Yellowstone River Picnic Area, from where you can set off on a 16-mile journey through eons of earth's history.

A climb of over 3,000 feet starts by winding gently along the Yellowstone River before ascending the sagebrush slopes of Specimen Ridge. A slow climb reveals the first layer of Yellowstone's geologic narrative: petrified forests. Ancient logs, turned to stone, are scattered throughout the landscape. Each log is a 50-million-year-old relic from the Eocene epoch.

Climb higher to enjoy transitions from sagebrush to pine and fir forests, opening into alpine meadows. Here, the ridge unfurls

Specimen Ridge features broad views, wildlife viewing opportunities galore, and even petrified forests.

before you, offering wide views of the Lamar Valley—a known hot spot for wolves, elk, and bison. Bust out the binocs: This is one of the best wildlife viewing areas in the park.

For those considering an overnight trip, several backcountry campsites are accessible from the trail (secure a backcountry camping permit from the park). Camping options include sites near Agate Creek and the upper reaches of the Lamar River. The park's nocturnal soundscape comes alive with everything from chirping crickets to keening wolf howls, and Yellowstone's dark skies light

stars ablaze on clear nights. Store food in bear-proof containers and carry bear spray; this is big-time grizzly country.

Farther on, the trail provides the option to summit Amethyst Mountain, where you'll enjoy an unparalleled overview of sprawling forests, meandering rivers, and distant mountain ranges both in and beyond the park.

Returning to the trail, you'll begin your descent back into Lamar Valley. The hike concludes near Soda Butte and the Lamar River, but you'll need to arrange transportation back to the initial trailhead or hike the trail as an out and back, doubling your mileage.

Mr. Bubbles, near the Bechler River, is the rare safe hot spring in Yellowstone.

HIDDEN GEM

Soaking in a Yellowstone hot spring is the least-relaxing thing imaginable. Most of the park's thermal features roil at temperatures hot enough to cook a turkey, and though it's illegal to approach them, more than twenty people have been boiled to death over the years from deliberately entering them or accidentally falling in. In 2016, one twenty-three-year-old man hell-bent on an illegal dip in Norris Geyser Basin fell into a 459-degree pool and dissolved before they could recover his body.

If you can get over that horror, there is one delightful exception. **Mr. Bubbles** is a backcountry hot tub perfect for soaking, and it's perfectly legal: 110-degree hot springs burble up from underground to mix with a 15-foot-wide, four-foot-deep swimming hole in the Ferris Fork Creek (technically, you're swimming in the river, which is allowed).

From the Bechler Ranger Station at the southern end of the park, hike 13.5 miles north past several waterfalls and great views of the Tetons to camp at the Ferris Fork backcountry campsite. From here, follow signs 0.25 mile more to encounter a soothing, aquamarine pool perfect for relaxing tight quads and calves. You'll need a permit to camp.

Crowds be damned, Yosemite Valley should be experienced at least once.

Yosemite National Park

California | nps.gov/yose | Visitation: 3,897,070

Let's get this out of the way: Everybody must see Yosemite Valley once. Drive through and get caught behind a shuttle bus or a kid's bike; injure your neck bending out the window to see the granite domes and walls roaring 5,000 feet overhead. Marvel at 800-foot waterfalls as they horsetail into mist on the valley floor. Drop your jaw to the climbers scaling the walls like teensy ants; imagine one of them is Alex Honnold while you wait in line for the bathroom. Ask yourself if the Merced is the prettiest river you've ever seen, but don't think about it too hard because you still have to pee. Then wave goodbye and never come back.

Yosemite Valley exhibits both the finest rewards and steepest penalties anywhere in the park system. It is clearly one of the most beautiful and humbling sights in the world. It is also maddeningly crowded and Disneyland popular—the antithesis of what it means to experience nature at its most pure. You still won't regret it.

Do it once—and then get to the good work of exploring the hidden corners of this massive crown-jewel park's 800 miles of trail on 750,000 wild acres. Yosemite Valley represents 1 percent of it, and most visitors never leave the closed box of its 7 square miles. Also, as great as the view from the bottom is, I prefer the view from the top. The onion-peeled granite monoliths, river-fed green valleys, and tumbling waterfalls look more imposing up close or from the high angles afforded on the rim.

Entire lifetimes have been dedicated to crafting tomes on every facet of Yosemite: geology, natural history, human history, ecology, conservation, advocacy, climbing, wildlife, and beyond. Mononyms can evoke visions of the park at a mere mention (Ansel, Muir). The damn place drips with a grandeur that signifies iconic "America" as surely as the Statue of Liberty, jazz, or baseball. You think I want to step into that arena?

OK, let's take a stab. Yosemite National Park is a sanctuary of stone and spirit. Let me take you on a journey through this colossal natural amphitheater, revealing tales etched in rock and whispered by the winds.

OK, barf. Let's try again. We'll start by trying to explain why this stretch of the Sierra Nevada stands out from the rest of that impressive 430-mile mountain chain. Our story begins some 10 million years ago, during a blip in the earth's overall timeline. That's when the Sierra Nevada began its dramatic rise, a result of tectonic forces compressing and uplifting the crust. The iconic granite cliffs—think El Capitan, Half Dome, and the Cathedral Rocks—began way before that as molten

North Peak, deep in Yosemite's backcountry.

rock deep within the earth, melty and fluid as Velveeta. This magma cooled over eons, forming large crystals of quartz, feldspar, and mica that give the granite its speckled appearance. Yet these monoliths didn't stand tall immediately; called plutons, they were buried under layers of overlying rock.

Around 1 to 2 million years ago, glaciers formed in Yosemite's high country—in some places 4,000 feet thick. Over centuries of grinding and carving their way through the canyons, they sculpted the granite into U-shaped valleys and domed peaks. Granite's hardness means the ice "exfoliated" the stone, peeling it in layers that created domes and sheer walls. As the glaciers receded, rivers and waterfalls took over to shape the valley. Further erosion by wind and rain leads to frequent rockfall even now.

The extreme elevation change in Yosemite—2,000 to over 13,000 feet—leads to a suite of ecosystems that vary widely and support a broad variety of flora and fauna. Most famous are the groves of towering giant sequoias in places like Mariposa Grove. These ancient trees, some over 3,000 years old, have witnessed civilizations rise and fall. The biggest are the largest living things on earth, period. Meanwhile, ponderosa pines, cedars, and firs add to the forested tapestry, each tree playing a vital role in this ecosystem despite being less impressive.

Meadows and grasslands function as the valleys' lungs. In spring, they explode in wildflowers—lupines, larkspurs, and monkeyflowers, to name a few. They are critical habitats for creatures like mule deer and numerous bird species. Ascend beyond the tree line, and the landscape transforms into an alpine world where tufted grasses, hardy wildflowers, and stunted pines reign. The air here is thin, the winds crisp, and the views of ragged peaks and glacially carved basins get sick.

Yosemite's wildlife inhabitants are plentiful, despite the park's popularity. In the meadows and forests, visitors may glimpse the curious gaze of a black bear, the agile movement of a bobcat, or the swift flight of a peregrine falcon. The Sierra Nevada bighorn sheep bounds across terrifying cliffs. Mule deer, coyotes, and numerous bird species like the American dipper and great gray owl merely scratch the surface of the animal cast of characters present here.

(*Note:* The bears of Yosemite are famously acclimated to humans and clever about scoring an easy meal. Take special care in camp to use bear-resistant containers or bear lockers, and guard your packs and snacks zealously. For serious.)

It's hard to talk about Yosemite without mentioning ardent champion John Muir, but his racist attitudes toward Black and Indigenous people require a necessary reassessment. Still, his relationship with Yosemite and his significant role in the conservation movement are deeply intertwined, so we must live in the complication. Yosemite captivated Muir in 1868, when he first set foot in the valley and came away drunk for life on its beauty and pristine wilderness.

His eloquent and vivid descriptions captivated readers and brought a newfound sense of enthusiasm for the natural world to an American culture previously enamored with unencumbered

Bears in Yosemite are acclimated to humans. Keep all food out of reach.

expansion and extraction. He recognized the pressing need for conservation and actively campaigned for the establishment of Yosemite National Park, which was granted protection in 1890. That advocacy in part laid the foundation for the national park system in the United States and conservation organizations like the Sierra Club, which he cofounded in 1892. Muir's philosophies emphasized the intrinsic worth of nature, arguing that it should be protected for its own sake, rather than solely for human use.

His impact reached the highest levels of government, as he corresponded with influential figures, including President Theodore Roosevelt. Muir's passionate letters and personal encounters with Roosevelt influenced the president's understanding of conservation, leading to the creation of additional national parks and the advancement of conservation policies.

But you can't fully appreciate Muir's precious "Range of Light" without going dark first. Yosemite was home to various Native American tribes for countless generations, and their presence and connection to the land predate the establishment of the national park. Most were removed prior to or during establishment of the park.

The Ahwahneechee people, a Miwok-speaking tribe, lived in the valley and surrounding areas, relying on the natural resources of the region for sustenance and cultural practices. The Ahwahneechee people understood the land, its ecosystems, and the seasonal cycles, which guided their hunting, gathering, and ceremonial lives.

Yosemite Valley, known as Ahwahnee to the Ahwahneechee people, held deep spiritual significance. It was regarded as a sacred place where they communed with nature and sought spiritual guidance from the granite cliffs, waterfalls, and wildlife seen as manifestations of their spiritual realm.

The arrival of European settlers and the subsequent establishment of Yosemite National Park ruined the Native peoples' connection to the land. The forced removal of Native communities from their ancestral territories and the imposition of new laws and regulations disrupted their traditional ways of life and severed their ties to Yosemite. Native people faced insurmountable challenges in maintaining their cultural practices and connection to Yosemite, as their access to the area became restricted. Ahwahnee, the domain of the spirits, is now the name of the park's most famous hotel.

Today, the National Park Service acknowledges the historical and ongoing presence of Native peoples in Yosemite. Collaborative efforts between the park and Native communities seek to honor and preserve Native American cultural heritage, foster educational programs, and promote Native voices in the interpretation and management of the park. This includes the recognition of sacred sites and the inclusion of Native perspectives in the storytelling and understanding of Yosemite's history and significance.

But most of what has been taken hasn't been given back, and that's worth thinking about as you enjoy the spectacular, "wild" wonders of a Yosemite that sheltered and supported a vibrant, successful Indigenous community prior to Eurocentric settlers' arrival and unilateral declaration of the meaning and purpose of nature. Let it weigh heavy on your mind and guide your choices.

Considering the ugliness that persists in the most beautiful place in the world is the least we can do.

HIKES

Gaylor Lakes

The 4.4-mile Gaylor Lakes Trail begins from the Tioga Pass Entrance on CA 120, east of the park. After entering the park, drive 2.5 miles and look for the signed Gaylor Lakes trailhead parking area on the left.

The Gaylor Lakes Trail showcases the captivating beauty of the Yosemite high country. As you ascend, the landscape transitions from lush meadows to rocky slopes adorned with colorful wildflowers during the summer months. Towering granite peaks surround the trail, creating a dramatic backdrop against the crystal-clear alpine lakes.

Start your hike from the Gaylor Lakes trailhead parking area. The trail begins with a steady climb, gradually gaining elevation as you ascend. The path meanders through picturesque meadows, where you may encounter vibrant wildflowers, including lupines, paintbrushes, and daisies. As you continue climbing, the trail becomes rockier, and switchbacks lead you up the slope. Along the way, enjoy stunning views of the surrounding peaks, including Mount Dana and Mount Gibbs, which stand majestically in the distance.

After 1.7 miles, you'll reach the lower Gaylor Lake. Appreciate the tranquil, shimmering waters and continue uphill for another 0.5 mile to reach the upper Gaylor Lake. This serene alpine gem rewards hikers with bigger views.

Mono Pass

Beyond the famed granite monoliths and cascading waterfalls of Yosemite Valley, the park's eastern realm beckons with less-frequented trails and high-altitude allure. Mono Pass rises above 10,000 feet and offers a journey through both time and terrain on an ancient trade route into the raw majesty of the High Sierra.

Mono Pass crests at over 10,000 feet.

Start at the Mono Pass trailhead, located on the Tioga Road (CA 120) 5.6 miles east of the Tuolumne Meadows Campground. Parking is limited, and given the trail's increasing popularity, an early start is advisable. Ensure you have a park map, plenty of water (or a filter to refill from streams), and provisions for changeable mountain weather.

From the trailhead, you're immediately introduced to the Sierra's subalpine realm. The trail meanders alongside Dana Fork, a shimmering creek fed by snowmelt, and gently ascends through a mix of lodgepole pines and mountain hemlocks.

At the Spillway Lake Junction fork at mile 1.3, continue straight, following the signs for Mono Pass. The path to the left leads to the serene Spillway Lake, a worthy side trip for those with time. As you climb, the terrain gradually opens, offering expansive

vistas of the surrounding peaks, including the giant Mount Gibbs and Mount Dana. The air gets thinner, the vegetation sparser and more stunted. Wildflowers, such as sky pilot and alpine paintbrush, punctuate the rocky terrain.

After 2.5 miles, you'll reach the historic Mono Pass at 10,600 feet. From here, gaze upon the Mono Basin to the east and the vast Sierra wilderness to the west. This was once a trade route for Native American tribes and later, miners seeking their fortunes in the 1850s. Most hikers opt to make the pass their zenith, finding a quiet spot to enjoy a well-deserved break with the marmots and pikas whistling amid the boulders.

Retrace your steps to return, appreciating the now downhill trajectory. The descent offers a fresh perspective on the landscape, with afternoon light casting a golden hue on the granite surroundings. Few trails offer such sweeping vistas with relatively moderate effort.

Kibbie Lake

In Yosemite's vast backcountry, there are trails that steal the limelight, and then there are those that remain improbably under the radar. Kibbie Lake, ensconced in the park's remote northwest corner, is one such treasure. This route gives solitude, pristine wilderness, and a taste of the Sierra's backcountry without the multiday commitment.

Begin at the Eleanor Lake trailhead, near Cherry Lake outside the park's official boundary. This location's remote nature usually means fewer crowds, but it does require a bit of a drive. Make sure to secure a wilderness permit if you're planning an overnight stay. The trail is best hiked from late spring to early fall, ensuring snow-free conditions and accessible roads.

Setting off from the trailhead, you're instantly welcomed by a mixed conifer forest of pines and cedars on a flat trail.

At mile 1, navigate your way across Eleanor Creek. Depending on the season, this could range from a gentle hop between stones to a more cautious wade. Past the creek, you'll climb a decent series of switchbacks with glimpses of Cherry Lake peeking out of the trees behind you. At mile 3, continue straight along Kibbie Ridge following signs for Kibbie Lake. The trail meanders through a medley of granite outcroppings, manzanita shrubs, and patches of vibrant wildflowers.

By mile 5, the trees give way to reveal Kibbie Lake's tranquil expanse. Tucked into a backdrop of white granite cliffs and sparsely dotted with islands, the lake is a pristine haven. The shores beckon, whether for a refreshing dip or a serene lunch spot. Keep an eye out for mule deer grazing in meadows and ospreys soaring overhead, eyeing the lake's trout.

If your legs still itch for more, a trail circumnavigates the lake, offering more perspectives and secluded nooks. It's also an idyllic basecamp for further backcountry exploration. If you opt to camp, the nighttime skies are spectacular.

The journey back follows the same route. With most of the ascent conquered in the morning, the return is quicker but no less scenic.

Wapama and Rancheria Falls

Yosemite is synonymous with waterfalls, but the falls in the Valley are choked with visitors. Not so on this pair located outside the less-trafficked Hetch Hetchy entrance.

Your quest begins at the O'Shaughnessy Dam parking lot, past the Hetch Hetchy Entrance Station. Before venturing forth, take a moment to absorb the panoramic views of Hetch Hetchy Reservoir—a controversial section said to rival Yosemite Valley in beauty before it was flooded by the dam.

Your first mile requires a trek across this impressive dam, offering sweeping views of Hetch Hetchy, Kolana Rock, and the distant

Wapama Falls crashes into Hetch Hetchy Reservoir.

Lembert Dome offers mellow hikes and challenging rock climbs.

Wapama Falls. Shortly after crossing the dam, you'll encounter a rock-hewn tunnel. Its cool interior and dripping condensation make for a welcome break from the sun.

Emerging from the tunnel, hug the reservoir's contours until you reach a series of switchbacks that weave through a mosaic of oak, pine, and chaparral. Around 5 miles in, you'll approach

Wapama Falls. Depending on the season, its waters might crash over the trail's footbridges, offering an exhilarating, misty crossing. Always exercise caution; avoid crossing if the flow seems too strong.

If you're satiated by Wapama's spectacle, you can turn back here. But if you crave a second cascade, press on for an additional 3 miles to Rancheria Falls. This section is quieter, meandering along the reservoir's northern shores, rewarding the persistent hiker with cascades and cascading pools at journey's end.

Retrace your steps to return (16 miles round-trip), taking in the landscapes from the opposite angle.

Lembert Dome and Dog Lake

From the gentle undulations of alpine meadows to the soaring heights of granite domes, Yosemite offers an abundance of soul-stirring landscapes. The trip up Lembert Dome and over to Dog Lake packs Yosemite's highlights into a compact hike.

Begin at the Lembert Dome parking area, found off Tioga Road in the Tuolumne Meadows area. Given its elevation and location, Tioga Road is seasonal, so ensure it's open for your intended hike dates. The loop in total covers roughly 4 miles, making it suitable for a leisurely morning saunter or a sunset jaunt.

From the parking, locate the signposted trailhead. The path starts relatively flat, meandering through picturesque meadows sprinkled with wildflowers in the warmer months.

About 0.5 mile in, the trail forks. To conquer Lembert Dome first, take the right. It's a steep, short climb, but as the ground beneath your boots shifts from soil to granite, your reward is a 360-degree view of Tuolumne Meadows stretching east and the high peaks of the Sierra crest rising to the west.

After soaking in the views, carefully descend the same route and, upon reaching the fork, continue toward Dog Lake. A gradual climb awaits, leading you through dense woods and past murmuring mountain streams. The trees soon part to unveil serene Dog Lake. For those seeking a chilly thrill, a dip here is both refreshing and invigorating. Complete your trip by taking the Dog Lake Trail south to reconnect with your original path, guiding you back to the parking area.

Lembert Dome features many climbing routes dotting its face, from beginner-friendly to more challenging ascents.

Given its elevation and relative isolation, the Tuolumne region offers some of the park's best stargazing. If you can, linger till dusk and watch the cosmos come alive.

HIDDEN GEM

Venture beyond Yosemite's iconic granite valleys and thunderous waterfalls, and you'll find landscapes equally deserving of awe. **Red Peak Pass Loop** is one such place—a challenging, rewarding trek through the wilder parts of the park's backcountry, replete with alpine lakes, lush meadows, and commanding vistas. Ready to delve into the heart of Yosemite's high country far from the Valley? Good.

Start and end your expedition at the Mono Meadow trailhead, located off Glacier Point Road. This loop covers 50 miles, so plan for four to six days, depending on your pace. Wilderness permits are mandatory for overnight stays—be sure to obtain yours well in advance, especially during peak season.

From the trailhead, descend to Mono Meadow—a wet, marshy meadow where early-season hikers might encounter muddy conditions. In summer, it dries out and sprouts brilliant, ankle-high wildflowers.

After leaving Mono Meadow, you'll gradually ascend toward Merced Pass, crossing through dense forests of red fir and lodgepole pine. Descending from Merced Pass, the trail meanders through a basin dotted with alpine lakes. Lower and Upper Ottoway Lakes are ideal for a chilly dip or a serene campsite.

Next, brace yourself for a challenging climb to Red Peak Pass, the loop's highest point at over 11,100 feet. The trail turns rugged, skirting boulder fields and patches of lingering snow. But atop, the world unfolds: a vast panorama of Yosemite's biggest peaks. After, head down, traversing subalpine meadows and passing trickling streams, reaching the confluence of Triple Peak Fork and the Merced River.

The route now meanders alongside the Merced River. Here, it's a far cry from the roaring force it becomes in Yosemite Valley.

Lower Ottoway Lake at dusk

Instead, it's a gentle, meandering waterway, perfect for refilling water reserves and enjoying a quiet moment.

The next stretch from Washburn Lake to Merced Lake offers a meditative trek alongside still waters and through thickening woods. Campsites are plentiful: With the hardest parts of the journey behind, it's an excellent time to slow down and immerse yourself in the wild (or possibly cast a line for trout).

As you approach Little Yosemite Valley, the signs of civilization begin to appear. If Half Dome is on your bucket list and you've secured a permit, this is your launching point.

The final leg takes you through well-trodden paths, past Nevada and Vernal Falls—two of Yosemite's crowning jewels. Soon, you'll rejoin the Mono Meadow Trail, retracing your initial steps to the trailhead.

The dizzying view from world-famous Angels Landing.

Zion National Park

Utah | nps.gov/zion | Visitation: 4,623,238

Located an hour's drive from St. George, Utah, Zion Canyon isn't the deepest or biggest canyon in the United States—but it might be the most scenic. As Yosemite is to mountains, Zion is to deserts: It demands pilgrimage. And pilgrims it gets: 4.7 million people visit its smallish 150,000 acres each year, giving Zion the bronze medal for crowds. But they can't diminish the glow of skyscraping Navajo pinnacles bathed in sunlight, or the serenity found in its hidden oases.

Zion is an ancient Hebrew word for "sanctuary" or "refuge," bestowed upon it by Mormon pioneers who encountered it. But originally it was called Mukuntuweap ("straight canyon") by the Paiutes who frequented the area (more on them in a bit). First, we must go deeper in the past.

Approximately 250 million years ago, the area that is now Zion National Park was a flat basin near sea level. Over millions of years, rivers carried sediments from the surrounding areas into the basin, layer upon layer, compacting into rock. The most distinctive rock of Zion is the Navajo Sandstone, a 2,000-foot-thick slab of rock notable for its sheer cliffs and cream-colored hue. The iconic red and pink layers seen in many of the park's cliffs, such as the famous Checkerboard Mesa, are a result of iron oxidation or "rusting." The vertical cliffs and high plateaus that characterize Zion today were formed by a process of uplift, erosion, and many of the geological forces we've been exploring for the duration of this book (except glaciation). In short, the Colorado Plateau uplifted the sandstone seabed as high as 9,000 feet, at the Virgin River's source. Zion Canyon is so steep because the river drops 71 feet per mile—leading to the dramatic narrow slot canyons and dynamic walls we see today.

People mostly come for those rocks, but it's full of life, too. Cottonwood trees line the Virgin River and its tributaries, with juniper and pinyon pine populating the drier areas of the canyon. Wildflowers pop in spring on the high plateaus, while prickly pears and cholla bristle in the open desert.

Home to more than 289 species of birds, 75 mammals (including 19 species of bats), and 32 reptiles, Zion is a relatively well-watered desert, defined by the Virgin River's seesawing flood cycles. On a fortuitous day, one might glimpse a soaring golden eagle, spot a flash of red as a vermilion flycatcher alights, or witness foxes, mule deer, or ringtails slinking in the underbrush.

Ancient Indigenous peoples lived in and around Zion for thousands of years. The earliest were the Paleo-Indians (8,000 to 6,000 BC) of whom we know little. Later, the Archaic people left their mark with unique rock art, featuring abstract designs that continue to intrigue historians. The Ancestral Puebloans inhabited the region from AD 300 to 1300, leaving behind fascinating remnants of their agricultural civilization, including pottery, granaries, and distinctive woven baskets and sandals.

By the late 1700s, Southern Paiute tribes occupied the area. European exploration began in earnest with the friar-led Dominguez-Escalante Expedition in 1776. The first settlers of European descent arrived in the 1860s, forming communities and introducing farming to the area. These predominantly Mormon settlers coexisted peacefully with Paiutes for the most part, but their cattle grazing destroyed traditional food sources, and they cut off water access, forcing out the Paiute. These Mormons originated the name "Zion," which in the 1900s would be preserved first as Mukuntuweap National Monument and then as Zion National Park in 1919.

Like Yosemite, hordes throng to Zion in every season (winter is a bit quieter, but it brings real cold, making paths icy and river travel untenable without frostbite). Like Yosemite, the vast majority of visitors pour into the 15-mile main canyon—but Zion lacks Yosemite's or Grand Canyon's vast backcountry to disperse into. This might make it the *most densely* visited western park. Discussions about limiting daily visitation à la Arches via a reservation or ticketing system remain ongoing. Visitors should expect extreme crowding more days than not.

But with a few clever moves, you can mitigate the crowds and amplify the experience. This is especially useful if you're hoping to bag one of Zion's twin marquee hikes—Angels Landing or the Narrows. Advice on the first: Skip Angels Landing. A new permitting system has reduced crowding some, but you're still waiting for your allotted time to stand in line while death-gripping a chain on the edge of a precipitous cliff littered with people who are frankly unprepared for or uncomfortable with extreme exposure. Folks fall to their deaths every year, but even if the Grim Reaper doesn't intrude on your day, it's a drag. An incredibly beautiful, scenic, life-list drag.

If you must, do the Narrows instead, which offers a tiny bit more flexibility and options. During peak months (May to November), visitors must park at the entrance or in nearby Springdale and take a park shuttle to access the inner reaches of the 15-mile canyon. Catch the earliest shuttle you can (they begin at 6 a.m. until September, 7 a.m. until November) and ride it all the way to the end of the park, where the peanut-butter-colored Virgin River pours out of the famous Narrows. This is the park's premier hike, but there isn't a trail. After a 1-mile, wheelchair-accessible path ends, hikers will wade into the rushing waters of the Virgin to trace its path as far as they dare. The Narrows are a thrill unlike any other: While you wade in calf-to-waist-deep water, canyon walls stained red, yellow, and black gradually close in until you reach Wall Street, a section where the sky is but a blue sliver a thousand feet above. Waterfalls pour off the canyon rim, feeding fern-lined grottos and catching the light like falling diamonds.

The sights of the Narrows are wholly unique, but they don't come easy. Filled with slick boulders and shoe-sucking mud, the Virgin riverbed makes for a challenging hike and virtually requires a stick or pole (if you've arrived early, you'll find a stack at the mouth of the canyon) and sturdy shoes. (If you need shoes, sticks, or more technical support, visit Zion Adventures at the entrance to the park.) You'll be constantly wet and often pinned between bone-chilling shade and scorching sun. Flash floods frequently close the Narrows, and they can strike without warning; they also kill people every year. Families with young children can always stick to swimming and playing near the mouth of the canyon, where the paved path ends.

But if you persevere, you will discover *Indiana Jones* levels of adventure with amusement-park access. And with a little preparation, luck, and moxie, you may get a once-in-a-lifetime experience. Several miles up the canyon, I once encountered a section of river roughly 7 or 8 feet deep that required I either turn back or swim across. Crowds had already thinned significantly at this point, but no one else wanted to test uncertain depths in water as clear as Dijon mustard, especially with cameras and phones in tow. I, however, had brought dry bags.

I chose the spooky swim and was rewarded with an empty back half of a legendary canyon, completely to myself.

Snow dusts the tops of the peaks surrounding undervisited Kolob Canyon.

ZONE OF INTEREST

Kolob Canyon

Plenty of folks beelining it for Zion don't know that the park has another "secret" or "hidden" canyon. Isolated Kolob Canyon is a scenic gem, nonetheless, that offers a unique and immersive wilderness experience without Zion's unavoidable bustle.

Located in the northwest corner of Zion National Park, a 40-mile drive from Zion Canyon, it features a separate visitor center and a 5-mile scenic drive that culminates at the Kolob Canyons Viewpoint. While Zion Canyon is closer to Springdale and the park's South Entrance, Kolob Canyons is accessed from I-15, making it less convenient for visitors who are primarily visiting the park's better-known sights like Angels Landing and the Narrows.

Hikes in Kolob Canyon provide a blend of stunning views, challenging climbs, and opportunities for solitude. Taylor Creek Trail and its Double Arch Alcove, La Verkin Creek Trail to Kolob Arch, Timber Creek Overlook Trail—these are a few standouts

The pools along the trail are known as "tinajas."

among many. At higher elevations, you'll tramp through groves of ponderosa pine, manzanita, and scrub oak; lower elevations showcase a desert ecosystem of sagebrush, rabbitbrush, and various cacti species.

This section isn't as lush or river defined as Zion proper, but on most trails you'll walk for entire stretches alone on sandy paths and sandstone ramps, which beats looking at them while crammed into a shuttle bus like an anchovy every time.

HIKES

Many Pools Trail

The Many Pools Trail, also known as the Root Canal Trail, is a 2.5-mile round-trip short-and-sweet jaunt that takes you through a landscape of slickrock and pinyon-juniper forest to end up at a series of clear pools that fill up after a rain to reflect the surrounding cliffs.

The trailhead is located off UT 9, on the east side of the Zion–Mount Carmel Tunnel. There isn't a designated parking area, but you can park along the road where space allows.

From UT 9, locate a drainage area on the north side of the road (to your left if you're coming from the Zion–Mount Carmel Tunnel). Follow the wash into the canyon. The trail isn't well marked, but you can easily follow the wash straight uphill. As you continue deeper into the canyon, you'll begin to encounter potholes scoured by erosion into the slickrock. These pools vary in depth depending on recent precipitation and can get quite deep after a rain. Some may contain water during dry periods. Resist the urge to swim, as they're an important watering source for wildlife, not to mention that getting out can be tougher than it looks.

After 1.25 miles, the canyon will split into two smaller washes. You can explore either or both washes, or you can choose to turn around here. To return, retrace your steps back to UT 9.

Wildcat Canyon

This secluded, tranquil canyon spurs off near the much more popular Subway Route in Kolob Canyon, far removed from the often-bustling main canyon. It's a moderate, 11-mile out-and-back trail that makes for a peaceful and rewarding half-day excursion. The trail ambles through a combination of high desert meadows, scattered pinyon-juniper woodlands, and high plateau terrain. As you wander deeper into Wildcat Canyon, sandstone walls will surround you.

Begin at the Wildcat Canyon trailhead, situated on Kolob Terrace Road. There's a small parking lot available.

From the trailhead, the trail descends into Wildcat Canyon, then gently rolls through meadows and ponderosa pine forests. Sandstone domes like Pine Valley Peak erupt from the wide-open expanse. At around the 2.9-mile mark, you'll come across a junction for the Northgate Peaks Trail. This can be a short detour to enjoy panoramic views, or you can continue on the Wildcat Canyon Trail. The trail becomes more rugged and rocky as it meanders through the canyon. It ends at the junction with the West Rim Trail. Retrace your steps to return to the trailhead.

The Wildcat Canyon Trail is part of the much larger Trans-Zion Trek, a challenging multiday backpacking route that crosses the entire park.

West Rim Trail

The West Rim Trail is one of Zion National Park's most breathtaking hikes, a blend of soaring cliffs, lush hanging gardens, and expansive vistas. It's a strenuous point-to-point hike that's typically completed as a two-day backpacking trip, but it can also be done in one long day by fit and experienced hikers. The West Rim Trail offers an array of landscapes, from high-alpine forests to expansive overlooks and narrow cliffside trails. You'll have stunning views over Zion's myriad canyons and cliffs, including Imlay Canyon, Phantom Valley, and the Great White Throne.

The full trail measures 14 miles, or 16.5 miles if you include a side trip to the famous Angels Landing (see above). All nine rim-top campsites are great, but site #6 is among the best in the park system, with mind-blowing sunsets where the red, pink, rust, and white of sky and cloud mirror the rock formations below.

The trail starts at the Lava Point trailhead in the Kolob Terrace section of the park, a high-elevation area that's a 1-hour drive from Zion Canyon. Many hikers opt to arrange a shuttle to the trailhead and leave a car at the front of the park.

From the Lava Point trailhead, follow the West Rim Trail as it gradually descends through a forest of ponderosa pines. The trail will pass the Sawmill Springs junction 1 mile in. Sawmill Springs, however, is not a reliable water source.

Continue along the trail, enjoying expansive views over Wildcat Canyon to the west. After 5 miles, you'll reach Potato Hollow, a forested basin with a small spring that's generally a reliable water source, though it can dry up in summer. This area also has a few campsites.

From Potato Hollow, continue south on the West Rim Trail as it begins a steep descent toward Cabin Spring, another potential water source. There are several campsites around Cabin Spring. Past Cabin Spring, the trail descends farther into Behunin Canyon, then climbs out to a plateau offering commanding views over Zion Canyon.

At the 7-mile mark, you'll reach the junction with the Telephone Canyon Trail. Sticking to the West Rim Trail here offers better views.

After another mile, you'll reach the junction with the Angels Landing Trail. This 2.5-mile round-trip detour is incredibly steep and challenging, with sheer drop-offs on either side of a narrow rock fin; it's not recommended for anyone with a fear of heights. The views from the top don't disappoint, but we don't think it's any better than views you've already seen from the West Rim (especially with the additions of heavy crowds).

The West Rim Trail offers some of the best views in Zion, high above the canyon rim and crowds.

From the Angels Landing junction, continue following the West Rim Trail as it descends Walter's Wiggles, a series of twenty-one tight switchbacks named for Zion's first superintendent, Walter Ruesch, then follow the cool, refreshing Refrigerator Canyon to the Grotto trailhead. This is your end—catch the shuttle back to your car at the park entrance.

Feeling more ambitious? Combining the West Rim Trail with the East Rim Trail forms the epic 48-mile Trans-Zion Trek, a multiday backpacking route that traverses the whole park.

Hop Valley and Kolob Arch

Part of the longer Trans-Zion Trek, the serene Hop Valley Trail offers striking sandstone cliffs, lush valleys, and a largely solitary hiking experience in 6.5 miles, with the option to continue at the junction of La Verkin Creek to see Kolob Arch, the second-longest and possibly biggest arch in the world (sorry, Arches) for a 14-mile round-trip. Some sandy sections can be tough to traverse, but the bigger annoyances are frequent stream crossings and the occasional cow pie (cows are allowed to graze here). But this helps keep the

Remote Kolob Arch soars high above the trail.

valley quiet, and it's arguably a more scenic route to Kolob Arch than the more popular La Verkin Creek route.

Start at the Hop Valley trailhead, located off Kolob Terrace Road. This is a remote trailhead with limited parking and no water or restroom facilities.

The trail descends from the trailhead into the Hop Valley, crossing a relatively flat area filled with sagebrush and native grasses. After 2 miles, the trail follows Hop Valley Stream, winding through a beautiful canyon floor that's contrastingly green and vibrant against the reddish cliffs. The trail crosses the stream numerous times (expect some wet crossings in spring or after heavy rain). It ends at the junction with the La Verkin Creek Trail. Turn around at this point for a mellow out-and-back hike, or turn left and continue on La Verkin for a short bit until you reach the Kolob Arch Trail. A 0.7-mile spur to the right leads on slickrock to Kolob Arch, a massive sandstone bridge high above you against the canyon wall.

Walter's Wiggles are a marvel of trail engineering.

Orderville Canyon is a stunning slot, but it requires canyoneering experience and a tolerance for cold.

The Hop Valley Stream runs alongside a portion of the trail, but the park service doesn't recommend drinking it because of the presence of cows. It is a potential water source, but it should be treated before drinking. Backcountry camping is allowed with a permit, and there are great designated sites available along the trail 5 miles into Hop Valley and along La Verkin Creek.

HIDDEN GEM

What if I told you that the famous Narrows of Zion had a secret sibling that was narrower, darker, and more mysterious? That's **Orderville Canyon,** an 8.5-mile wonderland of huge boulders, sculpted sandstone rock formations, side-trip slot canyons, and magical waterfall oases.

The catch is that Orderville Canyon isn't a hike: It's a light canyoneering route that requires comfort with scrambling over obstacles, downclimbs on slippery rock, frequent wading and potential swims in cold water, and two short rappels of 25 feet. You'll need to bring at least 50 feet of rope and be comfortable rappelling or using a handline; the two sections that require it look jumpable. Don't. You will break or twist an ankle and necessitate a slow and arduous rescue from this remote location. Little sunlight reaches this canyon, so it's always cold. Consider wearing a wetsuit on all but the hottest days. Wear closed-toed, protective shoes with great grip—the clay substrate deposited in the canyon can be extremely slick. Bring dry bags for any precious items; everything will get wet.

Any trip down Orderville requires a wilderness permit, and it frequently closes during periods of high flow or flash-flood risk. A high-clearance 4WD road leads to the Orderville trailhead. Once you've completed the dry upper canyon and the watery obstacle course of the lower canyon, you'll run into bewildered day hikers on the Narrows, 2 miles from the last shuttle stop in the main valley.

Photo Credits

Index of National Parks by State or Territory

About the Author

Ted Alvarez is *BACKPACKER* magazine's Northwest editor and was a National Magazine Award finalist in 2014. He is also the author of *The National Parks Coast to Coast: 100 Best Hikes*, *The Survival Hacker's Handbook*, and *The Wilderness Idiot*. Whether chasing grizzly bears in the North Cascades, fording an icy Alaska river, or drinking his own urine in the desert, he regularly goes to extreme lengths in pursuit of a good story. He lives in Seattle, Washington, where he survives on heroic doses of strong coffee.